SAINTS AND
REVOLUTIONARIES

STUDIES OF THE HARRIMAN INSTITUTE
Columbia University

The W. Averell Harriman Institute for Advanced Study of the Soviet Union, Columbia University, sponsors the Studies of the Harriman Institute in the belief that their publication contributes to scholarly research and public understanding. In this way, the Institute, while not necessarily endorsing their conclusions, is pleased to make available the results of some of the research conducted under its auspices. A list of the Studies appears at the back of the book.

Saints and Revolutionaries

The Ascetic Hero in Russian Literature

Marcia A. Morris

Studies of the Harriman Institute

State University of New York Press

Published by
State University of New York Press, Albany

© 1993 State University of New York

For information, address State University of New York
Press, State University Plaza, Albany, N.Y., 12246

Production by E. Moore
Marketing by Dana E. Yanulavich

Library of Congress Cataloging-in-Publication Data
Morris, Marcia A., 1952-
Saints and revolutionaries: the ascetic hero in Russian
literature / Marcia A. Morris.
     p.   cm.
Includes bibliographic references (p.   ) and index.
ISBN 0-7914-1299-7 (CH: acid-free).--ISBN 0-7914-1300-4
(PB: acid-free)
1. Russian literature--History and criticism. 2. Ascetics in
literature. 3. Saints in literature. 4. Heroes in literature.
5. Revolutionaries in literature. I. Title
PG2989.H4M6 1993
891.709'27--dc20   92-279
                                                     CIP

10   9   8   7   6   5   4   3   2   1

for Martin

CONTENTS

PREFACE

The genesis of this book can be traced to a conversation I had in 1983 with Dr. Deborah Martinsen. At the time I was engaged in preliminary research for a project on medieval Russian ascetics. Deborah very perceptively suggested that further investigation might yield interesting parallels between medieval saints and Rakhmetov, a character central to N. Chernyshevsky's novel *What Is to Be Done?* I pursued her idea and came very quickly to two conclusions: that certain features of Chernyshevsky's novel were, in fact, closely related to the saints' lives I was studying; and that *What Is to Be Done?* was only one of a number of nineteenth- and twentieth-century works that shared significant elements with the much earlier, medieval lives. I am beholden to Deborah both for the initial impetus for this study and for her advice and suggestions over the years I worked on it.

Professors William E. Harkins, Robert A. Maguire, and Robert L. Belknap read early versions of the manuscript, and I am greatly indebted to them for their comments and support. I also owe a debt of gratitude to my colleagues in the Russian department of Georgetown University, particularly to Valentina G. Brougher and Valery Petrochenkov for their suggestions regarding late twentieth-century realizations of the ascetic hero in Russian literature. I, of course, bear sole responsibility for all errors and deficiencies.

Finally, I would like to thank my family for its ongoing enthusiasm and encouragement. My husband, Martin J. O'Mara, has made numerous suggestions regarding source materials, devoted countless hours to proofreading the manuscript, and has been, through out, a pillar of support. Many thanks are due to Mary Lou Morris and Steve Payne, without whose computer expertise I would never have produced a readable manuscript. My sons, David and Daniel, have been a constant inspiration.

The transliteration used throughout this manuscript conforms to the Library of Congress system. Names of characters in medieval works, which often vary slightly from one manuscript to the next, have been standardized. The transliteration of names of well-known authors and critics reflects customary usage.

Where original Russian texts are quoted in English, translations are mine. Likewise, translations from other non-English sources are my own unless otherwise specified.

INTRODUCTION: THE NONRETURNING HERO

In one of the recurring story lines of Russian literature, we encounter a hero who is born into a large, well-to-do family. In his youth he studies hard, reads voraciously, and seems destined for great worldly success. He disappoints expectations, however, by taking his inheritance, distributing it among the poor, and embarking on a period of solitary wandering. When he finally comes to the city, he adopts a more sedentary way of life, but his fellows find him very odd: he engages in extremely rigorous ascetic practices and associates with others as rarely as possible. He seems to have some sort of secret knowledge, gained from a mysterious source.

As it turns out, he is a man with a message. He has a vision of the future, but it is dangerous for him to proclaim it, and the vision is only granted to him because he dedicates himself to it exclusively. He shows he is worthy of this vision or secret knowledge by suppressing all passions and mortifying his flesh.

Ultimately, led by an unbending will to achieve a great thing, he leaves the city and dedicates himself to preaching the advent of a great cataclysm. His fellows have only a vague sense of the nature of this cataclysm, yet they accept the wisdom of his decision. They too dedicate themselves to his cause, but although they admire him and seek to emulate him, none can match him. Instead, they flounder, caught in the web of everyday life. Unfortunately, he has set an example which few can follow.

This is the story of Avraamii Smolenskii, a thirteenth-century

saint from Smolensk. It is equally, however, the story of an altogether different man, Rakhmetov, the hero of Nikolai Chernyshevsky's
1863 novel, *What Is to Be Done?* Although Christian saint and socialist revolutionary might seem, in many contexts, to be as unlike
as two human beings could be, these two, at least, walk the same
path. And although recurring variations of a limited stock of story
plots lie at the very heart of literature and literary development, it
is nevertheless striking that *The Life of Avraamii Smolenskii* and the
Rakhmetov chapter of *What Is to Be Done?*, which share similar plot
structures, originate in such widely separated and seemingly dissimilar time periods. The genres involved, saint's life and novel,
are very different from one another, as are the world views which
inform them. And yet, for all that, the two works are very close,
even employing much of the same imagery.

The simplest explanation for shared features in two works separated by such a gulf of time and literary development might seem
to be coincidence, but yet coincidence does little to help us here.
The Life of Avraamii Smolenskii is not the only piece of early Russian literature structured around the career of a strong individual
who chooses a life of self-restraint. Nor, for that matter, is *What Is
to Be Done?* unique within the canon of nineteenth- and twentieth-
century fiction. Both must be seen within the context of any number of other works—works which, in the case of Old Russian literature,
enjoyed sufficient popularity to survive in numerous manuscript
copies even in the modern era and which, in the case of the later
period, were, and still are, celebrated as some of the most significant artifacts produced by Russian and Soviet culture.

An entire group of saints' lives traceable to the medieval tradition as well as numerous novels and stories coming out of the
modern period, then, share the same type of hero, a hero we will
refer to as the ascetic. But resemblances between these works go
well beyond the type of hero chosen. The very means chosen to
structure them are remarkably similar. Also, imagery is often the
same from one work to the next. Given that the genres in question
are so remote one from another, these convergences are nothing
short of extraordinary.

What can account for the high degree of likeness not only between works of the same tradition but also between those separated by a vast gulf in time? Although the areas of overlap are
numerous, there is reason to believe that the choice of an ascetic
as the literary hero is a critical factor in motivating other impor-

tant narrative strategies. For this reason we will investigate the convergence between medieval and modern literature through a typology of the ascetic hero.

Such an approach has been shown to be very fruitful when
dealing with works of medieval literature. In these works a close
interdependence between the type of hero chosen and the poetics
of the work can be definitely posited. D. Likhachev has stated that
the artistic means employed by an author follow inevitably from
the way he chooses to portray his hero.[1] In her study of the literary hero, L. Ginzburg notes that in "archaic" literature the characteristics of the hero are predetermined by the genre of the work.[2]
What is significant in these statements is not their disagreement as
to whether the primary motivating factor in a work of literature is
characterization of the hero, as posited by Likhachev, or genre, as
posited by Ginzburg, but rather their agreement that, for certain
types of literature, characterization, artistic method, and genre are
totally dependent on each other. Thus, the choice of a given hero
will necessarily involve the choice of a corresponding poetics.

There is an analogous interdependence of poetics and the particular type of hero chosen in certain nineteenth- and twentieth-century
works. A careful study of texts will show just how similar the modern
and medieval works are in this regard. This study will be based
primarily on a comparison of ascetic saints' lives with a number
of novels portraying the Russian struggle to achieve liberation from
the tsarist system. A small number of novels and stories outside
the revolutionary tradition yet structured around ascetics will also
be included.

Asceticism, the central motivating force in these works, can be broadly
defined as the voluntary adoption of poverty, fasting, and chastity; as a
principled denigration of the material aspect of life in favor of the spiritual. The ascetic apprehends the material and the spiritual as separate
and inimical forces and seeks to elevate the latter by debasing the former.

The behavior of our two illustrative exemplars of the ascetic
life, Avraamii Smolenskii and Rakhmetov, admirably reflects the
consequences of affirming a polar opposition between matter and
spirit. Both heroes are willing to turn away from the joys and re-
wards afforded by a wholehearted acceptance of the material world.
Both are engaged in a search for another kind of reward, an experience which sets their spirits free. Material goods and pleasures
serve to fetter their spirits; conversely, physical fetters encourage
their spirits to soar. This kind of behavior can only be explained

by the belief that matter and spirit are radically opposed to one another and that matter must be rejected in order to free the spirit.

Once the spirit is freed, of course, it is always loath to return to its earthly, material abode. The Russian ascetic hero, once he has abandoned his concern for his own material existence, is incapable of understanding others' concern and is neither very sympathetic nor helpful to them. This peculiarity of the ascetic's outward behavior is indicative of a deep underlying difference between his heroic career and those of other literary heroes. Most literary heroes follow a path defined by Joseph Campbell as one of separation-initiation-return:

> A hero ventures forth from the world of common day into a region of supernatural wonder: fabulous forces are there encountered and a decisive victory is won: the hero comes back from this mysterious adventure with the power to bestow boons on his fellow man.[3]

The ascetic, however, fails to "return." He keeps his mysterious, newly found powers to himself.

Let us examine the ascetic's realization, or nonrealization, of the separation-initiation-return pattern in more detail. Separation, the first phase of this A-B-A pattern, is achieved precisely through the hero's ascetic behavior. By adopting poverty, fasting, and chastity, the ascetic actively seeks to set himself apart from his fellow men and suppress his desire for material or "created" things. By spurning not just material things but also his own material nature, he frees his spiritual or "uncreated" self. He, in effect, achieves a double separation; he separates himself from his society, and he separates a part of himself from the whole.

Initiation involves integration into a new and presumably higher way of life. For the ascetic hero, initiation leads to attaining a state of perfection. Perfection may be defined variously: as a state to be achieved by the individual, or as a state to be achieved by mankind as a whole; as a state associated with a preexisting Supreme Being, or as a state associated with so simple a matter as the proper fulfillment of a task. For the ascetic, whose practices serve to separate him from the rest of society, however, the search for perfection is clearly an individual quest. In the Christian ascetic tradition, perfection is reached when the individual attains union with a transcendent God.

While union with God is the end to which medieval ascetics aspire, it is certainly not the goal of the ascetics of modern Russian literature, committed as they are to the establishment of an atheistic order. It is, nevertheless, an end which is most consistent with their means. Does not this disjunction between means and ends explain, in part, the underlying disharmony characteristic of many of the literary works in which it is found?

In most literary works, the return phase asserts the basic value of "the world of common day" from which the hero has separated himself. While the value of voyaging into the unknown is also recognized, the ultimate good still lies in returning. Jeffrey Perl notes this pattern and suggests that *The Odyssey* is fundamental in establishing it. He analyzes the basic plot movement of *The Odyssey* as one which achieves paradigmatic status by "encouraging the present [Telemachos] to seek out the past [Nestor and the other surviving heroes of the Trojan War]" and posits that by "unleashing the past to home towards the present, the Olympian council determines a longed for future."[4] In other words, in the overall frame of the work, the past (Odysseus, initially represented by his fellows-in-arms) must conquer the present (the corrupt order of the suitors) in order to reinstate itself. Odysseus breaks with home and the known values of the past so as to help reclaim Helen, the embodiment of beauty or the ideal. His quest takes him in unexpected directions and leads to rootlessness and ennui that can only be cured by renewed appreciation for the fundamental values of the past, or return.[5] The value of return, the reinstatement of "A," is paramount, and while neither Odysseus's long wanderings nor the siege of the suitors ("B") are entirely forgotten, neither is capable of exercising control over the newly achieved status quo.

The return phase is, of course, the phase which the ascetic hero realizes differently from the canonical hero. The ascetic rejects reintegration. The religious ascetic seeks to maintain his state of communion with the transcendent. His experience is one which is achieved only after he has fully perfected himself. He cannot show others the road to perfection; each must find it for himself. He is sometimes said to provide an example for others, but more often than not, he refuses to, withdrawing into a place of total seclusion such as a cave or a remote and wild area and avoiding all contact with others. Frequently he is followed by those who wish to learn from him, but he always withdraws into yet another place of seclusion. He continues his extreme ascetic practices and thereby continues his separation.

The revolutionary ascetic also experiences a transcendent moment. This is the moment when he realizes that the present is but an insignificant point in history's march towards a shining future and begins to live entirely for his vision of this future.[6] Once he is vouchsafed a vision of the future, he immediately eschews all further involvement in the imperfect present. Although he is also supposed to function as an example to others, he very rarely succeeds in imparting his wisdom to them. His followers are incapable of effecting such a complete rejection of the present. Some of them retain bourgeois attachments and emotions, while others reject the hero's vision altogether. Thus, the ascetic alone knows the all-embracing experience of transcendent reality.

The ascetic's idiosyncratic realization of the canonical heroic pattern bears witness to the fact that he does indeed constitute a discrete and legitimate type of hero. It also reveals a tension inside the hero himself. On the one hand, the ascetic hero achieves initiation through his mastery and eventual rejection of the material order. In thus mastering nature, he comes very close to the schematic, archetypal heroes of myth who are "conceived in human likeness and yet have more power over nature. . . ."[7] On the other hand, by selecting asceticism as his means of effecting initiation, he takes the first steps along a path which, as Robert W. Hanning has said, leads to the development of more individualized, multidimensional heroes who

> use their personal wit and ingenuity to shape their encounters with the world outside themselves to their own benefit, self-consciously and in ways that are often morally problematic.[8]

In other words, the ascetic hero combines elements of schematic, unidimensional, mythic heroes with those of more individualized, "modern" heroes. We shall have occasion later in this study to judge both the extent to which the ascetic shapes the world outside himself and the degree to which his efforts are morally problematic. For now, however, it is important to take note of the ascetic's mixed provenance. It is also helpful to note from the very outset Hanning's usage of the word "individualized," which can be profitably applied to medieval as well as modern ascetic heroes.

The very fact that the ascetic hero can be routinely fit into a schematic pattern of separation-initiation-nonreturn tells us something about the works of literature in which he is found. There cannot be a great deal of fantasy and fresh invention in a work which is bound by the constraints of the hero's nonreturn. Most fictive literature is characterized by carefully reconciled endings, in which the total withdrawal of the hero is hardly to be expected. Complete withdrawal is a rarely utilized device, and the factors which can lead to its coming into play are limited.

As will be seen, Russian works which depict the ascetic hero seem to explain his nonreturn by one or the other of two basic motivations—the urge to commune with God or the compelling desire to be numbered among the "saved" in the event of a cataclysmic, apocalyptic event. Given this limited stock of heroic motivations and the predictable outcome of the heroic career typical of Russian ascetic works, variety is severely limited. One ascetic work is much like other works of its own kind.

A concept which lends precision to the definition as well as the evaluation of works containing the ascetic hero is the "formula." The literary formula can be defined as "a structure of narrative or dramatic conventions employed in a great number of individual works," with the additional refinement that it combines or synthesizes "a number of specific cultural conventions with a more universal story form or archetype."[9] The formulaic work, from the perspective of analysis of the hero, is one which employs stereotypical characters in situations that are meaningful to a given culture.

In his study of the formulaic novel, John G. Cawelti makes several arguments which are applicable to a discussion of the literature of the ascetic hero. Cawelti suggests that the pleasure which a formulaic work gives its readers depends largely on how much it intensifies an already familiar experience. The reader of formulaic works, in Cawelti's view, uses literature to escape from the complexity of the real world into an ideal order, where ambiguity, uncertainty, and human limitations do not exist. There is, however, a danger that repeated exposure to this ideal world may lead to boredom; in order to forestall this possibility, formulaic works rely heavily on exciting plots. These plots usually revolve around violence, danger, or sex.[10]

The Life of Avraamii Smolenskii and What Is to Be Done? are joined by an entire repertoire of works, both modern and medieval, which create an ideal world order in which sex or violence are encountered and successfully overcome, culminating in the nonreturn of the hero. Many of these works, the modern ones more particularly, are little read in the West. They are considered implausible, awkward, and just plain poorly written. The close relationship of these modern works to medieval prototypes has not yet received the attention that it deserves, however. Hopefully, when the necessary relationships have been established, it will be possible to evaluate these works as members of a major and longstanding formulaic category rather than as examples of the mimetic art they have sometimes competed with.

It is a peculiarity of the literature of the ascetic hero that, although it does constitute both a major and a longstanding category of Russian literature, it nevertheless does not supply a consistent number of representative works for each and every period of Russian literary history. Rather, the popularity of the ascetic hero seems to wax and wane and, at times, diminish altogether.

A twice-recurring cycle, in which the ascetic hero struggles to attain recognition as a legitimate heroic type, then flourishes briefly, and finally loses popularity and vanishes, can be discerned in Russian literature. The first such cycle is attested to by saints' lives from the medieval period, while the second one begins with a number of works dating to the second half of the nineteenth century and continues on through the first three decades of the twentieth century.

The waxing and waning of these cycles and their recurrence after a centuries-long lapse must be explained as the outcome of complex literary as well as nonliterary processes. An aesthetic theory which would predict a cyclical return of certain types of literary forms is clearly part of any explanation of the literary factors affecting the fate of the ascetic hero. Just such a theory can be borrowed and adapted from the work of Wilhelm Worringer, a German art theorist of the early twentieth century.

Worringer posits the existence of two very different types of artistic creation, which he refers to as "naturalistic" and "non-naturalistic." Naturalistic art, as Worringer understands it, is produced at times when man enters into a "relationship of friendly confidence with the appearance of the outer world,"[11] in other words, in periods when man chooses to participate freely and openly in the life of the inorganic world and feels secure in it. At such times, man is in harmony with his natural environment and seeks to express his delight in it by representing it as faithfully as he can in his artistic creations.

Non-naturalistic art is created when man is "tormented by the entangled inter-relationship and flux of the phenomena of the outer world," when he is "dominated by an immense need for tranquility."[12] At such times the artist flees the seeming arbitrariness of the natural world and seeks refuge in a higher realm of abstract order. His art supplies "resting points, opportunities for repose, necessities in the contemplation of which the spirit exhausted by the caprice of perception [can] halt for a while."[13] Art of this type has been produced both during periods when primitive man has trembled in awe of the mystery and complexity of his world and during periods when a more sophisticated, religious man has rejected the multifaceted claims of the material order in favor of the values of the spiritual world. And although Worringer cautiously avoids examining the avant-garde art of the early twentieth century, he makes the tacit assumption that it, too, represents a manifestation of the non-naturalistic tendency.

In discussing non-naturalistic art, Worringer further states that its most salient characteristic is its urge to simplify the world by denying multidimensionality. Ever since the appearance of Lessing's powerful essay "Laokoon," it has been widely accepted that the graphic arts are forms which unfold in the dimension of space. Therefore, in its quest to simplify, non-naturalistic graphic art tends to deny spatial depth.

> It is precisely space which, filled with atmospheric air, linking things together and destroying their individual closedness, gives things their temporal value and draws them into the cosmic interplay of phenomena. . . . Space is therefore the major enemy of all striving after abstraction, and hence is the first thing to be suppressed in the representation.[14]

Literature, however, is traditionally regarded as an art form which is highly temporal. A literary work is apprehended by its audience only over the course of time, through the medium of time.[15] It stands to reason that in non-naturalistic works of literary art, *time* will be flattened out and deprived of depth. This is the most appropriate way for the literary artist to suppress multidimensionality.

As we will have frequent occasion to note, the literature of the ascetic hero is marked by a tendency to lift events out of their temporal framework and to refer them instead to the unchanging eternal order. This, in turn, has the effect of invalidating profane time, in the course of whose flow the complex events of daily life develop. Works portraying an ascetic hero seem, on the whole, to waver between complexity and simplicity. Depictions of the temporal order in all its variety are encountered, but, more frequently, the schematic, predictable atemporal order is found. The relatively high incidence of excursuses into the atemporal in ascetic works is a primary factor in deciding that the literature of the ascetic hero can indeed be considered a manifestation of non-naturalistic art.

Yet another factor is the audience's vision of the hero himself. The hero's unbending adherence to the separation-initiation-nonreturn pattern restricts the author to a set formula. The ascetic hero is mostly a type, only partly an individual. The need to uphold the type sets severe limitations on the possibility of detailed character development, and this serves as yet another indication of non-naturalistic art's urge to suppress depth and multidimensionality.

In light of what has been said, it seems reasonable to predicate that ascetic heroes will be produced only in periods in which non-naturalistic art forms flourish. The Middle Ages present a classic example of such a period, and, as we have noted, the first stirrings of abstraction in the late nineteenth and early twentieth centuries attest to yet another. These are, in fact, precisely the periods to which the Russian tradition of the ascetic hero can be traced.

It would clearly be incorrect, however, to say that because a given type of hero *can* be produced he necessarily *will* be produced. Periods of non-naturalistic art do not invariably produce realizations of the ascetic type; they merely allow for the possibility of them. In order to understand the forces which actively promote the creation of such heroes, it will be necessary to look to nonliterary factors, the subject of chapter 2.

For now we can say that the life of an ascetic can be differentiated from that of any other hero by the choice of nonreturn but also by an acceptance of extreme solutions to the problems of daily life. The hero's adoption of either of two motivations towards ascetic behavior—belief in the possibility of direct communion with God (the "vision of God") or belief in the imminence of a radical overthrow of the known order and its concomitant separation of mankind into the saved and the lost—is accompanied by certain actions on his part. First, the hero who gives himself over to exaggerated ascetic practices forfeits the possibility of participating normally in the society around him. His own "salvation" is more important to him than are the needs of others. Second, he is so driven in one particular direction that he necessarily fails to see other potential areas for self-development. The assurance that he is one with God or that he is numbered among the saved is the only thing he seeks. Finally, the ascetic hero becomes totally convinced of the efficacy of his practices. He feels completely assured that his sacrifices will, indeed, bring him the salvation he so steadfastly pursues.

An exploration of such extreme solutions to the problems of everyday life is rarely found in works of literature and tells us something important about the ascetic hero. We can best formulate this by using a scheme proposed by Victor Brombert. In Brombert's definition of the literary hero, a central role is played by three types of relationships into which the hero enters: relationships with the supernatural, with society, and with himself. By the hero's relationship with the supernatural, Brombert understands the tension in a work of literature between the hero's freedom and his subjugation to necessity. By his relationship to society, he understands the tension between the hero's private will and the collective will of a larger societal group. The hero is marked, on the one hand, by a propensity to *hubris* and a "megalomaniacal" need to assert his uniqueness and quality and, on the other, by the ability to sacrifice himself to a broader idea or ideal. Brombert understands the hero's relationship to himself as the tension between being and becoming. The more psychologically complex the hero, the more important is the dimension of becoming.[16]

These three relationships are closely connected to social milieu, that is, in our case, to the communities which fostered belief in the vision of God and apocalypticism. (In order to understand the tension between the hero's freedom and divinely imposed necessity, between private will and collective will, between being and becoming, it is necessary to know how a given society defines the terms "freedom," "collective," etc.) They are also connected to the three phases of the heroic career. They constitute, as it were, an extraliterary equivalent to our literary definition of the hero.

The ascetic hero's relationship to society, for example, can be profitably discussed in connection with his realization of the separation phase. In his separation phase, the ascetic hero directs his actions toward his own good. His salvation, be it defined in terms of communion with God or apocalypticism, is his primary concern. His actions neither impede others' quest for salvation nor do they contribute to it. The work of ascetic literature, rather than reflecting the tension between the good of the individual and the good of the larger societal whole, bypasses the entire predicament by deciding in favor of the individual.

The hero's relationship to the supernatural, or the tension between freedom and necessity, corresponds well to the initiation phase. For the religious ascetic, freedom can be defined as man's ability to live free from sin, and necessity as his inevitable subjugation to sin; for the revolutionary ascetic, freedom is the ability to live outside society's order, while necessity is subjugation to its laws. In the work of ascetic literature, the tension between freedom and necessity is resolved in favor of the former. The hero overcomes all temptations, be they sent by the devil or by tsarist agents, and comes to a state of grace in which the temptations cease and he is completely free. Once again, an extreme position on the continuum between two poles, freedom and necessity, is chosen.

The ascetic hero, likewise, mediates the tension between being and becoming by opting for an extreme—being. The ramifications of his choice are made clear through his nonreturn. In most works of literature, the main interest lies in the hero's "becoming," in working through complexities and gradually learning how best to live his life. In the work depicting the ascetic hero, however, the hero is presented as one who has already "become." The reader may be supplied with information regarding his struggles and the temptations he has overcome along the way, but the main focus of attention is on the hero in his perfected state, as he "is." Since the successful ascetic belongs to "the good" or the "saved," he denies the validity of the entire spectrum of values which lie between the good and the bad, the saved and the lost. By his nonreturn he denies the possibility that others might be in the process of "becoming," and that his knowledge might aid them in this process. For the ascetic, anyone who is not already among the saved must be among the lost, and there can be no point in trying to help those who already "are" damned.

The fact that the ascetic, by always adopting extreme yet simple solutions to complex problems, denies the tensions inherent in the careers of most modern literary heroes reminds us again that he is, in many if not all respects, a unidimensional creation. His denial of tensions is yet one more example of the many possible literary analogies to linearity in non-naturalistic art forms.

We have already noted Cawelti's contention that formulaic art, of which we have justifiably considered the literature of the ascetic a subcategory, combines specific cultural conventions with a story form or archetype. If a periodic return of non-naturalistic art forms provides us with some basis on which to explain the continuing survival of story plots and archetypes which were popular in the medieval period, it nevertheless says little about the cultural conventions which are and were just as important in creating these literary works from these plots. These cultural conventions lie outside the confines of aesthetic theory and yet are even more significant to a discussion of why it is precisely an ascetic hero who emerges in certain works of Russian literature rather than another type of non-naturalistic, unidimensional hero.[17]

I have already suggested that nonreturn, which is the hallmark and identifying characteristic of the ascetic hero, is explained in one of two ways in Russian literature: the ascetic has either entered into perfect communion with his God or has found some assurance that he can be counted among the "saved" in the event of an apocalyptic cataclysm. It is time to look at these two motivations for ascetic nonreturn in a bit more detail and to discuss some of their implications for Russian literature.

Chapter 1

ORIGINS

THE EARLY CHURCH

Ascetic practices are, of course, the common property of all cultures and all ages, and, clearly, many motivations for them must exist. Of interest to us however, are those factors which have influenced the Russian perception of the ascetic life. Russia's first documented and sustained contact with ascetic ideals can be traced to her conversion to Orthodox Christianity.[1]

Orthodox Christianity inherited the traditions of the early Church regarding asceticism. Although the earliest Church was not exclusively ascetic, it held within it a rich potential for the growth of ascetic movements. Peter Brown, a student of the religious world of late antiquity, has traced early Christian asceticism to phenomena broadly characteristic of the society of the Roman world. Throughout the second-century empire, there developed a belief, shared equally by both pagan and Christian circles, in "holy men," "exceptional human agents, who had been empowered to bring [divine power] to bear among their fellows by reason of a relationship with the supernatural that was personal to them, stable and clearly perceptible to fellow believers."[2] Although such holy men were recognized as exceptional beings, the boundaries between the human and divine remained fairly loose and fluid in the second century. If most citizens were denied direct contact with the divine, they could at least achieve an approximation of it indirectly through the holy man. By the late third and early fourth centuries, however, the boundaries were rapidly closing. For complex social and economic reasons, this era witnessed an upsurge in the ideal of "disengagement." Farmers, thinkers, and holy men alike cultivated self-sufficiency, living on their own and shunning cooperative ties with their neighbors.[3]

Monasticism, the Christian ascetic movement most pertinent to our present discussion, had its genesis at precisely this juncture and, in part, grew out of the widely current disillusionment with "the links that bound men."[4] While its roots lay in broadly accepted Roman ideas, it soon became a distinctly Christian phenomena. Fourth-century monasticism represented both an acceptance of the concept of the holy man as link between heaven and earth and a repudiation of the assumption that the heavens were open to all through his agency.

> The differences are radical, for pagan asceticism is founded on the idea of self-mastery and self-possession, a form of control available only to a few, and gained only through extensive learning, discipline, and culture. Pagan asceticism is a public and even a civic practice. Christian asceticism, by stark contrast, concentrates exclusively on the self, which is predicated to be corrupt in body and deceitful in thought. Christian asceticism enforced a sharp intensification of ascetic practices, but behind this difference in power lay a difference in kind, for the power situated in the eremite was not a product or function of culture. . . .[5]

Tracing the rise of Christian monasticism would be well outside the scope and purpose of the present work, but it is necessary to examine briefly certain key doctrines which played a part in this rise, if only because they form an essential part of our discussion of Russian ascetic literature.

If we ignore the many and varied social and economic factors in the rise of monasticism and concentrate instead on questions of Christian doctrine, we come upon a crucial and yet very controversial issue, the so-called *summum bonum*, the belief in the "vision of God." According to Kenneth E. Kirk, the *summum bonum*, one of the Church's first formulations of the goal of Christian life, was based on the promise of Mt 5:8, "Happy the pure in heart: they shall see God." Members of the early Church came to believe firmly that it was possible to see God and that the goal of life was the pursuit of this vision.[6] What precisely was meant by seeing God and how the seeker might best achieve this vision were not at first clear, however.

Certain Greek factions in the early Church came out of religious traditions (the Orphic or, in some cases, the Platonic, for example) which believed that seeing God meant realizing the divine in oneself. As new members of a Church anchored in Scripture, they were able to buttress this belief with Matthew's exhortation to become "perfect just as your heavenly Father is perfect." They saw in Matthew an implicit recognition of the fact that man and God shared a common nature. This nature was both divine and perfect. It was, moreover, spiritual rather than material, as the Father was an immaterial essence. Many Greek converts' understanding of the *summum bonum* was one in which "seeing" could be interpreted to mean "like communing with like" and in which likeness could be achieved through ascetic withering of the flesh and purification of the spirit.

The early Jews, however, acknowledged God as a completely transcendent being and recognized the existence of a great gulf between the Creator and his creation. To "see God" could hardly mean becoming God oneself. Although the prophets had seen Him, for most mortals the majesty of God was so great that to come into direct contact with it was to be destroyed. Thus, Jewish converts to the Church disagreed substantially with many of their Greek brothers regarding the meaning of the *summum bonum*.

Christian thinkers were faced with the task of somehow reconciling and synthesizing these divergent strains of thought concerning the vision of God. As Kirk has put it:

Christianity came into a world tantalized with the belief that some men at least had seen God and had found in the vision the sum of human happiness; a world aching with hope that the same vision was attainable by all. Men came into the Church assured that there, if anywhere, they would "see God"; and they brought with them all the diverse conceptions of theology and conduct with which the thought was invested in non-Christian circles. Their quest was primarily a selfish one; their motive to secure for themselves, either here or hereafter, an all-absorbing religious experience.[7]

The early monks were among the first to come to grips with the question of the *summum bonum*, to pursue the "primarily selfish" quest for an all-encompassing experience of God. Their movement, "the boldest organized attempt to attain to Christian perfection in the long history of the Church,"[8] arose as a protest or, rather, a series of waves of protest against the institutionalization of the faith.

The fact that monasticism originated as a protest against the recognized religious order is of some significance to our discussion of a hero whose methods are often perceived as being "morally problematic" and deserves further study. In its earliest days, the Church most certainly did not represent an established order. It lived in a constant state of expectation—expectation of the Second Coming of Christ and expectation of the end of the world. As the Second Coming failed to materialize, however, it became increasingly evident that the Church would continue its earthly sojourn for some time. The need for institutional structuring became more and more apparent, and the Church began, accordingly, to expand its hierarchical structure.

At the same time that the Church was developing its hierarchical structure, it was also becoming more committed to sacramentalism. This development contributed to the doctrine that grace came to the faithful through the mediation of the Church rather than through their own efforts. Some serious Christians felt that the Church lost in moral stature in proportion to its gains in institutional standing. They objected to the idea that God's grace came to them through the exclusive auspices of an organized institution. At the same time, they longed for a new age of martyrdom in which to test their mettle.[9] Monasticism enabled them to both protest the new trends in the Church and show the fervor of their faith.

In *The Life of Saint Anthony*, the founder of monasticism, we can easily discover many of the first monks' most pressing concerns. Anthony withdrew from social life and moved into a desert for a year. When friends came to check on him, he refused to see them. He persisted for twenty more years in lonely asceticism, after which time he was joined by others who sought to emulate him. Although he accepted their presence for a time, he eventually withdrew still farther into the desert to live in complete seclusion. Thus, Anthony separated himself not only from the world but also from the Church. As Herbert B. Workman has pointed out, it is unlikely that he received the Eucharist even once during his twenty years of solitude.[10]

In the first period of his life of renunciation, Anthony tried to imitate the deeds of experienced and virtuous men. Later, when he moved off into the desert by himself, the ever-increasing ascetic rigor of his life reached its culmination. He immured himself in a tomb, where devils came to him nightly and tormented him both psychologically and physically. Finally, when it became clear that the devils could never hope to sway him from his course, Anthony received his reward, a communication from God. The Lord came to Anthony and told him that He had watched him suffer and persevere and that He would now help him and glorify him. This communication was renewed at various times throughout his life, and his biographer, Athanasius, referred to it as a voice Anthony "was accustomed" to hear.[11]

It seems reasonable to assume that the goal of Anthony's life was to achieve this direct communion, or "vision" of God. Anthony himself referred to this experience, as had Greek interpreters of Matthew, as "perfection":

> Do not be fearful when you hear of perfection, nor be surprised at the word, for it is not far from us, nor does it exist outside of us; perfection is within our reach, and the practice of it is a very easy matter if only we will it.[12]

I would suggest that Anthony and many other anchoritic monks lived the way they did because they assumed that perfection, or communion with God in this life, was possible. They also assumed that only God would initiate this communion but that they themselves could achieve a state of being which was conducive to it. This state was described by Anthony:

> We need only will perfection, since it is within our power and is developed by us. For, when the soul keeps the understanding in its natural state, perfection is confirmed. The soul is in its natural state when it remains as it was created, and it was created beautiful and exceedingly upright.[13]

Anthony talked only of the soul, not of the body. He stated that the soul by itself was pure and worthy of communion with God. Although he did not explicitly condemn the flesh as the cause of the soul's fall from purity, it seems fairly clear that this is what he meant to imply. His own adoption of asceticism points towards a perceived need to subdue the material side of man's nature. In

Anthony's formulation, the possibility of achieving the vision of God depended on freeing the spirit through severe ascetic practices.

Anthony's extreme denigration of the flesh in favor of spiritual concerns brings us to the question of dualism. Dualism has been variously defined. In a very restrictive sense, dualism assumes that "the origin of Evil lies with matter itself, whose opaqueness and multiplicity are radically opposed to the spirituality and unity of God."[14] A broader and, ultimately, more helpful meaning has been proposed by Kirk, who suggests that dualism is present whenever man recognizes the existence of irreconcilable contradictions and attempts to escape from them as from a problem which has no solution.[15] Anthony must certainly have recognized "irreconcilable contradictions" in both the lay and the ecclesiastical life, contradictions severe enough to have motivated his unprecedented and permanent escape to the desert. His emphasis on a strictly spiritual type of perfection perhaps even hints at beliefs which reflect the more extreme definition of dualism.

If we take Anthony as our prototype for the Christian ascetic hero, and if we grant that his dualist approach to life's contradictions might well be viewed as "morally problematic" by an essentially monist Church, then we see more clearly how the ascetic hero fits into Hanning's characterization of the "individualized" hero. A major criterion for individualization, it will be recalled, is shaping encounters with the outside world in ways that benefit the hero but are often morally problematic.

Athanasius's *Life* of Anthony inspired many with its rejection of the idea that active participation in the life of the Church would bring closeness to God. It joyfully celebrated Anthony's claim of direct communication with the Creator, a claim which many believers could find blasphemous. Most importantly, as Workman has pointed out, although St. Augustine eventually helped to reconcile the cleric with the monk in the West through his teaching of the double form of Christianity—the visible kingdom and the inner kingdom of contemplation—no such reconciliation was effected in the East. The pronounced individualism of the ascetic monastic way competed both against the "collectivism" of the established Church and against the state.[16] Anthony had set a course which could never be entirely acceptable to the Church hierarchy and which would, therefore, put his followers at odds with the establishment for centuries to come.

Not all monks subscribed to the way of life that had been

inaugurated by Anthony, however. It is well known that monasticism split into two branches quite early. The cenobitic, or community-oriented branch was founded by Pachomius, partly as an alternative and partly as a corrective to the anchoritic variety. The informing philosophy behind cenobitism was that "to save your souls, you must bring them together."[17] Cenobitic monasteries emphasized communal work and participation in the liturgical and sacramental life of the Church. This emphasis on communal activities reflected Pachomius's fear that the lone anchorite ascetic might fall too easily to the devil's temptation.

Cenobitic monks, like anchorites, strove to attain "perfection." To some extent this goal was synonymous with attaining the vision of God, but the methods Pachomius's monks adopted to achieve this vision were very different from the anchorites'.

> The goal of all asceticism is union with God; but while cenobitism takes a defensive position, essentially avoiding mistakes, eremitism goes on the offensive, seeking to embody and exercise supernatural power. . . .[18]

Perfection also carried another meaning for these monks. In its second sense, it came closer to what John Passmore has termed "aesthetic perfection," which entails carrying out one's task perfectly within a system that functions as a flawless whole.[19] Each cenobitic monk strove to perform the tasks allotted to him so that the entire monastery would become a perfect, self-sufficient unit. In a broader context, the monastery itself also strove to perform its duty, which was defined as charity, so that the whole of society would benefit and function as a perfect image of the heavenly Jerusalem. Severe asceticism was neither condemned nor praised because it neither hindered nor promoted the achievement of the monastery's goal: "For, to be sure, neither eating nor abstinence is of any account, but it is faith which has extended itself to work done in Charity that counts."[20] The cenobitic monk engaged in moderate asceticism in order to discipline the flesh, but he never showed the outright hatred of the flesh which his anchoritic brother did.

A final and very important difference between the two branches of monasticism reflects, perhaps, the earlier, Roman belief in holy men as intermediaries or agents between heaven and earth. In the uncertain world of early Christianity, many believers craved some form of assurance that they were on the path to salvation. The anchorite, concerned only with mastery of the self, could not give them this assurance. Cenobitic monks, however, cultivated the "gift to search hearts."[21] They reached out to their fellows, monks and lay alike, comforting and sharing their powers.

Many students of asceticism have included both anchoritic and cenobitic monks in their studies of ascetics.[22] For my own part, I prefer to situate asceticism in the context of a dualist mentality. The dualism may be of an extreme kind, which specifically opposes spirit to matter, or it may be of a more general and tempered kind, which seeks an escape from irreconcilable contradictions of any type. In either case, the dualist world view is one in which life is shattered by disharmony. No amount of effort can mend this disharmony; man's only hope lies in transcending it. This dualist outlook was part and parcel of the anchoritic movement, as can be argued on the basis of evidence gleaned from Saint Anthony himself. It is in large part to anchoritic monasticism, and more specifically, to the anchorites' conviction that ascetic practices could bring a believer into direct contact with God, that we must trace the ascetic hero. We will have ample opportunity to test this assertion on the basis of material taken from Russian saints' lives.[23]

The other controversial early Christian teaching which eventually contributed significantly to the creation of ascetic heroes in Russian literature was apocalypticism, or the teaching of Christ's Second Coming and the subsequent end of the world. The Gospels had promised that Christ would return, and three things, at least, were known about His return: it was imminent; it would be heralded by cosmic disasters; and it would be a time when possessions and family attachments would not avail.

In times and places where the return of the Messiah and its accompanying separation of the wheat from the chaff were daily awaited, repentance became a byword. In the Book of Revelation, John had declared that "happy are those who have washed their robes clean, so that they will have the right to feed on the tree of life and can come though the gates into the city. These others must stay outside. . . . (Rv 22:14–15). The call to wash one's robes clean set off a wave of asceticism among certain Christians.[24] Whole communities participated in "collective endeavors to anticipate, produce or enter a realm of human perfection [which were characterized by] nervous anticipation, withdrawal from normal social commitments, and bitter renunciation of the established order."[25] Those who succeeded in cleansing themselves hoped they would be "saved" to enjoy a better life in a kingdom beyond time, while those who failed could only expect to be "lost."

Apocalyptic teachings, then, could powerfully influence believers to cleanse their souls at the expense of their bodies. And apocalyptic literature, too, was controversial enough to sometimes seem morally ambiguous. Well after the New Testament canon had been set, many communities within the Church refused to accept the Book of Revelation. What is surprising is that it was primarily the Greek communities which found it questionable.[26] Although dualism and the ascetic practices which accompany it were more typically manifestations of Greek than of Jewish currents of thought, asceticism generated by apocalyptic fears was rejected by the ancient Greek Church. In general, asceticism had been viewed by the Greek community as a means of perfecting oneself for union with God in the present life, while the aim of a more specifically apocalyptic asceticism was to prepare oneself for the destruction of this world and the advent of a new one. The unsettlingly otherworldly implications of apocalyptic thought probably explain why apocalyptic asceticism, like the anchoritic interpretation of the doctrine of the vision of God, failed to receive unconditional acceptance by all segments of the Church. Both teachings existed on the margin of mainstream, established Christianity, and this explains, in part, why the ascetic hero, motivated by one or the other of them, would also exist outside the mainstream and would be viewed with a certain amount of suspicion.[27]

Religious apocalypticism, like the doctrine of the vision of God, underlay the creation of ascetic heroes, but such heroes, motivated by the belief in an imminent religious apocalypse, are to be found almost exclusively among the ranks of the medieval saints. The religious strain of apocalypticism eventually came, however, to be overshadowed by a related phenomenon, revolutionary apocalypticism,[28] whose adherents also adopted an ascetic way of life. This movement too was characterized by a radical dichotomy between the "saved" and the "lost," although its goals were social rather than religious. It too was made up of a small group of dedicated believers, who followed their vision of the future and, accordingly, were unconcerned with the dross of daily existence. Revolutionary apocalypticism also served to motivate the actions of ascetic heroes in Russian literature—heroes, however, in the works of writers such as Chernyshevsky and Gladkov.

THE RUSSIAN WORLD

If we move our discussion of asceticism to a specifically medieval and Russian context, we must grapple with difficulties created by gaps in our knowledge of Old Russian life. The very existence
or nonexistence of asceticism in the earliest Russian Church is difficult to document. Our best extant literary sources for ascetic heroes, while sometimes reflecting much earlier events, date to the
thirteenth century. To this day, scholars continue to debate such
basic questions as whether the Russian Church of St. Vladimir's
time owed de facto allegiance to Byzantium, Bulgaria, or neither
of the two. It is hardly surprising that they fail to agree on the more
complex question of what form spiritual life assumed in the newly
converted land.

Certain bits of evidence may give us a basis on which to formulate tentative judgments regarding the nature and scope of asceticism, however. Such evidence comes in part from a study of
the Russian Church as an institution. In his discussion of Christianity in the Kievan period, A. Kartashev cites at least sixty-eight
monasteries founded before the Mongol invasion. Approximately
two-thirds of these were endowed by members of princely fami-
lies, while one-third were established by wealthy monks. Kartashev
suggests that so many monasteries could only have come into existence in the relatively brief centuries of Kievan Christianity if some
groundwork had already been laid for them. He posits the existence of a large number of "undocumented monasteries" which were
attached to parish churches and established even before the official baptism of Russia. He further suggests that the comparatively
small percentage of documented monasteries which were actually
established by monks themselves should be explained by the fact
that many monks preferred to live in these small and, presumably,
less strict parish monasteries.[29]

Igor Smolitsch, in an article proposing a scheme for the peri-
odization of Russian Church history, approaches the problem from
the perspective of the spiritual life of Kievan times. He considers
that true Christian life must always be based on a close relationship between a bishop and his flock. This relationship was broken
in Byzantine tradition, he claims, and Russia, greatly influenced by
Byzantine practice, suffered the consequences. Members of the Church
hierarchy failed to become involved in the educational and social
mission of the Church, leaving such matters to the monks. The distance

between bishop and believers grew over the centuries and was never bridged. Smolitsch concludes that the Russian bishops, monks, priests, and people never formed a shared spiritual community.[30]

Finally, we know that Feodosii Pecherskii, abbot of the Kievan Crypt Monastery, one of the largest and most influential monasteries founded in the pre-Mongol period, requested a copy of the Studite Rule. The number of his monks had grown greatly, and Feodosii felt the need of an organizational framework for their shared life. The Studite Rule was accepted by the Kievan Crypt Monastery as well as by many other Russian monasteries. It provided for a communal, cenobitic type of life.

When we try to synthesize these various pieces of information, we come to some interesting conclusions. We see that, on the one hand, the ascetic ideal, when preached at all, was probably preached more often by the monastery than by the parish church. On the other hand, most "documented" monasteries were run along cenobitic lines, and the cenobitic tradition was not productive of ascetics according to the strict definition we established above. Life in the "undocumented" monasteries of the Kievan period was probably even less rigorously ascetic.

This is not to suggest that there were no ascetics in the earliest period. Rather, my argument points to the likelihood that Russian ascetic monks were even less tightly linked to the official Church hierarchy than were their counterparts in traditions which retained closer bonds between bishop, monastery, and believer, and that even within the monastery, the uncompromising ascetic, as we have described him, was something of an anomaly. The Russian ascetic, as his brethren in the early Church, was outside the mainstream.

Extreme forms of asceticism did begin to appear in the monastery of the twelfth century, but they did not set a standard for monastic life. Smolitsch suggests that the Kievan Crypt Monastery began to feel a tension between a relatively worldly way of life and a very ascetic one at about this time. He attributes the growing spirit of worldliness to the monastery's increasing reliance on the Kievan princes for its maintenance. Asceticism arose as a reaction to this worldliness.[31] After Feodosii's death, the Crypt Monastery forgot the "golden mean" he had preached, and its members came to exemplify one of two extremes—an "overly-refined [überspitzte] asceticism or the degeneration of monastic life."[32]

Thus, the picture of Kievan Christianity which emerges is one of a mixed and divided community in which the highest leaders of the Church were, in all probability, further removed from the spiritual life of their monasteries than might be considered desirable and in which the monastery itself faced internal divisions on many basic questions. Clearly, asceticism was known and practiced, but what is equally clear is that it formed but one of many trends within spiritual life. Not every monk was an ascetic, at least not an inflexible ascetic as defined in this study.

Of our two motivations towards ascetic behavior, pursuit of the vision of God and anticipation of apocalypse, the second has left a stronger imprint on Old Russian documents. Kiev's Byzantine heritage provides a link between early Christian apocalypticism and the world of medieval thought. The apocalypse was much pondered in the eastern Roman world. Paul J. Alexander points, for example, to the existence of a large body of Byzantine material which "serve[s] as a continual bridge between ancient eschatology and the medieval Western world."[33] And the best variant of one of the most important examples of this material, *The Visions of Daniel*, has come down to us in a Slavonic recension.

Evidence of an Old Russian fascination with apocalypse abounds. N. Bonwetsch, in his bibliography of Slavic religious manuscripts, records a long list of texts which deal with apocalypse and which were preserved in Russian monasteries. These include the canonical Revelation, various apocryphal apocalypses, the Sybilline prophecies, and numerous commentaries.[34] A. Rubinstein mentions the thirteenth century as a likely date for the short version of the Slavonic Book of Enoch.[35]

An altogether different source, the usually business-like and straightforward Novgorod chronicle, also attests to the belief in an imminent and catastrophic end to human history. Under the year 1224 it records the first appearance of the Mongols on Kievan territory in singularly apocalyptic terms: "In the same year, for our sins, unknown tribes came; no one really knows who they are and whence they came, what their language is, what tribe they come from, what their religion is. They are called Tatars, but others say Taurmen, and still others Pechenegs. Yet others say that they are those of whom Methodius the Bishop of Patmos bore witness, who came from the Etrian desert, which is between the East and the North. For thus says Methodius, that at the end of time will appear they whom Gideon scattered, and they will subdue all the earth from the East to the Euphrates and from the Tigrus to the Pontus, excepting Egypt. God alone knows who they are and whence they have come. Wise men who know books know them well, but we do not know who they are and have written of them here in memory of the Russian princes and of the misfortunes which they brought to them."[36]

The Last Judgment, an event which was said to follow on the heels of the destruction of the world and which aroused less collective, more purely individual fears, was also much discussed in Kievan Russia.[37] Under the year 986 the Primary Chronicle relates a legend according to which Vladimir was approached by Bulgars seeking to convert him to Christianity. Germans preaching Roman Catholicism, Khazars preaching Judaism, and Greeks bringing Orthodox Christianity soon followed. A Greek emissary summarized Old and New Testament history for Vladimir and showed him a picture of the Last Judgment. Fear of eternal damnation, so convincingly and realistically portrayed, made the strongest impression on the Russian court and helped to tip it towards conversion to Orthodoxy. F. Buslaev suggests that this same fear, induced by terrifying visual representations of the Last Judgment, was instrumental in converting many other princes.[38]

Most likely this early attraction to apocalypse has its roots in the very nature of Russian Orthodox belief. N. Berdyaev has summarized a major difference between Eastern and Western Christianity in the following way, "The Church is not the Kingdom of God as St. Augustine asserted and as the majority of Roman Catholic theologians after him have likewise thought. The Church is only a pathway within earthly history." He adds that, "If we took a deeper view of history, we should be able to see that messianism, true or false, open or disguised, is the basic theme of history."[39]

Hope for the return of the Messiah and fear of the prophesied end of the world pervaded much of the medieval period, and we may take this fact as partial confirmation of Berdyaev's view. V. Sakharov traces apocalyptic fears through sermons, letters written by Russian metropolitans, and translated and original saints' lives all the way to March 1492, the year and month which Orthodox tradition decreed to be the end of the seventh millennium and, consequently, the end of the world.[40] Late fifteenth-century texts continued to debate whether the seventh age had really come to an end and questioned why the Messiah had tarried so long.[41]

The genesis of the doctrine of "Moscow, the Third Rome," a profoundly millenarian conception, will be taken up in a later chapter but deserves mention here as yet another proof of the continuing evolution of older, apocalyptic ideas. In time, the Old Believers came to build on this formula, insisting that Moscow, the final kingdom, had already fallen from grace. The end of the world must therefore be at hand. They cast, in turn, Patriarch Nikon, Aleksei Mikhailovich, and Peter the Great as incarnations of the Antichrist. They also contributed to a by now already well established tradition of ascetic withdrawal in anticipation of apocalypse.[42]

Echoes of millenarian beliefs can also be found in Russian folklore. Although it is impossible to definitively date works in the oral, folk tradition to specific periods of Old Russian history, there can be little doubt that many such works do, in fact, have roots stretching back to medieval times. Sakharov has carefully correlated individual passages from written apocalypses and commentaries with certain folk verses (specifically the "dukhovnye stikhi") and makes a convincing argument for the written texts' early influence on the folk tradition.[43] Other, later folk forms continue to echo millenarian themes, sometimes in the guise of visions of distant, wondrous lands, sometimes veiled as legends of saviors, both religious and secular, who return from far away to transform the lives of the people and punish their evil oppressors.[44] Although these later, utopian forms cannot, strictly speaking, be considered direct descendants of apocalyptic texts, they illustrate abiding and deeply held convictions. They reflect a preference for *radical* change and a belief that the existing world order must and shall be transformed,[45] views which continued to characterize certain segments of the Russian peasantry even into the twentieth century.[46]

Although Old Russia seems to have been particularly preoccupied with questions of apocalypse, we should not take this to mean that there was no place in the spiritual scheme of things for our other motivation towards asceticism—the pursuit of direct communion with God. Quite to the contrary, the Orthodox Church was very much attuned to the possibility of the vision of God and professed a doctrine which can be viewed as a lineal descendant of the earlier tenet—"deification."

Timothy Ware has defined deification in terms of the Johannine Gospel: "I have given them the glory you gave me, so that they may be one as we are one. With me in them and you in me, may they be so completely one that the world will realize that it was you who sent me and that I have loved them as you have loved me" (Jn 17:22–23). In explanation of this passage, Ware states, "the Greek Fathers took these and similar texts in their literal sense and dared to speak of man's 'deification.' If man is to share in God's glory, they argued, if he is to be 'perfectly one' with God, this means in effect that man must be 'deified': he is called to become by grace what God is by nature."[47] Along the same lines, Steven Runciman has claimed that the Western mystic seeks to know God while the Eastern mystic seeks to be God,[48] and Joan Mervyn Hussey has written, "to comprehend God is to be God, and it is this that the Greeks admitted, the Latins denied."[49] Evidence that at least some Russian religious figures also professed the doctrine of deification, or the vision of God, will come from our analysis of *The Kievan Crypt Patericon*.

THE ASCETIC CAREER

The spiritual world of Old Russia clearly produced the right conditions for ascetic heroes to arise. The potential for extraliterary factors (in this case, religious) to act in concert with literary ones (a period of non-naturalistic, simplified art forms) was great. At this point in history, both author and audience were able to appreciate a type of art which denied complexity and affirmed simplicity. This art created simplicity by holding to well-known patterns and minimizing innovation. The structuring of the work fell into a traditional mold, as did the heroic career. Some, though by no means all, authors and readers were also attuned to a dualist world view in which denigration of the flesh brought about a desired liberation of the spirit. They sympathized with the goal sought after by an ascetic hero and saw why this goal was consonant with the means he adopted to achieve it—extraordinary and severe ascetic practices.

Given the fact that the end which the ascetic hero pursued was always slightly suspect from the point of view of the establishment, it is understandable that he may have encountered a certain amount of resistance in being accepted as a legitimate heroic type. Even when the author of an ascetic work was convinced of the legitimacy of his hero's quest, there were readers who questioned whether a man could or, for that matter, should become one with the divine; could or should hold himself to be a member of a "righteous" minority which sought the end of the previously known order.

An author who recognized this problem could so construct his work as to "lure" his readers into accepting his convictions. A frequent consequence of this was that individual phases of the heroic career were not uniformly portrayed from work to work. Some ascetic heroes emphasized one phase, such as separation, over the other two. Sometimes this expedient was adopted because an audience which was unsympathetic to the goals of the ascetic might, nevertheless, be brought to accept him as a hero, if only the exact nature of the knowledge he was initiated into was kept vague. At other times one audience may well have been in sympathy with the ascetic's goals, while another audience, namely the censor, may not have been, and, again, the nature of initiation could not be spelled out.

Conversely, there were times when all members of the reading audience may reasonably be assumed to have applauded the hero and his goals. Ironically, this made the ascetic career even more difficult to pursue. When the ascetic way became popular, the uninitiated sought out the perfected hero, hoping for guidance. This created a situation in which it was very difficult not to "return."

Campbell's definition of return states that the hero must come back to the "world of common day," that is, to the world into which he was born. The ascetic who had been initiated into perfection never really rejoined the sinful, profane world, however. Even when he was surrounded by others, his metaphysical separation of one part of himself, the spirit, from the other, the flesh, continued undisturbed. In any case, the physical presence of others belonged to a physical order of reality he no longer recognized. Furthermore, his secret knowledge raised him to a purer level of existence, one which could not be touched by the sinful realia of the "world of common day." Sometimes such a hero served as a model for others, but he never communicated his deepest knowledge, gained at initiation, to them. As Brown has stated, "The monks sidestepped the ambivalences involved in claims to exercise 'heavenly' power in 'earthly' regions. They defined 'heavenly' power quite simply as power that was not to be used."[50] Since the ascetic hero never made a full and voluntary return to the life he had left, his nonreturn, however tarnished it may at first appear, was not, in the final analysis, compromised.

This kind of shift in emphasis—where separation may be emphasized over initiation, or nonreturn be made more complicated—is characteristic of the ascetic heroes of postmedieval literature as well. Although the extraliterary factor in their creation is more often political or social than religious, it is still subject to the same dynamic of audience acceptance.

Since ascetic heroes are created only in certain times and under certain conditions, and since each hero may emphasize one particular phase of his career over another, we are forced to recognize that the abstract category "ascetic hero" is a somewhat volatile one. Its subtly shifting realizations combined with its disappearance altogether for several centuries lend it an air of fragility. Nevertheless, concrete, recognizable heroes, manifestations of the ascetic category, persist in following their controversial quests in Russian literature hundreds of years after the original type has yielded to rather ridiculous and insignificant caricatures in Western literature.[51] The ascetic continues to provide inspiration to authors as dissimilar as Solzhenitsyn and Pasternak, and he thereby gives proof of his ability to maintain and strengthen his sometimes tenuous hold on the Russian literary imagination.

Chapter 2

KIEVAN ASCETICS: RESISTANCE TO THE TYPE

HAGIOGRAPHY AND THE POETICS OF THE ABSTRACT

The ascetic hero appears early in Russian literature, in works dating from the eleventh through the thirteenth centuries. He is not very frequently depicted in this early period, but the works in which he does appear—*The Kievan Crypt Patericon, The Life of Avraamii Smolenskii,* and *The Life of Feodosii Pecherskii*—are arguably among the finest examples of Old Russian literature extant.[1]

Each of these works belongs to the body of Old Russian hagiography.[2] To the best of my knowledge, there are no ascetics to be found in works of Old Russian secular literature. The implications of this are significant. It has already been noted that in analyzing the role of the hero in Kievan literature, Likhachev has claimed that he is "the central object of literary creation," that is, that each and every aspect of the literary work is connected to the way in which the hero is depicted.[3] The question which follows from such an assumption is whether works depicting different types of heroes will, in fact, have different structures. Will religious works be different from secular ones because their heroes are saints? Will the choice of an ascetic hero, for example, also involve the choice of a specific literary structure for the work in which he is portrayed? Put differently, does the uncompleted pattern of separation-initiation-return which distinguishes the ascetic as a religious figure also have literary analogues? How do the theoretical formulations we have already worked out regarding the literature of the ascetic hero find their specific application to works of Kievan literature?

Borrowing again from Likhachev, we can say that most works of Kievan literature treat the hero as a typical representative of his social group rather than as a self-valuable individual. He is a member of a certain feudal class, and his behavior reflects a code of conduct which is called forth by the norms of feudal society, not by literary requirements. Therefore, the depiction of the hero is closely connected to social milieu. And since we have established that the hero's depiction influences the poetics of the literary work, we must also recognize that this aspect, too, is connected to milieu.

Hagiographic literature, however, does not conform entirely to this general plan. As I suggested previously, saintly heroes have a position neither in the secular hierarchy of society nor in the official ecclesiastical structure.[4] "The conventions of their characterizations are different; they are totally dependent on a common body of Christian literature, local as well as translated."[5] In hagiographic literature the bond between the literary work and the specific social milieu from which it arises is comparatively weak.

When we place the origins of the saint's life in the broad Christian tradition rather than in Kievan society, two questions immediately come to mind: how, if at all, is the structure of the Old Russian ascetic work affected by the fact that the work is less contingent on a specifically Russian milieu and to what extent does the work continue to exist in the *Russian* literary tradition even though it is influenced by a transplanted culture? In other words, are the ascetic hero and the work of literature in which he appears alien to Russian culture? Answers to these questions lie in part in the poetics of Kievan hagiography.

The poetics of hagiography is informed both by the broad Christian models from which it evolved and by each individual Old Russian author's world view, which is to say by his understanding of the relationship between the profane world and its sacred counterpart. Thus, hagiographic poetics can be discussed from either the diachronic or the synchronic perspective.

In analyzing the diachronic aspect of the question, one student of the saint's life, the best-represented category of Old Russian hagiography, has traced the genre to dialogues between judges and early Christians on trial for their beliefs.[6] These earliest "lives" are strongly fictitious because their authors, writing from memory or from secondhand accounts, tend to fill in empty spaces in the narrative with details of their own invention. Another practice which promotes the introduction of elements of fiction is an author's tendency to emphasize edifying conduct over real-life behavior. As a result of these factors, lives from the early Christian period are often fairly antibiographical. As the genre evolves, some attempt is made to incorporate more specifically biographical material, but even at the time that the saint's life is passed from Byzantium to Kiev, fictive elements continue to exist side by side with concrete historical material. This commingling of presumed fact and fiction within the work is one of the most salient characteristics of hagiographic literature.

In his study of saints' lives, V. Kliuchevskii discusses the strong fictive element, which he terms "literary." He, however, explains its prevalence as a concession to formal concerns: "It is difficult to find another kind of literary work in which form could be said to dominate content to such an extent, subordinating the latter to its firm, unchanging rules."[7] Likhachev likewise notes the tendency of Old Russian spiritual literature to subordinate concrete information to formal considerations, referring to it as "abstraction." "And so, abstraction creates its own elevated, spiritual double of reality, a world which is maximally 'serious,' a world which is completely subordinated to literary etiquette . . . a sacred world wrapped [okruzhennyi] in reverence."[8]

Regardless of whether the "literary" or "abstract" is explained as a function of the historical development of the genre or in terms of the author's belief in the essential concordance of spiritual values and poetics, it occupies a central position in Old Russian literature in general and in religious genres in particular. This "literary" side of the life invariably works to portray and glorify a divine or sacred order, of which the profane world is merely a pale and flawed reflection. In effect, its presence drives out depictions of the world as it really exists and centers attention on the author's view of the world as it should be.

This normative system,[9] or "ascendancy of the abstract" must certainly have implications for the question of point of view. When discussing "point of view," I do not use the specifically literary meaning of the expression, that is, the relationship of the narrator to his story.

When discussed in these terms, almost all of Kievan literature falls into the category of third person narration. Old Russian literature knows very few instances of first person narration, and hagiography rarely expands its point of view enough to allow for an omniscient narrator, so that very little is likely to emerge from a discussion of the narrator's stance vis-à-vis his text. I therefore talk of point of view with the less technical meaning of "a given person's evaluation of the hero's acts." This person may be the narrator, but he may equally well be the reader or any character in the story, including the hero himself.

In those works of Old Russian literature where the author is under the sway of the abstract, most activities which take place in the profane world are portrayed as relatively unimportant. Only those acts which mirror the sacred world in some way are meaningful. Accordingly, the author judges his protagonist by the standard of how well his behavior conforms to the behavior of an ideal hero—a Church father or a character out of the Scriptures. Since the author is always tied to his unchanging ideal, he is free neither to portray his hero engaging in mundane daily tasks nor to show him developing over time. The hero, however, has the freedom to conform or not to conform to the Old Russian ideal. To the extent that he conforms, his interests converge with the author's. To the extent that he does not, his interests diverge from the author's and he is judged to be a villain. If the hero is informed by the same values as the author, he wins the author's complete and uncritical approval. As a result, there is no real distance between the author and his hero.

The audience, too, often lacks a critical, independent point of view. It is also presumed to share the same ideal as both the author and the hero. The Old Russian reader either approves of the hero and tries to emulate him or disapproves and tries to behave differently. Thus, literature's dependence on an abstract ideal which is shared by author, hero, and audience alike conduces to a situation in which point of view, understood as evaluation of the hero's acts, is uniform and predictable. The only exception to this is said to be the work of literature which depicts a villain, a rarity in hagiography.

Given the presumed identity of interests shared by author, audience, and hero, the only possible variable in the literary work is the ideal itself. Although within the context of hagiography this ideal is clearly a Christian one, Christianity, as has already been indicated, has not been as unified and homogeneous in its doctrines as it is sometimes said to be. Soviet critics in particular often assume that all Old Russian literature reflects the same unified ideal, but the simplicity of this assumption will be seen shortly, when we turn to our analysis of *The Kievan Crypt Patericon*.

A further feature which strikes the reader of Old Russian literature and, most specifically, of Old Russian religious literature is its treatment of time. Again, some explanation of terminology is perhaps in order. Discussions of time in works of postmedieval literature tend to focus on whether time is treated objectively or subjectively. Objective treatments present time as quantifiable and measurable, as something which always passes at the same rate. Subjective treatments recognize time as a dimension which exists only in the human context.[10] Time passes sometimes quickly, sometimes slowly, depending on the perceptions of the hero. Most works of modern literature mix elements of both the objective and the subjective views of time but tend to favor the subjective.

In works of Old Russian literature, however, the author rarely penetrates the inner world of his hero, and so subjective treatment is unlikely. This is not to say that an objective, scientific understanding predominates. Rather, the entire concept of time and its passing is less relevant to most works of Old Russian literature. The Old Russian writer is always aware of the reality of the heavenly order which exists beyond the world of everyday life. When he touches on this abstract reality, he removes himself briefly from earthly reality and consequently from the chronological frame of reference of earthly reality as well. As Likhachev puts it, "abstraction was called forth by efforts to see symbols and signs of the eternal, extra-temporal, spiritual, divine, in everything temporal and mortal, in natural phenomena, in human life and in historical occurrences."[11] Consequently, all day-to-day concerns as well as concrete, temporal information are banished from the work of literature.[12] The more closely the work is related to a religious function, the greater the tendency to escape from time into eternity.[13]

One method which is particularly conducive to lifting the work out of the temporal and into eternity involves focusing on events which recur cyclically, such as the liturgy, holidays, and saints' days. Such events have significance in the heavenly order, and whenever man celebrates them, he establishes contact with the divine and eternal and lifts himself above the world of temporality.[14] The Old Russian writer prefers to concentrate his descriptive skills precisely on such evocations of the eternal as commemoration of the liturgy or holy days and exegesis of readings from the Scriptures. Even those rare events which do unfold in profane time are meaningful only insofar as they serve as figures of other events which belong to sacred history. As Mircea Eliade summarizes it, the mystic and the religious man, like the primitive, live in a "continual present" which is connected through cyclical rites with "Great," or sacred time.[15] They fail to perceive any significance in the concepts "past" or "future." Accordingly, depiction of the passage of time in works of religious or primitive literature is very much weakened.

Literature which minimizes the element of time in favor of timelessness, logically enough, also tends to minimize development of the hero's character in time.[16] In Old Russian hagiography the hero tends to be a static character who retains the same basic features from childhood to old age. Rarely is an attempt made to depict insights or wisdom which he gains over the course of time. In contrast, in many postmedieval works, "[the hero] is a dynamic unity, and therefore neither his name nor the original setting with which he is connected can stop him from changing and developing, even if it be in an unexpected direction."[17] The Old Russian hero, however, is locked into his characterization. The possibility of inner development is ignored when the flow of time itself is ignored.

With the exception of historical literature, most Old Russian works are said to conform fairly narrowly to the poetic formulations outlined above. If they do in fact conform to them, the resulting literature must surely be exceedingly predictable and schematic. Such a system of poetics leaves scant room for artistic variation from one work of literature to another and presupposes the existence for each genre of a strict formulaic pattern into which different names and geographic locations can be inserted at will to distinguish the life of one saint from the life of another.

Fortunately for readers of Old Russian literature, this is somewhat of an exaggeration. Contrary to expectation, certain works of Kievan religious literature are more individualized and dynamic than the foregoing discussion might suggest.[18] It can be said that, to a limited extent at least, their events do unfold in time, and their characters do have different points of view from each other as well as from the author. An argument can even be made for a rudimentary type of character development in some works. It will be my contention that the "liveliness" of these particular works is a result of the fact that they depict the ascetic hero.

MONASTIC APPROACHES TO ASCETICISM:
PRO AND CONTRA

The Kievan Crypt Patericon (referred to hereafter as the KCP)[19] is central to our discussion of the ascetic hero. The KCP, an example of the so-called "genre-ensemble,"[20] is a work composed of many smaller, self-contained units, or *slova*.[21] Some of these *slova* depict the ascetic hero while others do not, so that if we compare the ascetic *slova* with the nonascetic ones, it should be possible to ascertain whether the choice of hero really does influence the poetics of the work.[22]

The KCP is not a unified work of art in the same sense that most modern, or even some Old Russian works are. Like many other examples of the "genre-ensemble," it represents the work of several authors who can be traced to different historical times.[23] As a result, subject matter as well as style may vary greatly from segment to segment. Moreover, a few of the *slova* are totally unsuited to a study of the hero, as they recount matters like the founding of the Kievan Crypt Monastery but do not focus on the founders. Their characterization is too little developed to allow for analysis. In contrast, Nestor's *Life of Feodosii Pecherskii*, which is traditionally considered a component of the KCP, gives an unusually detailed portrait of the hero. In fact, it is so much more complex and well developed than any of the other *slova* that it deserves separate treatment of its own. Discussion of the KCP will, therefore, be restricted to those *slova* which present a moderately detailed portrait of the hero, while analysis of the more complex *Life of Feodosii Pecherskii* will be reserved until later. The relevant *slova*, then, are those attributed to Polikarp as well as to Simon (excluding *slova* dealing with the building of the church) and one *slovo* which has been transplanted from the Chronicle into the KCP, the tale of Isakii.

There are two *slova* which do not treat the lives of monks but which nevertheless provide pertinent background information for the present discussion. They are the letter of Simon to Polikarp and the letter of Polikarp to *Hegumen* Akindin. Each of these works serves as a preface to its author's *slova*, and each sheds some light on his world view.[24]

Simon, bishop of Vladimir and Suzdal' and one-time monk of the Kievan Crypt Monastery, composes his letter as an admonition to Polikarp. He gives a detailed account of Polikarp's personal failings and outlines those qualities which he considers to be requisite to the ideal monk. From his condemnation of Polikarp and praise of others, it is possible to draw certain conclusions regarding his view of the monastic life.

Simon's stated reproach against Polikarp is the latter's ambition and haughtiness. Polikarp has coveted episcopal honors of his own and has criticized his elders in the Kievan Crypt Monastery as well. In a telling passage, however, Simon castigates him for behaving like an ascetic, thereby implying that ascetic behavior is every bit as evil as pride and ambition:

> And as to the fact that you have written to me about the wrong done to you—woe to you: you have damned your soul! I ask you, how do you wish to save yourself? *Even if you are a faster and sober in all things and indigent and never give in to sleep, but cannot tolerate reproof, you will not see salvation.* (p. 480, emphasis mine)

And further, "I have become convinced that you are a lover of rank and are looking for glory from men, not from God."(p. 480) Although Simon has not directly charged Polikarp with being an ascetic, he has accused him of excessive pride and individualism, the hallmarks of the ascetic, and has spoken of this unseemly pride as a logical concomitant to asceticism.[25]

In light of this harsh denigration of ascetic behavior, we can say with a good deal of certainty that Simon is not a representative of the ascetic ideal and that the exemplary tales which he composes for the KCP are unlikely to praise the ascetic way. His emphasis will rather be on communal life and obedience to one's superiors:

> Everything that you do in your cell is of little importance: whether you read the Psalms or sing twelve psalms—none of this can compare with one communal [s"bornyi] "Lord, have mercy!" . . . The Lord Himself said, "My house is called a house of prayer. Wherever," He says, "two or three of you are gathered in my name, I will be among them." If there is a gathering of more than one hundred brethren, you must believe even more that our God is there. (p. 476)

His ideal, as developed in the letter, recalls the earlier-quoted cenobitic admonition that to save one's soul, one must join together with others, and it reflects the monastic ideal prevailing in the Russian Church of his time.[26]

In keeping with the philosophy espoused by proponents of cenobitic monasticism, Simon defines the monk's goal as performing the
tasks allotted to him in a seemly and quiet manner. By doing this,
the monk contributes to the overall welfare of the monastery. The
monastery itself is praiseworthy because it commemorates events
which transpire on the sacred level. For example, the Kievan Crypt
Monastery sends forth its monks to guide the newly converted Russians
in the same way as Christ sends forth His apostles to shepherd His
people. Simon, then, understands the goal of monastic life as the
achievement of "aesthetic" perfection.[27] To achieve this end, each
individual must do his part to help the monastery fulfill its task
and become an icon of the heavenly Jerusalem. When each part of
the monastery functions properly, the greater whole transcends daily
reality and attains heavenly, or eternal, significance.

This emphasis on the transcendence of the heavenly order over
its earthly counterpart inevitably leads to the conception of time
which was described above as being typical of Old Russian religious literature. In other words, daily considerations are important
only insofar as they allow man to comprehend the sacred order.
The day-to-day passage of time is eclipsed and nullified when viewed
against the background of eternity. As Simon says, "One year's abode
in the home of the Mother of God is better than a thousand years
of everyday life. . . ." (p. 484). Thus, he gives voice to his belief
that within the walls of the Kievan Crypt Monastery, time is both
qualitatively and quantitatively different from profane time.

Simon's letter gives us a great deal of insight into his understanding of man and the universe well before we ever come to the
work which it prefaces. It also prepares us in part for Polikarp's
tales. Since Simon takes issue with Polikarp's way of life, it is fair
to assume that Polikarp does not profess the same views as the bishop.
Polikarp, at least at the time of Simon's writing, prefers to follow
his own individual path to salvation. Polikarp's path is one which
is marked by loneliness and hardships. From Simon's description
of this life, we are given to believe that the hardships are those which
are typical of the ascetic.

Polikarp's own letter provides us with a much more subtle
type of information regarding his philosophical and theological views.
It is relatively brief and fails to address the question of the ideal
way of life for a monk. Rather than providing concrete information, it radiates a strong rhetorical element. This rhetorical element

can be felt, for example, when Polikarp explains to *Hegumen* Akindin that he, Akindin, has requested a written account of the deeds of the holy monks of the Kievan Crypt Monastery; presumably Akindin is aware of his own request and needs no reminding.[28] It is also discernable in the fact that Polikarp bothers to write to Akindin at all; since both monks are living in the same monastery, there is no need to communicate by letter. Finally, it is evident from Polikarp's inclusion in his letter of the humility *topos*, a stereotyped protestation of the author's inadequacy and unworthiness. Although this is a common device in much of medieval literature, it is not mandatory, as is witnessed by the fact that Simon does not avail himself of it. Polikarp adds it as a strictly ornamental flourish. Both the content of this letter and its very existence are functions of Polikarp's perception of the need for a formal, literary preface to his work. Therefore, formal considerations play at least as important a role in the composition of his letter as informational ones.

Although Polikarp intends to continue Simon's work by adding to his exemplary tales, he proceeds from the very outset in a much different fashion from his mentor. The rhetorical element in his letter shows his interest in the form his work will take. At the same time, it allows no advance warning of the content or ideas which will presumably be expressed in Polikarp's tales.

This can be explained in one of two ways. First, it is possible that Polikarp is much more conscious of form than is Simon. This applies not only to his views on literature but also to his views on life. As Simon's letter shows, Polikarp seeks glory in the eyes of men, which is to say, in the profane world and ignores the judgment of God, which is made in the sacred world. He thereby betrays a preference for appearance over substance, form over content. Second, it may well be that Polikarp prefers not to lay out his ideas as openly as Simon has done. If his views differ significantly from Simon's, then they are also unlikely to be in strict conformity with the official teachings of the Church, and Polikarp may well be wary of announcing them too loudly. Either or both of these explanations may account for the emphasis in his letter on rhetoric and form over philosophy and content. Regardless of which explanation proves more accurate, Polikarp's interest in form suggests that his contributions to the KCP will be quite different from Simon's. Accordingly, there is a good possibility that they will differ from the prescriptive canons described earlier.

THESIS: MONK POLIKARP AND THE ASCETICS OF THE KIEVAN CRYPT PATERICON

N. Gudzy assures us that the very fact that Polikarp continues the patericon begun by Simon proves that he has taken the bishop's
criticisms to heart and changed his ways, but Polikarp's literary
contributions suggest otherwise.[29] Polikarp's work is "grim and
excessive; full of thaumaturgy and demonology."[30] It gives expression
to an extreme religious message and at the same time generates a
very unexpected poetics.

Eleven *slova* within the KCP are traditionally attributed to
Polikarp. Of these, four depict the ascetic hero, while two more have
heroes with strongly ascetic leanings. One of the more interesting
ascetic heroes created by Polikarp is Nikita *zatvornik*. Nikita asks
to be allowed to live as an anchorite in the monastery caves. At
first *Hegumen* Nikon refuses his request, reminding Nikita of the
misfortunes which befell Isakii, an earlier anchorite. Nikita insists
and is finally allowed to have his way. Soon a demon appears in
the guise of an angel and advises him to avoid prayer and to concentrate on reading books. Nikita gains a reputation for great erudition, but certain monks notice that he confines his knowledge to
the Old Testament and never studies the Gospels. They realize that
he must be possessed by a demon. After they exorcise the demon,
Nikita loses all his learning and can barely be taught to read again.
He leads such a virtuous life that he is made bishop of Novgorod.

If we adopt the expedient of discussing plot structure in terms
of "functions," or "acts which are significant for the course of the
action,"[31] we must conclude that by the standards of the KCP and,
indeed of paterica in general, the plot structure of this tale is rather
complex. The sequence of acts is as follows: the hero takes on a
task which is beyond his abilities; a tempter, posing as a mentor,
leads him astray; his true mentors intervene and displace the tempter;
and the hero takes on a new task which he fulfills admirably.

The tale seems at first to be a condemnation of asceticism. The
proud and willful ascetic is tempted and falls. He is saved only by
the efforts of a community from which he has withdrawn. This
interpretation does not follow logically from the facts of the story,
however. If this tale were a condemnation of asceticism, the new
task which Nikita takes on would have to be very different from
the original one. As far as can be judged from the text, this is not
the case. His new life is very much one of ascetic restraint. Fur-

thermore, his study of the Old Testament points to other, possibly unorthodox leanings which may be the true object of condemnation. Pagan ascetics, it will be remembered, achieved self-mastery in part through learning and culture. The early Christian ascetic rejected learning (often enough he was illiterate) and concentrated instead on mortification of the flesh. It is highly likely that in the early stages of the *slovo*, Nikita is meant to be perceived as an overly confident, aspiring ascetic, whereas later he becomes a true ascetic. Consequently, the condemnation is not of asceticism but of the monk who presumes to become an ascetic before he is ready. The tale of Nikita, then, suggests that the ascetic is a strong and tested man whose way is somehow higher than that of the nonascetic.

Polikarp presents just such a tested ascetic hero in Moisei the Hungarian. Moisei is taken captive by the Poles and is eventually ransomed by a beautiful young Polish widow. She begs him to satisfy her sexually, and he, of course, refuses. He also makes a point of scorning all but the most tattered clothing and of refusing anything beyond bread and water. The young woman offers him great wealth, but Moisei refuses it. When a holy man from Mount Athos secretly confers the tonsure on him, the woman reacts by having all the Orthodox monks driven out of Poland and by ordering Moisei to be tortured and emasculated. Moisei eventually escapes and returns to the Kievan Crypt Monastery, where he advises all those monks who are tormented by sexual passion.

The plot structure of this tale in many ways reverses that of the tale of Nikita. The hero does not embrace a great task but rather has one thrust upon him. A tempter tries to move him from his path, but he is not swayed. His mentor, the monk from Mount Athos, applauds his choice and strengthens him in his resolve. The hero perseveres and is rewarded by retirement from the world.

The difference in structure arises out of the fact that Moisei is a more perfected ascetic than Nikita. Unlike Nikita, he never presumes to seek out a great deed. When he is nevertheless called on to prove his worthiness, he gives the impression of acting primarily out of the desire to move closer to God. He parries suggestions, for example, that he should marry the young widow with the assertion that "a married man is concerned with pleasing his wife, while an unmarried man is concerned with pleasing God" (p. 548). He persistently rejects all those things which would bind him to the material world.

It is of some note that Moisei does not attempt to save his captors' souls—in fact he indirectly brings about their damnation. (The Polish people rise up when their rulers drive the monks out of the country and murder those who oppressed Moisei.) In contrast, several of Simon's tales feature captives who gain salvation by never thinking of themselves but by acting in such a way as to provide the occasion for their captors' conversion to Christianity. It is quite conceivable that Polikarp, by making his hero an ascetic rather than an exemplar of a more caritative type of faith, is reacting against Simon and positing an alternative path to salvation. And Moisei, although perhaps less overtly than Nikita, also is marked by pride. He gladly views his tormentors' damnation as a vindication of his own choice. This reinforces our supposition that pride and asceticism are intertwined one with another and that Polikarp is their champion.

Polikarp's third ascetic tale is the tale of Ioann *zatvornik*. Ioann is a rare and self-assertive exception to the Old Russian rule of the third-person narrator and tells his own story. Polikarp arranges the composition so that Ioann's experiences are unfolded in the form of advice to a younger, weaker brother. Ioann tells of the extreme lengths to which he goes in order to subdue the lusts of the flesh: he fasts, wears heavy chains, and remains in a narrow part of the cave for thirty years. When none of this avails, he buries himself up to his shoulders in the ground but still he cannot quench his passions. Finally, on the night before Easter, he is attacked by a fire-breathing dragon. Ioann prays to God and is vouchsafed a vision of the eternal light. He is told to pray to Moisei for relief from his passions, and from this time on, he is free from temptation and constantly bathed in God's light.

Ioann combines elements of both Nikita and Moisei. Like Nikita he consciously takes on a great task, and like both heroes he is subjected to the wiles of a tempter (in this case, the devil, who first attempts to snare him with passion and then tries to subdue him with pain). His relationship to his mentor has features found in both the other tales. On the one hand, Ioann's mentor, Moisei, strengthens him for the path he has chosen, just as the monk from Mount Athos strengthens Moisei. On the other hand, he comes to Ioann at a moment when the tempter has nearly broken his will, as happens in the tale of Nikita. Ioann's final reward, like Moisei's, is freedom from further temptation.

An important detail is Ioann's experience of the holy light. This is surely meant to be identified with the light which shone forth at

Christ's Transfiguration, and it signifies a direct contact or union with God. It is the only indisputable evidence in the tales being analyzed that the ascetic is indeed searching for a this-worldly reward, for personal contact with the divine.

Polikarp's final ascetic tale, the tale of Fedor and Vasilii, is one of the most interesting in the KCP because it combines elements of many other tales. Fedor gives up his wealth and lives as an anchorite in the Crypt Monastery. The devil interferes by causing him to regret the loss of his money. When Vasilii, one of the most perfect brothers in the monastery, learns of Fedor's worries, he offers him his own wealth. Fedor is chastened and repents of his greed, but the devil tempts him again. This time he adopts the bodily form of Vasilii and convinces Fedor that he should pray for new wealth with which he can do much good for others. Fedor does so and finds a hidden Varangian treasure. He is about to leave the monastery when the real Vasilii comes to him and convinces him to bury the treasure again. In his final assault against Fedor, the devil once again takes Vasilii's form and goes to Prince Mstislav Sviatoslavich. He tells the prince that Fedor is hoarding the Varangian treasure. The greedy prince has both Fedor and the real Vasilii seized and tortured. Both monks die without revealing the location of the treasure, but the prince also dies several days later.

As with the other ascetic tales, the plot is rather complex. The hero takes on a great task. A tempter brings about his downfall, but a mentor puts him back on the right path. The tempter again causes his downfall, and the mentor again saves him. The tempter tempts a fourth, previously uninvolved person, the prince, who takes the hero and his mentor captive. Both the hero and the mentor are killed. The captor dies without repenting.

The tale of Fedor and Vasilii is similar to that of Nikita. Like Nikita the hero falls after attempting a great task and is saved by a mentor. As in certain of Simon's tales, the mentor plays the role of a "true friend" who saves his brother's soul. (It differs from these tales, however, in that it concentrates on the fallen monk rather than on the mentor, or "true friend.") As in the captivity tales, there are both imprisonment and torture. Finally, as in Simon's tales of Erazm and Arefa, the hero despairs immoderately over his loss of wealth but is brought to see that his material loss is a spiritual gain.

One of the first things which strikes the reader about these tales of ascetics is the incredible difficulty that the hero encounters in effecting the separation phase. On the one hand, representatives of his community try to dissuade him from his chosen course. The *hegumen* at first forbids Nikita to go to the caves, and the Polish widow threatens and tortures Moisei in hopes of convincing him to marry her, while his friends support her by quoting him Biblical passages sanctioning marriage. On the other hand, a tempter, one who is certainly not a member of the Christian community, also tries to sway the hero from his path. Nikita, Ioann, and Fedor are all tempted by the devil, who assumes various guises (an angel, a fellow monk, a dragon) in order to lull them into sin or intimidate them. The hero's own weaknesses pose yet another difficulty for him. Ioann must constantly combat his own physical desires, and Fedor continues to mourn the loss of his wealth. As a result, there is difficulty in separating the self from the community as well as in separating the spirit from its material fetters.

This gives rise to a certain amount of confusion—in the Old Russian context, at least—with regard to evaluating the hero's actions. When characters who are meant to be judged positively, like the *hegumen* and Moisei's companions, disapprove of the hero's actions, they are, in effect, taking the same position as a character who is clearly evil, the devil. The hero, for his part, insists on the correctness of his choice, and the author agrees with him. The reader is meant to agree with the author, but we might question whether he always does. The sufferings which each ascetic endures—possession by a devil, castration, nightly attack by a dragon, and torture and murder—are so frightful that even the Old Russian reader must have paused to ask himself whether the hero could not have lived an acceptable life without having recourse to extreme ascetic practices. Polikarp seems to purposely dwell on the horrors of the heroes' privations. Although this concentration on hardship may function to accentuate the importance of the hero's triumph, it is also possible that Polikarp is leaving open the question of whether the Church's ambivalence towards asceticism is shared by the reader.

The difficulty of achieving separation has its effect on the perception of time. Although all of these ascetic tales are grounded in the eternal, and although some of them even highlight moments of communion with the sacred (most specifically, the tale of Ioann with its vision of the holy light), they are, for the most part, much more likely to also give expression to profane time than might be expected. The constraints imposed by the model of hagiographic poetics sketched out above certainly apply to them, but notable exceptions occur in each of them.[32] This is due primarily to the existence in each ascetic *slovo* of a tempter. The tempter offers very mundane enticements to the hero—sexual pleasure, wealth, the esteem of the community—which in no way refer the reader to any elevated events of sacred history (Christ's temptation in the desert, for example). The hero's difficulties are of the same order as those which confront the average man in his daily life. They ground him firmly in reality and form part of a series of events which occur in real, historical time.

Various visions which occur in these tales are also directed away from the heavenly, or sacred, sphere and towards the profane. Sometimes the vision may seem to present a messenger from the heavenly kingdom, but this is merely a subterfuge. The messenger is always the same—the devil. In effect, each vision is really an antivision; rather than directing the reader's attention towards the eternal kingdom of God, it focuses on the evil which constantly plagues the earthbound. Thus, one of the Old Russian writer's most important means of connecting the narrative to the sacred—use of direct visions of the divine—is either much curtailed or diluted in Polikarp's work.

Initiation is not very clearly spelled out in Polikarp's ascetic *slova*. Nikita gives us a hint of what he is searching for when he cries out, "Lord, appear before my very eyes, so that I may be able to see you," but we are not told whether his request is ever granted. No information is given at all regarding either Moisei's or Fedor's initiations. Only Ioann is said to be vouchsafed a vision of "divine light like the sun." This is followed by an actual conversation with God. Seemingly, initiation, if and when it is portrayed, marks a moment of direct contact with the divine.

Although no moment of initiation is supplied for either Moisei or Fedor, each of these heroes, out of all those discussed so far, is able to work miracles. Each is given the ability to command the devil, his former tempter. Moisei drives him out of monks who suffer from physical lust, while Fedor harnesses him to do chores for the monastery. This suggests that the hero has been granted certain divine powers. For each of these ascetic heroes, an implied deification marks initiation as a union with God.

I would not like to suggest that Polikarp is actually aware that his works overemphasize the separation phase and, accordingly, depict profane, historical time to a greater degree than is usual in Old Russian literature. Therefore, I will not explain the weakness of the initiation phase in ascetic *slova* as a conscious attempt to further direct the work away from the atemporality of the sacred order.

Nevertheless, initiation is the moment when the action of the narrative is most closely connected with eternity. When initiation is either underemphasized or only implied, the most obvious opportunity to show the hero's transcendence over the accidental and transient is missed. Although these ascetic *slova* are all products of the medieval world view and are, in essence, tightly bound to the atemporal, Polikarp's peculiar and idiosyncratic realizations of the separation and initiation phases have the *de facto* result of bringing the reader somewhat closer to an "objective" perception of time.

Return, in the literary work, implies coming back to one's starting point. The canonical hero, to be sure, is changed by his new-found knowledge, but he nevertheless comes back to his previous life. For the ascetic hero, separation means moving away from the community and from material desires. Polikarp's ascetics neither return to the communal type of monastic life they once led nor allow their flesh to reclaim its rights. Moisei and Ioann live out their lives in isolation. The many community-oriented tasks which a monk like Feodosii Pecherskii engaged in have no place in their lives. They do advise others as to how to subdue their passions, but their advice is not the product of their own experiences. Rather, they give the afflicted monks a "magic tool," a relic of some sort, and they are immediately cured. This is not the same as communicating the secret knowledge gained at initiation, knowledge which in the Christian ascetic tradition represents a power "not to be used." Both of these heroes keep their knowledge to themselves. Fedor, for his part, dies at the end of his *slovo*. Therefore, he too fails to return. Only Nikita, who becomes a bishop, could be said to be in a position to help others. Whether he does so, thereby completing the separation-initiation-return pattern, is not recorded.

Thus, all of Polikarp's ascetic tales have certain shared features. His heroes, for example, experience neither change nor development. They may gain deeper insight into the truth through their ascetic practices, but they know from the outset that the ascetic way is the only correct one. They come into the narrative forearmed with the knowledge that usually constitutes heroic initiation. These tales are also similar in that their separation phase is always achieved with great difficulty, their initiation phase is rarely depicted, and their return phase is either completely missing or is not alluded to. As a direct result of these peculiarities, the possibility of conflicting points of view arises, and concrete, historical time gains a firm foothold in the narrative.

I will now turn briefly to two of Polikarp's tales which present heroes with ascetic traits but do not consistently focus on these traits. The tale of Prokhor is about a monk who eschews all possessions. He even refuses monastery bread, baking his own from *lebeda*, a bitter grass. During a great famine he gives freely of his bread, and those who receive it from his hands find it sweet and wholesome. Those who steal it, however, find it bitter and unpalatable. Besides baking bread, Prokhor makes salt from ashes during a salt shortage. Prince Sviatoslav steals this salt, but it changes back to ashes. This miracle terrifies the prince, and he repents.

From the point of view of plot, this tale is both quite different from those analyzed thus far and quite simple. The hero takes on a great task. His success in this task is rewarded by the ability to work miraculous transformations. Two examples of miracles are given: sour bread becomes sweet, and ashes become salt.

Prokhor combines ascetic and caritative traits. The ascetic traits predominate earlier in the tale, while the caritative become more pronounced as the tale progresses. This suggests one of two things: either that the ascetic can and should rejoin a community when that community needs him or that even caritative qualities depend on ascetic living. I prefer the second explanation, as it follows more logically from the structure of the story; Prokhor's generous acts are based on his ability to create the necessities of life from dross, and this ability is a reward for a life of restraint.

The second partially ascetic *slovo* features Pimen, a monk who leads an ascetic life more because circumstances force it on him than because he actually wills it himself. He is born sickly and from childhood hopes to receive the tonsure. His parents object to this wish, but a group of unidentified holy monks perform the necessary rituals over him in secret. From this time on Pimen remains ill by his own desire. He prays constantly that his sufferings will continue. When his fellow monks begin to avoid him, he prays that they too will fall ill. After twenty years of suffering, Pimen is miraculously cured in token of his impending death. He bids his brothers farewell and asks pardon for having burdened them for so long with his needs.

This is a tale, like that of Moisei, in which a great task is thrust on the hero and in which he, like Moisei, perseveres in his task. It differs from the tales of most ascetics, however, because there is no tempter. It differs radically from any tale seen so far in that its hero, in a fit of spite, burdens others with his task. Structurally it resembles neither those tales that center on an ascetic nor yet those that present a hero who performs a social service.

Pimen's story is permeated by an extraordinary contempt for the flesh. Other ascetics in the KCP go to great lengths to subdue their bodies, but none pray for them to rot. The overall tone of the tale is reminiscent of the Gnostic dualism which permeates the apocryphal Gospel of Thomas.[33]

The tales of Prokhor and Pimen only partially fit the pattern established by Polikarp's ascetic *slova*. Prokhor's separation is achieved without the disapproval of his fellows which is a characteristic element of most ascetic tales, and he is never faced by a tempter. His ability to perform miracles, indicating that he has acquired some attributes of the divine, does fit into the ascetic mold. He breaks the pattern again, however, by turning to a life of community service, which constitutes a type of return. Pimen, on the other hand, separates with difficulty, as is witnessed by his parents' objections to his chosen way of life as well as by the aversion his fellows feel towards him. He also gains miraculous powers. A type of return is implied, however, by his transformation, however brief, into a healthy man. Return is further evidenced by the fact that he begs his brothers' pardon in an attempt to reintegrate himself into their fellowship.

Prokhor's tale presents the more serious violation of the ascetic pattern. Because so few of the hero's functions are typical of the ascetic, the poetics of the work is also at variance with that of ascetic tales. There is, for example, no disparity in point of view. No one hinders or doubts Prokhor, and the only character who tries to take unfair advantage of him, Prince Sviatoslav, is clearly perceived as an evildoer and is immediately punished. The episodes in which various characters try to benefit from Prokhor's miraculous talents, however, do lend the work a greater sense of realism.

Pimen's tale is closer to the ascetic pattern and, accordingly, shows more of the features common to ascetic tales. Unity of point of view, for example, is infringed on perhaps even more than in any of the more typically ascetic tales. The evil of which Pimen is guilty necessarily influences the reader against him. Although Polikarp means him to be just as much a model hero as the other monks presented in the KCP, he is clearly not.

Polikarp's remaining tales do not touch on ascetics at all. It is curious to note, however, that the heroes of these tales are still the creations of Polikarp's spiritual world. These heroes' powers are exerted to produce an effect in *this* life, as are the ascetics'. Their efforts to control the material world parallel, to a certain extent, those of their ascetic brothers. Their quest for mastery over matter is but a shift in emphasis from the ascetics' quest to free themselves from matter's mastery over them. The juxtaposing of man with matter is central to Polikarp's work.

ANTITHESIS: THE REJECTION OF ASCETICISM

Polikarp's work merits so much of our attention because it so often depicts the ascetic hero. The larger part of Polikarp's *slova* have heroes who either totally or partially fulfill the necessary criteria for inclusion in the ascetic category. Of the two motivations towards the ascetic life—desire to commune with God and apocalyptic expectations—the first seems more applicable to these tales. In two *slova* this desire is explicitly referred to. While the other tales omit such a reference, there is too little of the spirit of repentance which accompanies apocalyptic works to allow us to posit this as the motivating factor.

It is fair to say that, within the Old Russian context, Polikarp's ascetic heroes are morally problematic. Their behavior is too extreme to fit smoothly into the mainstream of Old Russian Christianity; for although the desire to commune with God and to achieve a state of deification is, in and of itself, perfectly acceptable in the Orthodox Church, this desire is most frequently fulfilled through a combination of moderate asceticism, community activity, and participation in the sacraments. Polikarp's ascetics are noticeably weak with regards to community service. In most cases there is no mention of this aspect of monastic life at all. Participation in the sacraments is also uncertain. The monks who choose to immure themselves in the monastery's caves are never present at the liturgy and presumably also dispense with the Eucharist. The only remaining path towards deification, asceticism, is overemphasized: Polikarp's ascetics subject themselves to emasculation and rotting of the flesh, neither of which is encouraged by the Church. At the same time, however, they continue to live within the Church and to profess their orthodoxy. So although Polikarp's monks fail to develop as personalities and are, therefore, schematic and unidimensional characters, they do act as representatives of extreme beliefs within the larger community of the Church and are, therefore, the vehicles for introducing a more multidimensional view of reality.

The fact that asceticism was considered suspect by some Orthodox readers may well be connected with the deep antipathy of the official Church hierarchy of Old Russia to one of the most radically dualist Gnostic systems known to the Middle Ages, Bogomilism. Bogomilism took the Balkans and even Byzantium itself by storm. Its major tenets, as reported by Theophylact, were the following: God was identified as the "Creator of Light," while the demiurge who was responsible for the creation of the material world was referred to as the "Creator of Dark"; the Old Testament was rejected as a product of darkness; and the human or material nature of Christ was disputed, resulting in a denial of the real presence in the Eucharist.[34] The Bulgarian priest Cosmas described, in part, the moral teachings which flowed out of these beliefs. In order to achieve unity with God, material things were to be avoided as much as possible. Baptism, the Eucharist, Confession, and the liturgy were all rejected, as was the clerical hierarchy.[35] The Bogomils were strict ascetics who often eschewed marriage as well as meat and wine.

In a very broad sense, ascetic anchoritic monasticism and various heresies, including Gnosticism, shared a common ideological direction. Both were, generally speaking, biased against the more specifically Jewish-oriented traditions of the Church.[36] In a more specific sense, Orthodox asceticism sometimes bore a suspicious resemblance to Bogomilism. Cosmas, in his *Sermon Against the Heretics*, had accused certain Bulgarian monks of adhering to beliefs which were similar to Bogomil doctrines, and Obolensky has suggested that the geographic proximity of the centers of both Bulgarian anchoritic monasticism and Massalianism, a Gnostic sect related to Bogomilism, may have fostered a certain amount of reciprocal interchange between the two.[37] Certainly, both anchoritic monks and Bogomils shared a common goal, union with God, and both followed an ascetic path in their pursuit of it. They were also linked by a jointly held disregard for the sacraments and the clerical hierarchy of the Church. This is not to say that all orthodox monks were covert heretics or that the resemblances between them and the heretics were much more than superficial; it is also not to ignore the fact that no direct contacts between the Bogomils and Kievan Russia have been proven to exist. I would merely like to suggest that the institutionalized Church, which in earlier times and places had felt misgivings about anchoritic asceticism, became even more suspicious of it in Kievan Russia when it was seen to share certain heretical practices and tendencies.

If we return to Polikarp's ascetics, it is not difficult to find a connection between their perceived moral ambiguity and the Old Russian fear of heresy. Obolensky suggests just such a connection between the tale of Nikita, in which the Old Testament is very much disparaged, and Bogomilism which, like other Gnostic systems, rejected the Jewish components of Christian doctrine.[38] The sweeping rejection of marriage seen in the tale of Moisei may also reflect Bogomil doctrines.[39]

Thus, we can partly explain the difficulty of the separation phase of Polikarp's ascetic tales by virtue of extraliterary factors: the institutionalized Church has frequently had reason to find this type of separation suspect. Therefore, all the forces of an organically religious community have been arrayed against the hero. At the same time, structural factors also come into play. Each ascetic tale features a tempter, who is in fact the devil. His main function within the narrative is to hinder the hero whenever he can. Whether Polikarp is conscious of it or not, he parallels literary and extraliterary elements and thereby sets them equivalent to each other. This has the disturbing effect of equating the motives of the Church with those of the devil. Is this perhaps why he fails to lay out his views of the monastic life in his letter to Akindin?

Regardless of the doctrinal reasons which lead Polikarp's heroes to experience such difficulty with separation, the literary realizations of them—the various delaying tactics engaged in by the tempter—are striking. Descriptions of the devious dealings of the lusty widow in Moisei's tale, to take just one example, serve to present human nature as it really is, not as it should ideally be. Other hindrances to separation, such as Fedor's grief at losing his wealth, also show us what one individual man really feels when he undertakes a great task. Ironically, although Polikarp's heroes aspire to escape the fetters of material existence and become one with the uncreated divinity, the tales in which their aspirations are played out present life in a relatively concrete and realistic manner.

The same cannot be said for the nine *slova* dealing with monks composed by Simon. Each of these *slova* is relatively short and simple in structure and reflects the philosophy developed in Simon's letter. Only in one *slovo*, the tale of Afanasii *zatvornik*, does Simon write about an ascetic. Afanasii dies after a long illness, but his body remains unburied. He is so poor that no one wants to perform the necessary rituals over him. The *hegumen* is reproached in a dream for allowing this to happen, and when he goes to look into the matter, he finds that Afanasii has come back to life. Afanasii's only words to his brothers are a warning to be steadfast in their obedience to the *hegumen*, in their repentance for their sins, and in their prayers to the Virgin and to Antonii and Feodosii. Their most constant wish must be to die in the Kievan Crypt Monastery, for this will guarantee them salvation. Following these words, Afanasii disappears to his cell, where he lives in great poverty for twelve more years. Before his death he calls the brothers and repeats this same message. His remains cure the sick, and the brothers take this as a sign that his strict life has pleased God.

Structurally this tale is quite simple. The hero dies, returns to the same kind of life he led before his death, and dies again. The interpretation of the tale, however, is more complicated. Although it is clear that Afanasii has chosen the ascetic path to salvation, it must be asked whether he reaps the benefits he expects from it. If the ultimate good he strives towards is to be saved in the next life, then his return to an earthly existence can only be seen as a punishment. I would suggest that this tale illustrates Simon's belief that asceticism is not an adequate way of life for a monk. Afanasii's poverty and isolation are such that he is rejected by his fellows; he has, in effect, been placed outside the sacramental life of the Church. He forfeits his right to burial, a ceremony which connects the dead with both their community and their Church, by refusing to involve himself in communal activities during his lifetime. And by losing burial, he also loses the reward he seeks, death, which brings a new and higher life in God. His response to being brought back to life convinces the reader that this is a negative experience: ". . . in the morning the *hegumen* with all the brethren went to the dead man, and they saw him sitting and weeping." (p. 496) It can be concluded that salvation is found through communal life (obedience to the *hegumen* is certainly connected with establishing social order in the monastery) and prayer, not severe ascetic practices.

The only *slovo* of the nine related by Simon which pretends to treat an ascetic greatly downplays the ascetic element. Afanasii's ascetic practices are never actually described since the tale opens with his death. His original separation from both the secular and religious communities as well as his initiation are never referred to. If, however, his death at the beginning of the *slovo* is understood as a second repetition of the separation phase, then the knowledge he gains beyond the grave must constitute a new initiation. His return to life completes the threefold pattern in a very literal realization of the return phase. The purpose of his return is to share the knowledge gained at initiation with his fellows. From this it can be concluded that Simon, dissatisfied with the actual facts of Afanasii's life, with its presumed leanings towards ascetic practices, has chosen to give him a new biography, one which fills the requirements for a good Christian life as Simon understands it. Therefore, even this tale, which ostensibly describes an ascetic, is restructured into a nonascetic one.

One other *slovo* in the KCP, the tale of Isakii the Cave-dweller, should be mentioned. It is the work of neither Simon nor Polikarp but is taken rather from the *Primary Chronicle*. Isakii is sometimes discussed in the context of *iurodstvo*, or folly for Christ's sake, but there is equal justification for placing him among the ascetics.[40]

The tale opens with Isakii's decision to leave his flourishing business and enter the Kievan Crypt Monastery. Under the guidance of Antonii, he adopts the most severe asceticism, clothing himself in a goatskin, taking only small quantities of bread and water, and walling himself into a small cell in the monastery's caves. After passing seven years in this manner, he is approached by two youths who command his worship by proclaiming themselves messengers of Christ. Isakii prostrates himself before them and in so doing falls into a profound state of sin. The youths are devils who have sensed Isakii's weakness—the pride which inevitably results from an isolated, ascetic way of life. For two years Isakii lies as if dead and is finally brought back to life by Feodosii. Although he continues to fast, he remains above ground and lives within the monastic community.

Isakii's tale, like Polikarp's tales of ascetics, begins with a task which is interrupted by a tempter. A mentor, in this case Feodosii, helps the hero to overcome temptation, and the tale ends with Isakii's complete triumph over the tempter. From the structural point of view, this tale is identical with Polikarp's tales of Ioann and Nikita.

Although the tale has the same basic plot structure as Polikarp's tales, the correspondences between this structure and the structure of the heroic pattern are different from those found in Polikarp's *slova*. In Isakii's tale the difficulty of the separation phase is not touched on, while initiation is described in detail: "Suddenly in the cave a light shone forth like the sun's . . . and two beautiful youths with faces shining like the sun approached him and said, 'Isakii, we are angels, and now Christ is coming towards you with His angels'" (p. 608). The catch is, of course, that these youths are really devils. Isakii's initiation is a false one, and he is punished for his presumption.

Isakii's punishment is very like a death sentence. On seeing him, Antonii thinks, "He has probably died," and the community marvels that he neither eats nor drinks for two years. When Isakii returns to life, he is like a babe newly born. He is unable to walk, talk, or eat.

Isakii's two-year trance marks a clear break in the tale. The first half of the tale includes the task and tempter and realizes the ascetic pattern of separation-initiation-nonreturn. The second half, in which Isakii's *iurodstvo* is described, includes the mentor and triumph and has its own heroic pattern which ends in return. The second separation phase corresponds to Isakii's decision to play the fool, a decision which earns him the contempt and scorn of his fellows. The second initiation phase occurs when Isakii realizes that salvation is achieved not through his own efforts but through God's grace. ("You, demon, tempted me while I sat in one place; therefore I will no longer be walled in a cave but will defeat you by God's grace as I walk abroad in the monastery" [p. 610].) This initiation is indeed followed by return. Isakii accepts service in the kitchen and teaches his fellows to respect his way of life by performing miracles which attest to his holiness.[41]

Although the tale of Isakii the Cave-dweller was composed earlier than either Simon's or Polikarp's *slova*, it can be read as a summation and judgment of the possible paths to salvation. The author seems to imply that the ascetic path is too difficult. It entails severe temptations which few can withstand. Work in the community, regardless of how humble, leads more surely to the desired end.

SYNTHESIS: THE MIXED ASCETIC

The eleventh-century *Life of Feodosii Pecherskii* by Nestor can be read as an uneasy synthesis of two opposing views, Polikarp's strident advocacy of asceticism and Simon's rejection of it.[42] The work fails to present as complete a picture of the ascetic as do Polikarp's contributions to the KCP, but its hero nevertheless incorporates some ascetic characteristics.

Much has been made of Feodosii as a representative of the "golden mean" in Russian spiritual life.[43] Although his *Life* bears witness that asceticism is not foreign to him, it also testifies to the fact that it constitutes but one of several currents in his thought. Feodosii is capable of secluding himself in a cave for weeks at a time, but he also devotes much of his time to manual labor and social work and undertakes to move the monks' cells above ground, away from their original site in the caves. His *Life* presents only a partial realization of the ascetic pattern.

The *Life* itself is a very complex and detailed work, and since Feodosii is not a perfect example of the ascetic hero, only a brief outline of it will be given here. Feodosii is a gifted young boy who becomes aware of a calling to the religious life very early. He tries several times to make pilgrimages to the Holy Land and also sets off for various monasteries. Each time Feodosii leaves home, however, his mother follows after him in great anger. She leads him back, beats him, and locks him up. Eventually Feodosii succeeds in making good his escape and finds his way to Antonii and Nikon who are living in caves not far from Kiev. Some time after this, Feodosii's mother discovers him, but he convinces her to become a nun in a nearby women's monastery.

The *Life* goes on to describe many incidents in Feodosii's long life as well as happenings of note in the Crypt Monastery's history. An intriguing picture of Feodosii emerges. On the one hand, the saint spends his nights exposing his naked flesh to mosquitoes and constantly repeating prayers in order to keep himself awake. He drops out of communal life from time to time and secretes himself in the caves. On the other hand, Feodosii dines with the local princes and mixes in their feuds. He chops firewood for the communal dining hall and makes plans for a new stone church. Periods of ascetic rigor alternate with periods of social involvement, charitable works, and almsgiving. Clearly, Feodosii's life *does* incorporate a number of different spiritual currents.

Another character in the *Life*, Varlaam, the survivor of a short but dangerous skirmish between the spiritual and profane worlds, is of particular interest to the present discussion. Although his story is briefly and succinctly told, its structure mirrors that of the much more detail-filled *Life* of which it forms a part. Varlaam is the son of the Kievan prince's most important retainer. He asks to be allowed to live with Antonii, Feodosii, and Nikon in the caves, and Nikon gives him the monastic tonsure. Varlaam engages in the strictest asceticism until his father discovers his whereabouts, dresses him in costly clothes, and leads him back home on horseback. Varlaam rolls off his horse into the mud in order to dirty his clothes, and he refuses to eat the luxurious dinner prepared for him in his father's house. He ignores his wife, who begs him not to abandon his duties towards his family. Eventually his father relents and allows him to return to the monastery. At this point Antonii retires to his cave, Nikon leaves Kiev for Tmutorokan, and Varlaam becomes *hegumen.* He erects a church, the first of the monastery buildings to appear above ground.

The same curious blend of ascetic and nonascetic elements which marks Feodosii's career can be found in Varlaam's. Each hero takes on a great task, but even before the devil is able to work his usual mischief, the hero's family intervenes. Thus, the tempter is replaced by a family member, who, however, urges the same behavior on the hero as the tempter. The hero triumphs, just as he does in ascetic tales which include a tempter, and he is allowed to continue his ascetic life. At this point, however, Varlaam and Feodosii part ways with their ascetic brethren. Their careers are distinguished by "social advancement," which cuts their ascetic lives short through promotion to a position of leadership within the monastery. Each of them must abandon his solitary existence, however reluctantly, and take on responsibility for the larger community. Although the great majority of the events in the remainder of the text could be said to result from this social advancement, the great task interrupts from time to time and tries to reassert itself as the controlling element. It is always overridden by social advancement, however; the hero repeatedly abandons his ascetic life in favor of a life of community service.

From the point of view of plot structure, both the *Life* and the short tale of Varlaam begin in the same way as works which depict the ascetic. Midway through the narrative, however, a shift towards a different type of structure takes place. This same shift can be noticed when an analysis of the heroic pattern is made.

The hero undergoes an extremely trying separation phase. He has such great difficulty in effecting a separation from the secular, profane world that no mention is even made of his struggles to overcome the bonds between spirit and flesh. This difficulty in separation is, as we now know, typical for tales of the Kievan period which depict the ascetic hero. Typical again is the absence of a clearly demarcated initiation phase. The reader is never provided with so much as a hint as to Varlaam's goal. In the case of the *Life* as a whole, it is true, various miracles are attributed to Feodosii, from which we may at least assume that he *has* been initiated and has received certain divine powers. The shift away from a typically ascetic pattern and towards the canonical heroic pattern takes place when the hero returns. He reintegrates himself into the monastic brotherhood and performs various services which benefit all. He thereby affirms the cenobitic belief that a community-oriented life will most surely lead the monk to salvation.

What is interesting is the vacillation between one pattern and the other. At first the hero seems to abandon his original task (although there is never any mention made of a conscious decision on his part to do so), and a new path is chosen. Eventually, however, he seems to conceive a longing for his previous way of life and picks it up again, even if only temporarily.

Two different factors are at work here. First, Nestor is portraying real-life figures who have their own views and opinions. Varlaam and Feodosii really do represent the "golden mean." They mix both ascetic and caritative qualities together in order to achieve a balanced view of the religious life. Since even the canonical Old Russian religious work mirrors reality to a certain limited extent, the *Life* is, in this case, reflecting the actual facts of Varlaam's and Feodosii's lives. This explanation of the hero's vacillation between two paths is quite legitimate, but it rests on assumptions which have more validity for the religious historian than for the literary critic.

Of greater interest is a structural impasse motivated by the previously mentioned fact that Old Russian society viewed the ascetic life with a good deal of suspicion. This suspicion is clearly reflected in works of art which portray the ascetic. We have seen how works featuring ascetics are distinguished by the complexity of their separation phase. A further indication of the uneasy position which asceticism occupied in Kievan Russia is the existence of a kind of competition within a given literary work between two mutually exclusive determinants—the great task and social advancement. Adoption of either one precludes adoption of the other, but the author seems to be caught between the two, unable to make a clear-cut choice between them.

Thus, the short vignette about Varlaam, as indeed the *Life* as a whole, illustrates yet another ramification of the choice of an ascetic hero. If the author is unable to commit himself wholeheartedly to his choice, his work will reflect his indecision. It may be characterized by a pattern in which one sequence of actions will regularly alternate with another, but no resolution of the two will be possible. In this case the work will end on a note of vagueness because important structural differences will not have been resolved.[44]

Hagiography and the Poetics of Resistance

We have looked at two works of Kievan literature and have concluded that both portray ascetic heroes or semi-ascetics. Both works share other important features.[45] The casts of characters are similar. The hero is a saintly ascetic who is contrasted with one or more characters who oppose his way of life. These characters always include people who are God-fearing and well-meaning but misguided (members of the Church hierarchy and parents, for example). They frequently include figures who are truly evil (most often demons). Although it is not uncommon for a work of hagiographic literature to show its hero engaged in some type of battle with the forces of evil, it is rare that a character or characters who are actually good people nevertheless act in a way which hinders the hero. The inclusion of such "misguided" characters, whose points of view are firmly and even judiciously grounded in official Church doctrine, is one distinguishing feature of Kievan literature of the ascetic hero. This structural feature is tied to a peculiarity of the poetics of the work, namely a primitive but nonetheless noticeable break in unanimity of point of view.

The inclusion of "misguided" characters is also tied to another structural feature of the literary work. These characters act in ways which significantly increase the hero's difficulty in separating himself from his community. Were his difficulties exclusively products of the devil's machinations, his course of action would be clear and unambiguous. Since they result, in part, from the interference of well-meaning people, however, the hero must proceed by half measures, remaining outwardly a part of their fellowship while trying secretly to persuade them to accept his choice. Thus, the separation phase is more complex and protracted than is usual in Old Russian literature.

The initiation phase in all these works is very weak. As was previously established, initiation is the phase in works of hagiographic literature with which contact with the divine is most firmly connected. Because works featuring the ascetic hero so often have exaggeratedly complex separation phases, they provide exceptional opportunities for describing real life. Because they have underdeveloped initiation phases, they miss at least one important opportunity to counter the injection of material taken from real life by pointing out the ascendancy of the sacred world over the profane. As a result, time is portrayed in a manner which, although still at variance with modern practice, nevertheless approaches it more closely than might be anticipated.

Return is, by definition, either missing or else weakly expressed. In the case of Feodosii Pecherskii, who is not a pure example of the ascetic hero, there is a return, but there is nevertheless a certain ambivalence about this phase. Feodosii constantly alternates between service to the community and ascetic isolation. In general, if a return phase is included in the work, it is only because the hero is not a consistent ascetic. Furthermore, this return will not provide a convincing sense of closure to the work. The possibility of an alternative career, which would not end in return, is always present.

The factor which unites these two works is not genre. Although the concept of genre is certainly operative in Old Russian literature, and although it can be invoked to provide important information regarding both works, it seems in the present connection to explain very little. It is important only as a gauge by which to measure the degree to which the *Patericon* and the *Life of Feodosii Pecherskii* differ from other hagiographic works. Neither do the philosophical and theological ideas which underlie the works explain their structural peculiarities. Polikarp's contributions to the *Patericon* are informed by a desire to commune with God, while Nestor's *Life* seems to be much less the product of a consistently dualist thought system; it espouses a more moderate philosophy. The controlling factor is the type of hero chosen. The pattern of heroic actions, which is, to be sure, based on certain philosophical and theological assumptions and which can be applied only to a limited number of genres, determines the structure of the literary work.

We can say with some confidence that the ascetic hero is not alien to Russian literature. On the one hand, he appears in the earliest period of Russian literary history in several works which would continue to enjoy many centuries of popularity. On the other hand, we can note the relative abundance of features in the works in question which ground them in social milieu. This moves the works closer to more secular literature, such as historical tales, which are more specifically Russian, and removes them somewhat from the body of religious literature which is shared by all of Orthodox Slavdom and, indeed, by the early Christian Church as a whole.

Yet in another sense, these works are, if not alien, then at least strange. They are meant to be works of hagiography and are unquestionably recognized as such, and yet they fail to meet certain genre expectations. Their structures and poetics are at variance with the canons of hagiography.

We can perhaps gain greater insight into these works through looking at certain ancient narratives which exhibit curiously similar features. In his discussion of Greek and Roman literary chronotopes (a term used to describe "the intrinsic connectedness of temporal and spatial relationships that are artistically expressed in literature"[46]), Mikhail Bakhtin includes the "adventure novel of everyday life," a form which treats time very similarly to Polikarp's ascetic tales. Bakhtin's adventure/everyday time is, as its name implies, of mixed nature. Novels which utilize it depict, on the one hand, a metamorphosis of the hero that "unfolds not so much in a straight line as spasmodically, a line with 'knots' in it, one that therefore constitutes a distinctive type of *temporal perspective.*"[47] There is no gradual evolution in the hero; rather his career progresses as a series of extraordinary moments. On the other hand, this type of novel features descriptions of everyday life, of the world in which the hero's metamorphosis is transacted. The two orders of time interact with each other almost accidentally. "The course of [the hero's] life is uncommon, outside everyday life; one of its stages just happens to be a progression through the everyday sphere."[48]

Bakhtin's "metamorphosis" is very like the ascetic hero's initiation—a radical and sudden change in the hero's status which occurs in a privileged order of time outside the everyday. The major difference between the two is that, for Bakhtin's adventure hero, this special order of time is governed by fate or chance, while for the ascetic, it is governed by sacred, transcendent forces. In either case, however, it is intersected by episodes taken from everyday time, "which is sharply different from cyclical time—cut off from nature and its cycles [and] depicts the seamy side of life—sexuality, violence, thievery, fraud, beatings."[49]

According to Bakhtin, the hero of the everyday adventure novel belongs solely to the privileged order of time. "Everyday life is that lowest sphere of existence from which the hero tries to liberate himself, and with which he will never internally fuse himself."[50] In other words, as long as the hero remains in his metamorphosed state, he will remain apart. Again, we see an analogy with the nonreturn of the ascetic hero. The "adventure novel of everyday time" may well provide a prototype for the treatment of time in Polikarp's ascetic *slova*.

The sense of strangeness about these works can also be attributed to the fact that the ascetic hero remained on the margin of the official religious world which brought literature to Russia. Although Russian culture itself may have been receptive to him, certain segments of the Church continued to look askance at him. His presence in works of literature which were meant to illustrate Church teachings was inevitably perceived as an intrusion.

Just as the Church resisted many of the ascetic's beliefs, so too did the work of literature resist his pattern of behavior. His unusual manner of realizing the phases of the canonical heroic pattern was perceived as foreign and new. The work of literature had to change its own structure in order to accommodate its hero's peculiarities. Boris Tomashevskii describes just such a situation with his statement that "new devices startle [the reader] by their unusualness, especially if they are taken from the repertory of things which have been forbidden up until now."[51] Certain features of asceticism were clearly perceived as verging on "the forbidden," and, therefore, the work of ascetic literature did startle the reader with its use of unexpected devices.

In the Kievan period, the ascetic hero was a new and fresh creation of the literary imagination. He was also, however, a very important creation who could not easily be ignored. Even Simon, who rejected him completely, felt compelled to grapple with his controversial way and voice his objections to it. *The Life of Feodosii Pecherskii*, a work of major importance to the Russian literary tradition, also took the ascetic into account, seemingly accommodating and resisting him at the same time. Thus, Kievan literature never came to a definite consensus regarding the ascetic's literary career. But although many of the most influential thinkers of the day resisted him, the ascetic nevertheless became established as a type, and his popularity spread even beyond Kiev. Few literary works of non-Kievan origin have survived from the early centuries, so it is doubly significant that at least one of them, *The Life of Avraamii Smolenskii*, presents a striking portrait of the ascetic hero. This will be the subject of chapter 3.

Chapter 3

VISIONS OF THE END: *THE LIFE OF AVRAAMII SMOLENSKII*

A LIFE OF RESTRAINT

Thirteenth-century Smolensk provides us with a work of major importance to the tradition of the ascetic hero, Efrem's *Life of Avraamii*.[1] This life supplies the first medieval example of a Russian hero whose adherence to ascetic purification is motivated by eschatological anticipation of the end of the world.

Although some students of Russian apocalypticism trace its roots to the first flowerings of the doctrine of "Moscow, the Third Rome," we have already seen that familiarity with apocalyptic literature considerably predates the sixteenth century. In George Fedotov's assessment, Avraamii Smolenskii himself deserves study as an early teacher of eschatological doctrines.

> Saint Abraham of Smolensk stands apart not only among pre-Mongolian saints in general. . . . But the contents of his teaching, which was for him a personal religious call, is very Russian. . . . His eschatology remains, for all time, an outstanding feature of the Russian religious mind.[2]

Fedotov speculates that Avraamii's familiarity with eschatology may well be traced to his marked preference for the work of another preacher of eschatological doctrines, Ephraim the Syrian.

The Life of Avraamii Smolenskii may certainly be read as a work which testifies to an Old Russian interest in eschatological teachings. More specifically, however, it represents a channeling of these teachings into the confines of what is known as an "apocalyptic movement." An apocalyptic movement has been defined as any movement which "endorses a 'world view' in which supernatural revelation, the heavenly world, and eschatological judgment" play essential parts.[3] As the following brief summary of the Life will reveal, supernatural revelation and eschatological judgment are, in fact, major controlling elements in its narrative.

The author of the Life, Efrem, relates that Avraamii is marked for a great mission even before his birth. While the saint is still in his mother's womb, a holy nun is granted a vision in which she is told to seek out and baptize a newborn infant. When she finds him, she also glimpses a mysterious woman bathed in shining light (the Virgin, perhaps?), who holds out clothing "as white as the whitest snow" for him. The nun awakens and goes to Mariia, the mother of the infant in her vision. Mariia, who already has twelve daughters, tells the nun that she has just felt new life stir in her womb. In time she gives birth to a son, Avraamii. The child is exceedingly virtuous, a fact which Efrem repeatedly mentions, as if in confirmation that he is indeed the one for whom the white clothing was foretold.

Years pass, Avraamii's parents die, and the youth calls to mind the biblical injunction to take up the cross and follow Christ. He gives away all his wealth and begins to lead a life of iurodstvo, or folly for Christ's sake. After a period of wandering, he comes to the Virgin's monastery, receives the tonsure, and gives himself over to thoughts of the Holy Land and Christ's grave. While in the monastery, Avraamii excels in both book learning and rigorous asceticism ("The blessed one's face and body were much wasted, so that his bones and joints could be distinguished. . . ." p. 78). All is as it should be; the hegumen rejoices in Avraamii's virtuous life, and laymen flock to him to hear his exegesis of holy texts.

Suddenly, however, the first note of disharmony is sounded. Avraamii's virtuous way of life has drawn unwelcome attention. The devil, perpetual hater of all that is holy, determines to combat Avraamii's influence over the townspeople. In order to do so, he uses the local clergy. They turn against Avraamii, complaining to the *hegumen* that his beliefs are pernicious. The hegumen orders Avraamii to refrain from teaching and forbids him to say mass. Avraamii, undaunted by the devil's machinations, leaves the Virgin's monastery for the Holy Cross monastery, where he continues to preach. There he also paints two icons; the first portrays the Last Judgment, and the second the heavenly tollhouses, way-stations through which the soul must pass as it ascends towards heaven. Even in his new monastery, however, the priests and hegumen turn against Avraamii. Their antipathy turns into violent hatred, and they incite the crowd against him. He barely manages to escape being murdered.

At this time, a drought falls on Russia, and the people are faced with ruin. Various members of the clergy, fearing that they have wronged Avraamii and angered God, beg his pardon. Avraamii forgives them and prays for rain. God immediately grants his request, and he is vindicated. The bishop declares Avraamii innocent of all wrongdoing and gives him his own monastery, where the saint continues to preach to his followers. The *Life* ends with an elaborate variation on the humility topos by Efrem.

KNOWLEDGE AND CATACLYSM

Avraamii is unquestionably an ascetic hero. Like all ascetics, he renounces worldly goods and physical passion and spends his time in prayer and extreme fasting. In fact, asceticism is so important a component of Avraamii's message that a standard *topos* of most Russian saint's lives is violated in order to accommodate it. Medieval saints' lives almost invariably make mention of the hero's physical strength and beauty, but Efrem breaks this convention and paints his saint quite differently. Avraamii fasts so strictly that he becomes extremely gaunt and wasted.

It is important to note that Avraamii really does stand apart from most Old Russian saintly heroes by virtue of his ascetic life. Aside from Polikarp's monks, no other extreme proponents of the ascetic way can be found among the heroes of the literature extant from the first centuries of Russian Christianity. Just as Simon's heroes are very different from Polikarp's, so too are Feodosii Pecherskii and the princes Boris and Gleb, the heroes of the other surviving early saints' lives, very different from Avraamii Smolenskii.

What causes Avraamii to take up a life of such markedly severe ascetic restraint? Are his reasons similar to those of his ascetic brothers in the KCP? In attempting an answer, we are at first in some difficulty. In the segment of the *Life* which recounts Avraamii's first decision to leave home and dedicate himself to following Christ, motivation is very unclear. On the one hand, Avraamii is said to become a *iurodivyi*, although his period of *iurodstvo* is never described. And, as we have seen from the example of Isakii, *iurodstvo* is sometimes perceived as antithetical to strict asceticism. On the other hand, the growth of Avraamii's reputation as a learned man would seem to suggest that he has abandoned *iurodstvo* at some point, even though a definite decision to change his way of life is never alluded to. For reasons which are not at all clear, the introductory segments of the *Life* fail to supply the reader with any idea of the motives which underlie Avraamii's asceticism.

As the *Life* moves away from its somewhat muddled image of the hero's early achievements, however, a more definite picture begins to emerge. From various details supplied by Efrem, we come to realize that Avraamii is a man obsessed with fate, both the fate of mankind as a whole and that of man as individual.[4] More specifically, he is obsessed with what will happen when the world comes to its prophesied end. Many times we see the saint contemplating manifestations of this end—a river of fire which will destroy the earth, the pain the body will feel when it is torn away from the soul, and the sins of the Russian people which will inevitably bring these sufferings to pass. Particularly indicative is Avraamii's icon of the Last Judgment, which Efrem dwells on at some length.

Avraamii's obvious fascination with questions of final judgment and retribution does much to explain why he becomes an ascetic. Moments of supernatural revelation and intercession, which interrupt the flow of the narrative, help to explain why the reader applauds his decision and sides with him against the clergy of Smolensk. Such moments include the revelation of Avraamii's impending birth as well as a call from on high to a citizen of Smolensk who sets off and saves Avraamii from the raging crowd. So, although unmediated supernatural revelations to Avraamii himself are not recorded, the text nevertheless evidences a combination of eschatological anxiety and knowledge gained through supernatural intervention which points directly towards an apocalyptic movement and allows us to posit belief in a cataclysmic end of the known world order as the extraliterary factor which motivates Avraamii's asceticism.

It is significant that the organized Church objects vehemently to Avraamii's teachings and subjects him to repeated censure. There can be little doubt that the Church's persecution reflects its rejection of the apocalypticism inherent in Avraamii's views. There is never any mention, for example, of a putative concern that Avraamii is acting out of excessive pride, a charge often levied against ascetics in the KCP. Nor is there any implication that Avraamii is seeking personal union with God in the here-and-now. Thus, the acceptability or unacceptability of such union remains moot and can hardly be the cause of controversy. Avraamii's adversaries never suggest that he should spend more time working within the community. This indicates that Avraamii's contemporaries do not particularly prefer Simon's more caritative type of Christianity to asceticism.[5] On the contrary, in fact. Everyone seems to take great pride in the rigor of Avraamii's life. It is unlikely, therefore, that the same kind of objections that were made against Polikarp's ascetics form the essence of the clergy's condemnation of Avraamii.

Rather, the trouble lies with the content of Avraamii's teachings. The first evidence for this is found in Efrem's description of the outbreak of persecution against him. The reader is informed that "some called him a heretic, and others said of him that he read *glubinnyia* books. . . ." (p. 81). Fedotov, one of the few scholars who has devoted serious attention to the *Life*, speculates that these *glubinnyia* books, for which no adequate explanation or translation into either English or Russian presently exists,[6] represent some form of Bogomil literature.[7] Since there is no obvious connection between Avraamii's thought and the teachings of the Bogomils, however, it seems more plausible to posit that they are connected, instead, with the saint's major interest, the Second Coming and the end of the world. In justification of this suggestion, we should note that the populace also accuses Avraamii of physical license and alleges that he has already corrupted their children. It is very unlikely that such charges would be made against a Bogomil, as the Bogomils were strict ascetics who totally eschewed the sexual act. Furthermore, Efrem notes that some members of the crowd call Avraamii a prophet. Traditionally, apocalyptic literature has cloaked itself in the form of a heavenly revelation to a prophet. The crowd's designation as prophet of a man whose major interest is the teaching of the end of the world would seem to indicate that apocalyptic knowledge underlies both the *glubinnyia* books and the Church's condemnation of Avraamii.

If it is indeed Avraamii's teaching of apocalypse that brings about his condemnation by the clergy, we are justified in asking the reasons why. Several possible answers present themselves. First, it should be remembered that the Eastern Church was much later in accepting Revelation, the only canonical biblical apocalypse, than was the Western Church. It is probable that the canonicity of apocalyptic teachings was still somewhat dubious in thirteenth-century Russia, surviving Old Russian manuscripts of apocalypses notwithstanding. Second, although Avraamii never insists that apocalypse is imminent, contenting himself instead with the assurance that it is inevitable, the behavior which results from his belief in apocalyptic inevitability is undesirable from the Church's perspective.[8] In Avraamii's view, the people of Smolensk are facing certain disaster. In such a situation repentance is essential—the noun "repentance" and the verb "to repent" are repeated constantly throughout the *Life*. Little else seems to matter to Avraamii. He does, to be sure, show a great reverence for the celebration of the mass, a sentiment lacking in Polikarp's work, but he exhibits scant regard for the institution which had developed around this sacred rite — the Church. Efrem, for example, allows himself numerous diatribes against Smolensk's priests, and Avraamii presumably shared his sentiments. Efrem subtly develops a feeling in the reader that the Church, rather than promoting mankind's salvation, hinders it by persecuting prophets like Avraamii. It is likely that Avraamii's lack of interest in the Church as an institution, which is a logical extension of apocalyptic doctrines, also alienates Smolensk's clergy from him.

LITERARY RAMIFICATIONS

Although the extraliterary factors which determine the ascetic behavior of the hero of *The Life of Avraamii Smolenskii* are quite different from those which apply to the ascetics of the KCP, the actual plot structure of the *Life* is quite similar in many respects to the structure of Polikarp's ascetic tales. In their broadest outlines, both the *Life* and the tales are built around the following sequence of actions: a hero takes on a great task—to live as a strict ascetic. A tempter, the devil or his surrogate, tries but fails to sway him from his course. Finally, the hero triumphs over the tempter.

This one basic sequence occurs a total of three times in the *Life*. In the first sequence, Avraamii leaves home, strong in his determination to imitate Christ. He begins his new life as a *iurodivyi*, however, and seems to come no closer to his goal. I would suggest that the seeming incompatibility of asceticism and divine folly observed in the tale of Isakii is a real one and that Avraamii is "tempted" away from Christ's path by the less efficacious pursuit of divine folly. He surmounts this temptation by entering a monastery and adopting a life of severe fasting and penitence.

When the sequence recurs, Avraamii's *hegumen* takes on the part of tempter, by urging Avraamii, on pain of being barred from celebrating the liturgy, to cease his teaching. Avraamii triumphs over this temptation by moving to a new monastery. In the third repetition of the sequence, Avraamii is still struggling with the same task—that of becoming a perfect ascetic in the apocalyptic tradition. Here the tempter slot is filled by members of the local clergy. Avraamii's triumph is manifested when he ends the drought and receives his own monastery. We see that although the *Life* is much longer than any of the *Patericon slova* and supplies more details from its hero's career, it shares the same basic plot determinant, a tempter, as Polikarp's ascetic tales. The plot's seemingly greater complexity is strictly illusory; in fact, one simple plot repeats itself over and over again.

Given the presence of a tempter, it comes as no surprise that the hero's separation phase is very difficult. Avraamii is assailed by the devil in all his many guises: he comes as a lewd and beautiful woman, as a terrifying lion, as a fierce warrior. These temptations of the devil represent the passions, desires, and fears over which the ascetic must establish control. In order to triumph, the saint must first vanquish his material self—his lusts, his fears. Separation is further hindered by various social groups. Members of the ecclesiastical hierarchy rise against Avraamii and inflame the masses to do likewise. Here we see the stumbling blocks to separation which are set by the community.

I define initiation in the apocalyptic tradition as the hero's awareness that he is in fact among God's elect. In a certain sense, Avraamii undergoes initiation even before he is born. He is the thirteenth child and only son of a God-fearing couple, whose conception and birth are foretold by a mysterious, unnamed nun. Efrem emphasizes that Avraamii's mother is not infertile, but she *is* incapable of giving birth to a male. She prays constantly for a miracle, a son who will be her true fulfillment. Thus, the birth of Avraamii represents a kind of personal fulfillment for his mother. On a more elevated level, of course, he is born to preach the cosmic fulfillment of apocalypse. The nun's vision indicates that from the moment of his conception, Avraamii has been marked by God.

Avraamii's more obvious and conscious initiation takes place later when he is rescued from the crowd which has turned against him. A certain Luka Prusin hears a voice from on high which warns him that "they are leading my blessed servant to the assembly with two of his servants and are going to torture him" (p. 82). With this statement, God himself explicitly identifies Avraamii as one of His elect. Even after such impressive proofs of Avraamii's election have been given, however, the clergy still harbors doubts. The saint is placed under strict guard, and no one is allowed to see him. A local priest, Lazar', warns that if this persecution persists, a great punishment will fall on Avraamii's oppressors. Several priests do in fact die suddenly and inexplicably. Then a terrible drought falls on Smolensk. Avraamii puts an end to the disaster through his prayers, and all doubt as to his election evaporates. This, his first miracle, confirms the fact that he has been chosen, and therefore, initiated.

The return phase is missing from the *Life* just as it is from the *Patericon*'s tales of ascetics. Far from reintegrating themselves into the masses of the condemned, Avraamii and his followers continue to withdraw from life. Once Avraamii is settled in his own monastery, he increases his asceticism and meditates even more on the separation of the soul from the body which will take place after death.

In *The Life of Avraamii Smolenskii*, we note many of the same infringements on the Old Russian literary canon which mark the KCP. Just as in the *Patericon*, there are a host of difficulties and complications to the hero's spiritual separation both from his community and from his material nature. Just as in the *Patericon*, these complications have a perhaps unintended but nevertheless palpable effect on the poetics of the work. Again, a unified point of view is shattered, and the elevated tone achieved by establishing correspondences between this world and the heavenly kingdom is lowered from time to time by descriptions so concrete as to verge on the naturalistic.

Unified point of view is violated in the same way as in the KCP. One group of characters, which includes Avraamii's *hegumen* and bishop, seeks to hinder Avraamii's separation. These figures belong to the category of positive characters, characters who share the same Christian values as the author. In fact, Efrem takes great pains to assure his reader of their holiness. At the same time, the devil also acts to hinder Avraamii. Thus, the actions of both positive and negative characters converge. Although the author sides with his hero, other holy men, unwittingly to be sure, side with the devil. The reader is left to sort out the resulting ambiguity.

The intermingling of temporal and atemporal elements in the text is also a direct result of the difficulty of separation. On the one hand, Efrem constantly seeks to elevate his text by linking the events of the hero's life to sacred history. Many times biblical passages are cited and subjected to Efrem's exegesis in order to establish a parallel between the actions of his saint and those of renowned sacred heroes. Efrem makes constant reference to the sacraments as well, another technique to connect the profane with the sacred. Visions and voices abound. On the other hand, however, very forceful and vivid descriptions of everyday reality intrude into the narrative. An outstanding example is the scene in which the crowd turns against Avraamii. "Everyone in the city, from the smallest to the largest, came together against him. Some said that he should be imprisoned, some that he should be nailed to the wall and burned, and others that he should be taken through the city and drowned" (p. 80). Nailed to the wall and burned! This is the most graphic suggestion imaginable. It returns us immediately from our sacred heights to mundane, sinful reality. This scene is followed by an even more distressing spectacle. "And so it came to pass that God softened the hearts of the authorities [vlastiteliam], but the *hegumens* and priests, if only they had been able to, would have eaten [Avraamii] alive" (p. 82).[9] We witness an extreme divergence in opinion, where one segment of educated society supports or, at least, tolerates Avraamii while another thirsts for his blood.

Efrem interweaves the temporal and atemporal in more subtle ways as well. In the middle of describing Avraamii's misfortunes, he breaks off to cite similar dark moments in the lives of renowned saints of the early Church. He relates, for example, how those who persecuted John Chrysostom were punished after his death.

And after the blessed one passed away, the prophecy of the holy apostles regarding those who had persecuted the saint and had driven him away was fulfilled, so that death overtook some of the bishops, while purple pustules appeared on the legs of others and began to burst. The leg of another one swelled and began to fester, and when it brushed against his other leg, the contagion spread, and he died in three years time. . . . (p. 86)

This passage, which continues at some length, makes reference to events of divine history and at the same time depicts in graphic, almost grotesque detail a very human, coarse thirst for revenge. While its ostensible purpose is to raise the events of Avraamii's life to the level of sacred significance, it paradoxically functions to connect the two saints' lives in a way which lowers the sacred character of Chrysostom's. The misery which overtakes Chrysostom's persecutors is exactly what Efrem wishes to call down on Avraamii's enemies. Its all too macabre character contrasts markedly with the spirit of peaceful reconciliation which the Gospels enjoin us to seek.

A similar technique seems to be at work in the final segment of the *Life*, Efrem's elaborate protestation of his unworthiness.

> And I call myself a monk, I who cannot even name myself among the least, because the evil deeds I have committed are manifest and terrifying. Therefore I say that during the life of the blessed one I was the least of his followers, I who in everything failed to follow his life, his patience, his humility, his love and prayer, his ways and his customs. I was always drunk and made merry and was distracted by unworthy things; in truth I was idle. (pp. 96, 98)

Efrem goes on to say that he frequented feasts and banquets, that he enjoyed music and dancing and that he favored rich and beautiful clothing. All of Ephrem's frivolous delights and desires are, of course, contrasted with the saintly restraint practiced by Avraamii. Although protestations of humility are a standard *topos* of the saint's life, this particular protestation verges on the grotesque. We can hardly be expected to believe that Efrem was constantly engaged in merrymaking, music, and drinking, and yet his lengthy descriptions of such activities attract us and lead us to dwell on them to a greater extent than is, perhaps, appropriate. We become witnesses, as it were, of Efrem's vision of a world in which "the laws of statics, symmetry, and proportion are no longer valid,"[10] a world familiar to those conversant with apocalyptic revelation. Apocalyptic literature imagines the moment immediately preceding cataclysm as fraught with a terribly heightened contrast between the just and the damned. Presumably Efrem places himself among the damned in order to glorify Avraamii, his example of the just man, through grotesque contrast. The overall effect of this juxtaposing of the sacred and profane, however, is to portray the profane much more convincingly than the sacred and to lend it a stronger attraction.

SEPARATION AND THE POETICS OF RESISTANCE

It is apparent from the foregoing discussion that *The Life of Avraamii Smolenskii* shares many features with Polikarp's tales of ascetic monks. The overall plot structure is the same, as is the ascetic-heroic pattern of separation-initiation-nonreturn. Similar, too, are the mechanisms which lead to a degree of diversity in point of view and an escape from eternal values. This is not to say that either the *Life* or Polikarp's segments of the *Patericon* present the distancing of author from hero or the "realistic" depiction of life which are typical of postmedieval literature. Rather, we must say that in comparison with Simon's work as well as with the two other major lives of the period, those of Feodosii Pecherskii and of Boris and Gleb, the ascetic works often present a greater sense of ambiguity and drama. Although they are written to certain genre patterns, they constantly bump up against the limits of these patterns and in certain instances exceed their limits.

What makes the close similarities between the poetics of these two works astonishing is that their heroes are so very different from each other in their motivations. As we have seen, the ascetic who proceeds from the desire to see God acts in accordance with very different principles from the ascetic who seeks to cleanse himself in preparation for the Second Coming. Therefore, although both share a dualist world view and a conviction that the individual can perfect himself in this life, each comes to these beliefs in his own way.

It seems to me that the deciding factor in the closeness of the two works is the pronounced difficulty in achieving separation which is encountered in them. Although nonreturn defines the ascetic as a discrete type of hero, it has no major ramifications for the poetics of the work. Separation, however, is the phase which can call forth a tempter, who in turn acts in a way which invariably necessitates the introduction of the *realia* of everyday life. It is the introduction of elements of everyday life which ties the works to the social milieu of Old Russia and makes them so lively.

In *The Life of Avraamii Smolenskii*, we once again find justification for Likhachev's suggestion that depiction of the hero determines the shape of a literary work in Old Russia. Assuming that the difficulty of the hero's separation is indeed responsible for the unique plot structure and relative "realism" of the works under discussion, we must recognize that it is precisely because the hero is an ascetic that the separation phase assumes the form that it does.

Since the ascetic stands outside the mainstream tradition of the Church, the degree of difficulty of his separation is increased. What links the *Life* and the KCP, then, is the ascetic hero. The philosophies which underlie the two works—the possibility of the vision of God and the inevitability of the Second Coming—are quite different from each other and do not constitute the determining factor. The genres of both works are also different and cannot account for their structural similarities. [11] Therefore, the structures of the works being considered must in fact be determined by the type of hero depicted.

The Life of Avraamii Smolenskii is the last medieval ascetic work we will look at which is characterized by the immense difficulty of achieving separation. A combination of factors—changes in the cultural and religious life of Old Russia, together with the Old Russian reading public's increasing familiarity with the ascetic ideal as well as its literary manifestations—spells an end to the period of resistance to the ascetic, the first phase of the medieval ascetic-heroic cycle. The next phase of the cycle, the Muscovite period, abounds with examples of ascetic heroes, but these heroes are slightly different from their southern predecessors. A shift in emphasis towards phases of the heroic pattern other than separation begins to become apparent. With changing social conditions come new approaches to old problems, and although the ascetic hero himself remains the same, his chroniclers as well as his audience can be observed making new demands on him.

Chapter 4

ASCETICS OF THE NORTH: STABILIZATION AND DECLINE

EXTRALITERARY CONVERGENCES

We have seen that the ascetic hero makes his debut very early in Russian belletristic history and that his presence in literary works strongly influences their structures. We have likewise seen that the powerful influence exerted by the hero on literary structure in the Kievan period is a result of several factors, literary as well as extraliterary. The ascetic hero continues to be prominently featured in hagiographic works of the post-Kievan period, particularly in the so-called "northern Russian lives." We shall see that in these lives, just as in the lives of the Kievan period, the ascetic hero plays a determining role in the literary work in which he is found. We shall also note that once again both literary and extraliterary factors contribute to this phenomenon.

The fall of Kiev created a definite, if difficult to define, break in Russian cultural history. On the one hand, literary production was affected by the fact that those who would normally be engaged in intellectual pursuits were much occupied instead with questions of day-to-day survival.[1] On the other hand, the continuing decline of political power in Kiev and its eventual resurgence in Moscow brought accompanying shifts in many facets of Russian spiritual life, which in turn exerted an influence on literature in general and hagiography in particular.

As Russians attempted to come to terms with both Tatar incursions and geographical displacement, they inevitably evolved new social forms to fit the circumstances of their changing lives. One manifestation of this was a shift in emphasis within the monastic movement. Whereas early Russian monasteries were located in established urban centers and were predominantly cenobitic,[2] later ones were founded in the "desert" (pustyn'), or wilderness, of northeastern Russia. In the first years after their establishment, they showed many features of anchoritic monasticism.[3]

The change in cultural life has important ramifications for the literature of the ascetic hero. The brief hiatus in literary production in this period accounts for the fact that Kievan works featuring ascetic heroes were no longer perceived as strange and new. They belonged instead to a past whose concerns were no longer clearly understood. They were accepted as part and parcel of the Kievan legacy and were, therefore, venerable and worthy of emulation. The shift from cenobitic to anchoritic monasticism also contributed to a wider acceptance of ascetic heroes. As the ascetic anchorite ceased to be an exception and came to represent a norm of religious life, he encountered fewer objections from his society to the way of life he had chosen. As he pursued salvation through ascetic means, he gained the respect rather than the enmity of most of his fellows.

At the same time objections to the ascetic life were losing currency in Old Russia, new spiritual tendencies which reinforced the dualist world view characteristic of asceticism came to the fore. The late thirteenth, and the fourteenth and fifteenth centuries were marked by an upsurge of apocalyptic fears and expectations. Concurrently the Hesychast school of spirituality gained a foothold in Russia. The Hesychasts believed that direct contacts with God, in the form of visions of divine light or "energies," were possible.[4] Although Simeon the New Theologian and Gregory Palamas, the religious figures most frequently associated with the Greek Hesychast movement, advanced neither dualist nor ascetic views, their followers in Russia did.[5] Most importantly, these two paramount motivations towards the ascetic life—apocalyptic expectations and the desire for the vision of God—tended to converge with one another in these

intensely spiritual centuries. Doctrines which were originally unrelated to each other were more and more frequently found coex-
isting in the minds of religious thinkers. The thirteenth through fifteenth
centuries marked the high point of Old Russian asceticism.

Many different factors were responsible for the upsurge in
apocalyptic fears. In a very general sense, the fall of Kiev to the
Tatars was one of these factors. The carnage and devastation which
followed military defeat were viewed as manifestations of God's
wrath. There was a strong feeling that this was the final period of
destruction which was to precede the establishment of the millennial
kingdom.[6] It is ironic that, although these fears gradually began to
recede as the population accommodated itself to its new circumstances, they reappeared just as Moscow was shaking off Tatar control.
The major impetus for their reemergence was the previously mentioned fact that the calendar used by the Old Russians extended
only to 1492. Since the world was expected to endure for 7,000 years,
and creation was said to have taken place in 5508 B.C.[7] the waning
years of the fifteenth century were fraught with apocalyptic significance.

In the years immediately preceding the fateful, final one, new
factors arose which kept apocalyptic fears current. The heresy of
the Judaizers appeared in the 1470s. Although none of the Judaizers'
own writings have survived, we learn something of their beliefs
from invectives launched against them by their critics. These critics, highly placed members of the institutionalized Church like Iosif
Volotskii and Bishop Stefan of Perm, vehemently protested the
Judaizers' attacks against and rejection of the official Church. It is
clear from this that the Judaizers sought to undermine the established Church wherever possible.[8] A favorite means of doing so was
to show that Christian Scriptures were inaccurate and, therefore,
not divinely inspired. One inaccuracy which they seized upon with
particular glee was the prediction that the world would end in 1492.
When this did not occur, they proclaimed the fallibility of Scriptures.[9] The Church combated this heresy by commissioning a new
translation of the entire Bible.[10] For the first time, previously unknown works such as the Apocalypse of Ezra became available. The
translation of yet another apocalypse contributed in and of itself
to a resurgence of eschatological anxiety. The Apocalypse of Ezra
had a further role to play, however. It was instrumental in formu-
lating and justifying one of the most significant apocalyptic teachings to arise in the entire course of Russian history—the doctrine
of Moscow, the Third Rome.[11]

Many traditions and historical events coalesced in the doctrine of Moscow, the Third Rome. Of seminal importance was the understanding of the significance of Rome itself. The Book of Daniel identified Rome with the fourth beast of the apocalypse, while the Apocalypse of Ezra identified it with the third head of the apocalyptic eagle.[12] There was some uncertainty in the early Church as to just how these identifications were to be interpreted. Was Rome the kingdom of the Antichrist, or was it the kingdom by whose power the Antichrist was held back? Byzantium and Russia, in turn, saw themselves as Rome's heirs but were also unsure as to the meaning of the legacy.[13]

Another basic element in the Russian formulation of Moscow, the Third Rome, was the Byzantine equation, borrowed in a somewhat altered form, of Church and empire. If the Church existed only in conjunction with the empire and Byzantium lost its empire, could it still retain its position as center of the Eastern Church? As D. Strémooukhoff shows, this question was a persistent one for Russian thinkers. When Byzantium did actually fall, three possible answers suggested themselves: either Moscow must free Byzantium and restore its sanctity; or the claims of the Western empire must be recognized; or Russia must now constitute the new empire. The first alternative was given serious consideration for some time, while the second was rejected out of hand. The third position, however, was the one which was finally adopted.[14] The decision to abandon Byzantium while arrogating its prerogatives was made under the influence of such factors as the wave of anti-Greek sentiment which followed Byzantium's acceptance of union with Rome at the Council of Florence-Ferrara and Moscow's growing aspirations to nationhood and rejection of dependence on Byzantium.[15]

Thus, Moscow came to see itself as heir to the traditions of Rome, but its citizens were divided on the question of what this meant. Was the growing Muscovite empire the empire of the Antichrist,[16] or was it the final kingdom which preceded him? Although the first view had obvious eschatological implications, even the more optimistic appraisal had eschatological overtones of its own. If Moscow was the third and final kingdom, then history would come to an end with its fall. The disturbances of the seventeenth century, including the temporary fall of Moscow to the Poles, seemed, when viewed in this light, to be harbingers of total annihilation.[17]

Although various factors led to the rise of apocalyptic fears at various times, it is important that the imminence of the end of the world was a constant and growing possibility in Russian minds after the fall of Kiev to the Tatars. The fate of the doctrine of the vision of God, the other teaching which generated ascetic behavior, is simpler to unravel. Its continued development on Russian soil owed much to courageous monks who transplanted the monastic heritage of Kiev to the frozen wastes of the north. These monks, who lived in complete solitude, developed methods of contemplative prayer which were closely related to the type of prayer practiced by the Hesychasts. When engaged in prayer, they were frequently vouchsafed visions of the uncreated light of the Transfiguration.

N. Nikol'skii speaks of monastic penetrations of the north under the auspices of Novgorod as early as the beginning of the eleventh century,[18] but the true inspiration for most of the "northern" monks was Sergii Radonezhskii. In rejecting what he perceived as the corrupt life of already established monasteries and striking out on his own, Sergii set a precedent which was followed by several generations of monks.[19] In selecting a remote and totally unsettled region in which to live, he took upon himself "a harder task—one necessarily connected with contemplative prayer, [which elevated] spiritual life to a height not yet achieved in Russia."[20]

As Sergii's fame spread, more and more monks abandoned the settled life of the southern monasteries and set out for the north. This led to the establishment of such great centers as the Kirillo-Belozerskii, Solovetskii, and Ferapontov monasteries. The irony in this, however, lies precisely in the fact that they did become "established." Once monks began to flock to these previously unsettled regions, the atmosphere most conducive to contemplative prayer was, from the anchorite's point of view, dispelled. Those monks who were truly in quest of the type of spiritual life experienced by Sergii pushed even farther into the wilderness on their own. If they were successful in their quest, however, their fame invariably spread, and they were once again inundated by waves of disciples. Thus, the ascetic was subjected to a forced reintegration into his community. No matter how often he tried to escape his followers, he was in most cases found out.

Given the way in which the ascetic hero has been defined here, it may seem at first that none of these northern monks could be considered true ascetics. I would argue that there is a major difference between them and imperfectly realized ascetics like Feodosii Pecherskii, however. Feodosii Pecherskii completed the return phase of the heroic pattern because he chose to. Ascetics like Sergii returned because they were forced to by circumstances outside their control, and although they were surrounded by the energetic life of great monastic communities, they resisted the attempts of others to incorporate them into this life and continued to lead solitary and ascetic existences, rather like those of Polikarp's monks, who also lived in large monasteries. There were also those like Nil Sorskii who allowed their fellows a degree of communal living but yet accepted no compromises on the question of their own ascetic solitude.

The medieval tradition of seekers after the vision of God culminated in Nil Sorskii and the Transvolgan elders. Nil was the major Russian exponent of Hesychasm, with its rich traditions of direct contacts with the divine energies. He was also a severe ascetic who spurned any direct involvement in the institutionalized life of the Church. Ironically, however, although Nil's life marked a new high point in asceticism in Old Russia, he was also one of its last representatives. His ideas were not fated to dominate Russian spiritual life and were superseded by those of Iosif Volotskii, the great proponent of social service.[21]

So it is that Russia's golden age of asceticism saw a deepening both of apocalyptic anxiety and of the conviction that direct contact with God was possible in this life. Furthermore, there is evidence that both of these beliefs informed the thinking of some of the foremost religious figures of the times. Nil Sorskii, for example, whose primary concern lay in establishing communion with his creator, first became embroiled in the ecclesiastical controversies which made him famous when he was called on by Iosif Volotskii to give his opinion regarding the prophesied end of the world in 1492. Kirill Belozerskii, a follower of Sergii Radonezhskii, and hence a seeker of divine visions, also contemplated the possibility of apocalypse. A poem discovered in one of his collections of private readings clearly foretold the imminent Second Coming.[22] Thus, judging by the abundance of material connecting Old Russia with apocalyptic thought and Hesychast teachings, we are well within our rights to posit, as do Iu. Lotman and B. Uspenskii, that Old Russian culture rested on a profoundly dualist conception of life.[23]

Now that we have ascertained that conditions are ripe for the creation of ascetic heroes in this period, we must ask whether these heroes are more likely to resemble their Kievan brothers or to differ from them. The fourteenth and fifteenth centuries supply ample material on which to base our discussion. Saints' lives abound.[24]

Some of the best of these are written in an ornamental style known as word weaving, a style which is characterized by the repetition of adjectival epithets. A sense of repetition is also achieved by means of synonyms. Likhachev suggests that the use of synonyms is an essentially dualist technique. In order to create synonyms, the author often has recourse to negating the antonym of the attribute in question. This forces him to think in terms of polar opposites. Likhachev further believes that the stylistic dualism implicit in word weaving is based on the more pervasive philosophical dualism which is characteristic of the age as a whole.[25] It stands to reason that an age which produces numerous saints' lives and which is permeated with a dualism that affects both the form and the content of these lives will be richly endowed with ascetic heroes. This is indeed the case.[26]

LITERARY CONSIDERATIONS AND THE SPLIT CHRONOTOPE

In discussing the similarities and dissimilarities between Kievan and northern lives of ascetics, we must keep in mind that the hero's difficulty in achieving the separation phase is a distinguishing feature of the earlier period. This difficulty leads to the disruption of certain literary canons, as is most clearly evidenced by the depiction of time and the treatment of point of view. Difficulty in achieving separation is much less of a problem in works written in the later period, however. Since the need for ascetic separation is evident to one and all, the community rarely attempts to sway the hero from his choice. Metaphysical difficulties in achieving separation, most frequently realized in the Kievan period as temptations by the devil, are also less common in the later literature.[27] Therefore, although northern ascetics do exert a certain amount of effort in achieving the separation phase of their careers, they are subject to many fewer obstacles than their predecessors. As a result, there is almost no disruption of point of view. Author, reader, hero, and peripheral characters evaluate the action of the narrative in the same way. A further consequence of the lack of obstacles is a difference in the depiction of time. There are fewer episodes taken from daily life which, in the Kievan era, served to divert attention from correspondences between the action of the literary work and the life of the sacred world. The author makes allusions to the sacred sphere, and the force of these allusions remains relatively undiluted by the trivia of daily life.

Although the lives of northern ascetics are less likely to depict the flow of historical time than are Kievan lives, they seem to compensate for this by a greater freedom in depiction of space. Although separation is no longer as difficult for the hero, the need for it is nevertheless more pressing. As Old Russian thinkers became more absorbed in teachings which entailed ascetic behavior, the monastic life became more popular. This led to excesses and corruption within the monastery, and true ascetics were forced to abandon traditional houses of God and strike out on their own. The lives of northern ascetics are filled with journeys into the virgin wilderness as well as visits to remote hermitages. The difficulties encountered by laymen during pilgrimages to holy ascetics also serve to emphasize the vast expanses in which the action of the narrative takes place.

This indicates that a different chronotope is being used to structure the work, one that occupies the middle ground between Bakhtin's "adventure novel of everyday life" and his "adventure novel of ordeal." Adventure time in classical literature fills in the temporal hiatus between two poles of plot movement, the first meeting of a boy and girl and their marriage. This hiatus is marked by adventures which separate the two and serve as obstacles to their attainment of union. Importantly, these adventures are totally unrelated to objectively verifiable, linear time. The characters who pursue them never change or evolve, and chance rather than human initiative steers their course. Large expanses of space are required for the enactment of such adventures. Bakhtin defines this space as "alien," that is, devoid of any specificity.[28]

Northern lives feature a similar simple, nonbiographical concept of time. They also make use of broad expanses of space. The two temporal poles which frame the action, however, are the hero's moment of initiation and his death. Although the ascetic's strong will has brought him to the moment of initiation, and his separation is a consciously willed act, the events which follow separation and make up the essence of the life are outside the hero's control. They constitute a series of hindrances to his continuous experience of initiation in the same way that the adventures of a Greek novel preclude the lovers' happy union.

The space in which events are played out is strongly emphasized, as in the novel of ordeal, but with the difference that the locality is not at all alien. Rather, it is the specific, well-known territory of northern Russia. In this respect the northern lives bear a closer resemblance to the novel of everyday life. This type of novel "fuses the course of an individual's life (at its major turning points) with his actual spatial course or road—that is, his wanderings."[29] According to Bakhtin, the road runs through familiar territory, there is nothing alien or exotic about it. Although the hero's surroundings are those of everyday life, however, the hero himself remains separate from them.

> Everyday life is that lowest sphere of existence from which the hero tries to liberate himself, and with which he will never internally fuse himself. The course of his life is uncommon, outside everyday life; one of its stages just happens to be a progression through the everyday sphere.[30]

Thus, the northern lives differ significantly from earlier lives of ascetics in their chronotope. They are, on the one hand, simpler and more consistent in their use of time—they take place in adventure time, unalloyed with everyday time. They depict, on the other hand, a more concrete, less alien type of space.

Northern lives also differ from Kievan ones in that their initiation phase is developed in detail. This is hardly surprising. Whereas the motivations of the ascetic were suspect in Kievan Rus', a society newly converted to Christianity and extremely sensitive in its proximity to the centers of the Bogomil heresy, they aroused fewer suspicions in a world which was nervously awaiting the end of creation. The ascetic's search for personal perfection was understandable to one and all, and the author's depiction of the moment when this perfection was achieved was an inspiration to those who would also save their souls in the same way. Depiction of the actual moment of initiation ties the life of the hero to the life of the eternal and sacred and, once again, separates it from the life of the Kievan ascetic.

Finally, the return phase of northern lives is different from the nonreturn of Kievan lives. Separation for the northern ascetic is defined by the vast expanse of virgin space into which he escapes. As disciples find him out and build their own cells near his, his space begins to be filled. When the virgin expanse gives way to an established monastery, which has the same worldly needs and requirements as any complex institution, separation is perforce ended and the saint must turn his attention to mundane administrative questions. To be sure, he continues to lead his own intense inner life and is still separated from his community, which constitutes "everyday life," that "lowest sphere of existence . . . with which he will never internally fuse himself," but separation by virtue of spatial distancing is ended.

Thus, we see that the tradition of ascetic saints which begins in Kievan times is continued in the post-Kievan period, but the literature of the northern ascetic is marked more by its focus on space and less by a unique approach to time. In this it foreshadows the literature of another intensely apocalyptic age, the early Soviet period, which also dwells on physical space. Both the separation and the return phases of such works are contingent on the availability of large areas of open and unsettled space.

THE LIFE OF SERGII RADONEZHSKII

The *Life of Sergii Radonezhskii* comes to us in a large number of redactions.[31] Which of these redactions should be assigned to Epifanii Premudryi, the original author of the *Life*, and which to Pakhomii Serb, its later editor, is still much disputed.[32] For the purposes of the present discussion, however, this is not important. What is important is to select a version of the *Life* which has survived in a large enough number of copies to have influenced later literary works and later depictions of the ascetic.[33]

The version of the *Life of Sergii Radonezhskii* which I have chosen to analyze is very tightly and deliberately organized. The principle around which it is built is one of triple repetition. This organizing principle is established very early in the *Life*, when a miraculous prophecy is made—the child Varfolomei,[34] as yet still in his mother's womb, will one day grow up to praise and glorify the Holy Trinity. Devotion to the Trinity is, at this time, still relatively unknown in Russia, and its mention in such a notable context immediately attracts the reader's attention. The triune nature of the Godhead functions as an organizing device for the entire *Life*, an assertion which is borne out by the fact that almost all of the most significant structural elements in the *Life* are repeated three times.

Sergii's close personal relationship to the Trinity is symbolized by his position within his own familial triad—he is the second of three sons. He thus occupies the same position in his family as Christ occupies in the divine Trinity. This underscores the fact that Sergii is born to carry out a salvific mission—the revitalization of Russian monastic life.

It is clear from the prophecy made before his birth that Sergii is among God's chosen, but his status as one of the favored is emphasized still further by thrice-repeated visitations by angels. The first such visitation occurs while Sergii is still young; as he is wandering about the environs of his home, he becomes aware of a stranger who is engaged in prayer. He tells the stranger of his difficulty in learning to read, and the stranger promises to intercede for him with his prayers. The stranger reiterates the earlier-made prophecy regarding the Holy Trinity and becomes invisible, a sure sign that he is an angel. Later, when Sergii has already become both a monk and a priest, one of his companions notes that an angel stands next to him as he offers up the Mass. This second mention serves as a means of informing the reader that what was foretold in the first visitation has indeed come true; Sergii has devoted himself to the Trinity and found favor with God. The third visitation is more abstract in its realization than the other two. When Sergii dies, his fellows gather to look at him one more time. Epifanii says that at this moment his face glows like the faces of the living, but then he corrects himself and declares that he looks more like an angel than a man. I interpret this to mean that the angels who have accompanied Sergii throughout his earthly life have now taken up their abode in him. These three visitations function to reassure the reader, deeply concerned in these troubled times with the question of salvation, that Sergii is indeed one of God's chosen.

The three revelations that Sergii is one of God's favored are balanced by three occasions on which this status is denied. First, one of Sergii's followers questions the saint's motives in forbidding begging and implies that the community will starve if it obeys his injunction. Sergii asks the brethren to wait and see what the new day will bring, and he is vindicated when a cart laden with provisions arrives. Next, a peasant arrives at Sergii's monastery seeking advice from the great saint. He refuses to believe that the indigent man pointed out to him is in fact the renowned saint and reviles him. Later he witnesses a prince humbling himself in front of Sergii and comes in fear and trembling to beg Sergii's pardon. Finally, a Greek bishop journeys to Russia to see the saint who has been so much talked about. He is filled with doubt, however, because he refuses to believe that a man of such holiness could live in a land as savage as Russia. He is struck blind in punishment for his doubt, but Sergii cures him.

Once the nature of Sergii's mission has been established and his status as one of the chosen has been confirmed, the *Life* moves on to describe the moment when Sergii decides to dedicate himself totally to God, which is to say, the moment of separation. When Sergii announces his intention to leave home and find a secluded place in the wilderness, his parents intervene. They remind him that his two brothers are married and that there is no one to look after them in their old age. Sergii willingly agrees to postpone his plans until after their death. In this way Epifanii indicates that separation is not totally free of difficulties.

When Sergii actually does set forth into the wilderness, he is accompanied by his brother Stefan, who has recently been widowed and has taken monastic vows. The reality of life in the wilds is too daunting for Stefan, however, and he returns to his monastery. The impression is given that Sergii too may have to abandon the secluded life of the forest. He perseveres in his course, however, and remains in his lonely hut. Although Stefan's desertion is a second impediment to Sergii's separation, it, like the conditions placed on the saint by his parents, is easily surmounted. Once separation is decided on, there is very little real resistance made to it.

Later in the *Life*, when Sergii is in charge of a flourishing monastery and is practicing asceticism as well as tending to the needs of the brethren, his brother Stefan returns. He sows discord in the community by protesting that he has not been shown the deference due him. Sergii, rather than refuting his brother's claims, secretly leaves the monastery and searches out a deserted place nearby. This incident marks a third challenge to the saint's way of life, but it too is easily overcome. The brethren find him in his refuge and beg him to return. He willingly does so and resumes his usual ways. Thus, token resistance is thrice made to the ascetic's separation by close family members. Epifanii's pattern of triple repetition is retained in his treatment of the separation phase.

On three separate occasions Sergii is granted mystical visions—he sees a radiance brighter than any natural light, he beholds the Mother of God,[35] and he witnesses a flame passing through a chalice. These visions mark moments of initiation. The radiance Sergii observes is surely the light of the Transfiguration, while the flame passing through the chalice is the action of the Holy Spirit. Since Orthodox tradition decrees that the Father can never be seen, the third member of the Trinity is absent. A vision of the Mother of God is substituted instead. These experiences of initiation are consonant with a definition of perfection as being the achievement of the vision of God. They are repeated, as might be expected, exactly three times.

The return phase, which is somewhat ambiguous in the northern lives, is also alluded to three times in the *Life of Sergii Radonezhskii*. On three separate occasions outsiders come to Sergii and require him to take actions which compromise his ascetic isolation. First, a monk-priest arrives to confer the monastic tonsure on him. Given that Sergii's choice of the wilderness as a dwelling place is indicative of his rejection of the monastic standards of his times, this arrival must be viewed as an invasion of his ascetic solitude. Second, when the priest who celebrates mass for the monks dies, the brothers urge Sergii to accept the priesthood. Sergii's bishop, Afanasii, likewise encourages him to be ordained, and he eventually assents. Sergii's ordination compromises his separation because it forges a tie between him and the institutionalized Church, which he has hitherto avoided.[36] The third compromise of Sergii's ascetic isolation occurs when representatives of the Greek patriarch arrive and suggest that Sergii form a community along cenobitic lines. Up until this point, the monastery has functioned as a loosely organized group of anchorite hermits. Once Sergii introduces cenobitic rules, the status of his monastery as a frontier outpost of ascetic living is subtly changed. Although this third compromise seems the most serious, we must remember that it affects the monastery as an institution much more than it affects Sergii, its founder. In his personal life, Sergii remains an ascetic, dedicated to the pursuit of personal perfection.[37]

We have seen that Epifanii constructs his *Life of Sergii Radonezhskii* around the principle of repetition. This is a common structuring device in Old Russian literature, as we have noted in the context of our analysis of the *Life of Avraamii Smolenskii*. Epifanii utilizes repetition in a complex and sophisticated way, however. Efrem, in his *Life of Avraamii Smolenskii*, creates a complete pattern of separation-initiation-nonreturn and then goes on to repeat this pattern several times. Epifanii mixes the three phases with each other without regard for completing one discrete sequential pattern. Return may be touched on before initiation is specified, or two incidences of initiation may occur in close proximity to one another without any other phases intervening between them. Thus, Epifanii is able to utilize a time-honored medieval structuring device and yet create a work which is new and fresh in its narrative strategies.

It is not difficult to determine why Epifanii chooses three as the dominant of his text. Sergii's special devotion to the Trinity is the most obvious explanation. Three is used significantly in various accounts of Christ's life as well. The number is clearly one which is rich in spiritual associations for medieval Christians. The *Life*, of course, reflects spiritual values to a much greater extent than do more secular works of medieval literature. Rich as it is in miracles and wondrous events, it cannot help but lift the reader's attention to the world of sacred history which supplies an ideal model for the profane world. Epifanii is not satisfied with merely providing an edifying content, however. He composes his work in such a way as to make its very structure reflect the triune mystery which is his God.

Epifanii creates a direct linkage between the elements of his hero's career and the events of sacred history. This linkage is rarely broken. In the variant of the *Life* which I have chosen to analyze, one brief break in the chain of carefully forged correspondences between the sacred and the profane worlds occurs when the saint meets a wild bear. The description of Sergii's relationship with the bear occupies the structural slot in a saint's life which is usually reserved for describing temptations by the devil.[38] In this case a short vignette which has strong overtones of folklore is substituted. Although the story of the bear clearly breaks the elevated mood so carefully wrought by Epifanii, it does so very briefly and does not interfere with the completion of any of the significant stages of the hero's career.

There are other incidents which "lower" the elevated tone of the work, such as Stefan's moment of dissent and the peasant's abuse of Sergii. None of these episodes seriously affects the relationship established between events in the sacred and profane spheres, however. In all cases the deeds of the evildoers are clearly recognized as evil, and the entire community bands together to repudiate them and to reforge the link with the heavenly kingdom. Within the context of the poetics of ascetic literature, the *Life of Sergii Radonezhskii* differs from the lives of Kievan saints. It consistently maintains an aura of timelessness and achieves a definite unanimity of point of view.

Predictably enough, the *Life* also differs from the lives of Kievan ascetics in its treatment of space. In Kievan works dealing with the ascetic hero, space is enclosed. The monks of the Kievan Crypt Monastery live either in the cells built by Feodosii and his successors or in the caves dug by the first ascetics. Avraamii Smolenskii moves from one monastery to another, but his *Life* gives no strong sense of the natural setting of any of them. Because the process of separation is so difficult in these works, more attention is lavished on descriptions of the saint's struggles than on the what or the where of his actual achievement. This is definitely not the case with the *Life of Sergii Radonezhskii*. Concrete descriptions of the monks' huts, their cultivated fields, and especially the forest surrounding the monastery abound. Space is even seen as changeable; its characteristics can be altered over the course of time. An area which is forested today is cultivated tomorrow; an expanse of uninhabited waste yields to a flourishing village. In the northern lives, the setting in which the saint performs his deeds becomes much more important.

The *Life of Sergii Radonezhskii* is full of accounts of the miracles performed by its hero. Most of these miracles involve situations which can only occur in the context of the vast expanses which are described in the *Life*. A child dies in the midst of a journey to Sergii's monastery, for instance, and Sergii brings it back to life, assuring its father that it was never dead at all; it was merely frozen from the rigors of the journey. Or, the brothers complain to Sergii that he has chosen a bad site for his monastery; it is located far from a source of fresh water. Sergii apologizes for his oversight and creates a spring near the brothers' cells by praying over a pool of standing water. We have noted before that the hero's ability to work miracles is a sign that he has won favor with God and that he has acquired certain of God's attributes. This being the case, we can say that one of the most important of God's powers must be the ability to overcome space. Sergii first triumphs over space when he penetrates the wilderness in order to build a hut, and he continues to show his power over it by performing miracles which abolish the resistance that it offers to others.

Finally, the *Life* mentions many journeys to distant hermitages and monasteries. Sergii frequently leaves his monastery in order to dedicate churches which have been built in the wilds. Other characters undertake similar journeys: Prince Dmitrii travels to the Tatar horde; and Stefan of Perm passes by the monastery on his way to Moscow. By describing such journeys, which are invariably successful, Epifanii emphasizes that the characters who undertake them stand apart from the usual order of mankind; they are able to overcome the power of nature.[39]

If we ask the question that we posed in previous chapters—whether the literature of the ascetic hero has a place in the Russian cultural tradition—we must again give the same answer—that it does. Literature of the Kievan period finds its place in the tradition because it is dependent on the social milieu out of which it springs. The *Life of Sergii Radonezhskii* is also at home in the Russian tradition because of its connection to milieu. In this case, however, milieu is something slightly different. It must be construed in a physical sense, as the harsh forces of nature which shape the Russian view of the world. The most salient feature of Russian nature—the abundance, indeed the superabundance, of space—is given extensive treatment in the *Life*. It is one of Epifanii's most important themes.

A hypothesis can be made on the basis of the conclusions just reached. The literature of the ascetic hero, be it Kievan or "northern," is defined by its characteristic pattern of heroic nonreturn. The separation phase, however, is the phase which determines the more specific poetics of the work. In Kievan lives, the *difficulty* of separation affects the way in which time is depicted. In northern lives, the intense *need* for separation dictates a emphasis on the depiction of space. Those lives which concentrate on the temporal dimension, unexpectedly depicting time in its historical flow, fail to develop the spatial dimension, while those which concentrate on space are very conventional in their treatment of time. It seems that no single life of an ascetic hero can combine innovative approaches to both time and space.

The way in which a given work approaches time and space is very important because the relationship of these two dimensions creates movement in literature. Likhachev formulates this in the following way:

> . . . space in literary art is directly linked to artistic time. It is dynamic. It creates the milieu in which movement takes place, and it itself changes and moves. This movement (in movement space and time are united) may be easy or difficult, rapid or slow, it may be connected with a well-known resistance of the milieu and with cause-effect relationships.[40]

In a work like the *Life of Avraamii Smolenskii*, where the depiction of the passing of time sometimes approximates what we understand in modern literature as "passing," movement is inhibited because we have no sense of the milieu in which time unfolds. In a work like the *Life of Sergii Radonezhskii,* where physical milieu is described in detail, movement is inhibited because we have no sense of the temporal framework in which events unfold. This is not to say that there is no literary movement in works featuring the ascetic hero, but rather that movement in such works is severely circumscribed.

A circumscribed sense of movement in a work is a purely literary phenomenon, but its underlying causes are a function of religious perceptions. Eras in which asceticism is viewed with suspicion seem to generate works with an underdeveloped spatial dimension, while eras in which asceticism is admired produce works which are deficient in the temporal realm. As we must reiterate, lives of ascetics are characterized by a tight interdependency of literary and religious factors.

THE LIFE OF KIRILL BELOZERSKII

We shall test our hypothesis regarding time and space by turning to another well-known work, the *Life of Kirill Belozerskii.*[41] This life, which was written shortly after the *Life of Sergii Radonezhskii,* is generally regarded as the most artistically developed original work composed by Pakhomii Serb. It nevertheless suffers from numerous aesthetic flaws, chief among which is an overemphasis on the description of miracles worked by the saint. Over one-half of the *Life* is dedicated to recounting healings and exorcisms. Since these miracles are, for the most part, uninspired repetitions of one or two identical story plots, I propose to exclude them from my analysis of the *Life.*

The *Life of Kirill Belozerskii* represents a fairly straightforward account of biographical facts. It describes how Kirill is orphaned and left in the care of an influential relative who opposes his desire for the contemplative life of the monastery. It tells further of how Kirill disobeys his guardian and receives the tonsure, of how he enters the Simonov monastery, and of how he learns the discipline of strict obedience from Mikhail, his mentor. The saint is sent to work in the monastery's kitchen, a seemingly mundane and irksome assignment. In the kitchen, however, he begins to meditate on the fire in the oven and comes to realize that it presages the eternal fire of damnation. He braces himself to endure the kitchen fire so that he may escape the more terrible fire to come. At this time he becomes acquainted with Sergii Radonezhskii and enjoys his special favor.

Kirill throws off the yoke of discipline for a brief time and gives himself over to divine folly. He is placed on a strict fast in punishment for his foolishness but rejoices that he now fasts on someone else's command and not from his own proud desire. When his *hegumen* realizes the saintly motives behind Kirill's behavior, he releases him from kitchen duty and sends him to copy manuscripts.

Eventually the *hegumen* is promoted to the position of archbishop of Rostov, and Kirill becomes *hegumen* in his stead. He finds the position cumbersome, however, and gives it up in order to devote himself to solitary asceticism. The man who replaces him as head of the monastery envies his reputation for holiness and erudition and intrigues against him. Kirill leaves Simonov and moves briefly to another monastery. There he is granted a vision in which the Mother of God instructs him to set out for the North. He is shown the site where he must settle and witnesses a brilliant burst of light.

Kirill sets off with a fellow monk, Ferapont, finds the place indicated in his vision, and builds a cell. Very early on, he and Ferapont begin to disagree on how their new life is to be organized, and Ferapont leaves. Kirill remains alone to build a chapel to the Mother of God. In due time others come to share his lonely life, and a community is formed. Several attacks are made on the new monastery by nearby boyars and peasants, but the monks are saved by the Virgin's intercession. As Kirill's fame spreads and the monastery grows, the need for formal organization becomes evident. Kirill establishes very severe rules governing every aspect of the monks' lives. In his strong emphasis on discipline and nonpossession, he remains true to his early training at Simonov. The *Life* ends, as has been mentioned, with an elaborate recounting of the many miracles worked by and associated with Kirill.

It is clear even from this brief summary of the *Life of Kirill Belozerskii* that Pakhomii's work is distinguished by little of the sophistication which characterizes Epifanii's *Life of Sergii Radonezhskii*. Nevertheless, there are important similarities between the two works. Both depict a hero who only truly achieves separation when he sets off for the wilderness, and both show how this separation is compromised when the wilderness is settled by the hero's disciples.

Kirill first attempts to separate himself from his community when he asks his guardian's leave to enter a monastery. Although the guardian protests Kirill's decision, he eventually accedes to it. Once the hero enters the monastery, separation proceeds smoothly.

A mentor teaches him the ways of ascetic restraint, and he masters them joyfully.

Initiation is heralded by a sign that Kirill has been chosen by God. Sergii Radonezhskii arrives at Kirill's monastery in order to confer with the *hegumen*, but he is discovered, to the surprise of one and all, in deep conversation with Kirill instead. Pakhomii portrays Sergii as one whose holiness is unquestioned. He is a vessel of divine grace and blessings. By singling out Kirill for special attention, Sergii indicates that God's particular favor rests on the young monk.

Immediately after this revelation of divine favor, Kirill undergoes his first initiation. He suffers the heat of the kitchen fire in order to preserve himself from the eternal fire to come. This scene is not sketched out in detail. It seems possible, however, that the episode with fire is meant as an allusion to the approaching apocalypse. Fire is the destructive force which Russian apocalyptic thinkers dwell on in greatest depth, and the idea that present suffering will win the believer recognition as one of the chosen is also central to apocalyptic thought. Significantly, Kirill's experience of the fire is coupled with the assertion that he is particularly assiduous in his ascetic restraint at this time. Thus, it is possible that Kirill undergoes initiation as a believer in the imminence of apocalypse.

Kirill's separation comes to an end, however, when he becomes *hegumen* of the monastery. Although Pakhomii omits concrete descriptions of Kirill's duties and thus preserves the elevated tone of his work, he nevertheless indicates that they are hindrances to the saint's pursuit of salvation. Kirill steps down from his high office, but the life he seeks still evades him. He has been reintegrated into the life of the Church against his will.

True ascetic that he is, Kirill resists the snares and entanglements of daily life. Rather than submitting to the distractions which plague him, he prays to the Mother of God to show him a new path. In his prayers he, therefore, already contemplates a second separation. This second separation is granted to him in his vision of the Virgin. The Mother of God urges separation on him in a most concrete way ("Kirill, set forth from here and go to the White Lake. There I have prepared a place for you where you will be able to find salvation." pp. 14–5).

The announcement of a second separation is conflated with a second initiation. After the Virgin shows Kirill her special favor, a dazzling light appears to him. It fills him with great joy, but at the same time it indicates the site of his future monastery. The eminently practical function of locating the new monastery shifts Kirill's attention away from his daily cares and ties his vision of light to the new separation phase, while the more elevated function of renewing the wearied saint belongs to initiation.

We note that the second initiation is very different from the first. The first initiation, it will be remembered, is an apocalyptic one. The second has none of the anguish and repentance characteristic of eschatological experiences. It is inspiring and uplifting and symbolized by light. This indicates that, although Kirill has retained an ascetic way of life, he is now moved by a new quest—the pursuit of the vision of God. In the *Life of Kirill Belozerskii*, we have a perfect opportunity to observe that the ascetic life remains the same regardless of the spiritual tradition which motivates it. Kirill's way of life is consistent and unchanging. In fact, the one theme that ties the disparate threads of the *Life* together is the hero's strict adherence to ascetic principles. Kirill's faithfulness to ascetic forms replaces Epifanii's elaborate system of formal repetition as the unifying force in the work. The urge to asceticism must be very strong indeed if it is capable of reconciling the hero's apocalyptic fears with his quest for the vision of God.

Regardless of the factors which motivate the hero's second separation and initiation, the second return phase is very like the first: it is only a partial return and it is enacted against the hero's will. Like Sergii Radonezhskii, Kirill establishes himself in the wilderness and dispenses with the help of his fellow monk, Ferapont. In this way he signifies his intention to live in complete isolation. His disciples soon find him, however, and decide to settle nearby. As more and more monks arrive, Kirill loses the solitude he has so ardently sought. Once again the ascetic's space becomes peopled, and this imperils his separation.

Pakhomii's *Life* is marked by the same preoccupation with space as Epifanii's. In fact, Pakhomii emphasizes the spatial dimension even more strongly than does Epifanii. He recognizes that Kirill's first initiation is inadequate to his spiritual needs and grants him a second one. This second initiation is achieved only by overcoming the rigors of nature. Pakhomii thus implies that Kirill's ultimate reward comes to him because nature exercises no power over him. The importance of space is also underscored by the violence of the attacks which Kirill's neighbors make on the monastery. They perceive the monastery as a direct threat to their livelihood because more and more of the land available for cultivation is donated to the monastery by wealthy patrons. On several occasions they try to burn down the settlement and drive the monks away. At the heart of the dispute between the monastery and its neighbors lies the issue of who will master the land and what form this mastery will take. Will the ultimate victor be Kirill, for whom nature is a transparent, nonresisting medium, or the boyars, for whom nature can be overcome only by exerting great physical effort?

It is fair to say that the *Life* is informed more by the hero's need to remove himself physically from others than by his need to justify his way of life, which is to say, that it is more strongly colored by depiction of the spatial dimension than by depiction of the temporal. The one possible exception to this generalization is the section of the work in which Pakhomii introduces the theme of land disputes. The tension between the monastic and secular estates is a sociohistorical phenomenon which, incorporated into the *Life*, threatens to disrupt its elevated, spiritual tone and underscore the role of historical time. Although the topicality of the disputes cannot be denied, it must be argued that they do not impinge on the overarching correspondences between the action of the narrative and the life of the sacred sphere. In Kievan lives, the acts of characters like Feodosii's mother and Avraamii's *hegumen* are understandable and perhaps even pardonable. They are motivated by natural human desires and emotions rather than by greed. In the *Life of Kirill Belozerskii*, however, this is not the case. Those acts which most disrupt the harmony of the order created in the work are truly sinful, and their evilness is recognized by the reader and the author as well as by the other characters. The doers of these evil deeds are, in fact, villains, whose depiction always differs from the canonical representation of Old Russian heroes.[42] Their acts represent not so much a disruption of the tone of the work as an opportunity to show how God intervenes in the affairs of men. After each attack on the monastery, the man responsible for it comes to Kirill and begs his pardon. The man always becomes a model Christian and serves the monastery loyally for the rest of his life. Thus, although these acts seem at first to negate the elevated tone of the *Life*, they in fact lead to its confirmation.

THE LIFE OF ULIANIIA OSOR'INA

A final, late-blooming realization of the northern ascetic type occurs in the *Life of Ulianiia Osor'ina*.[43] This *Life* retains elements of the lives of ascetics and yet betrays signs of an entirely different genre—the family chronicle.[44]

Ulianiia is quite clearly not a typical ascetic hero. First of all, she is a woman.[45] Second, she is a wife and mother and is responsible for running a large and well-to-do household. Finally, she never enters a monastery, although she would very much like to. This having been said, however, it is also possible to note certain aspects of Ulianiia's career which have definite ascetic overtones. Although she accepts her duties as wife and mother, Ulianiia secretly longs for a different life. She asks her husband to allow her to enter a monastery, and when he refuses, she persuades him to give up sexual relations. In this way she fulfills one criterion of ascetic separation—abstention from the sexual act. Although she is mistress of a wealthy household, she constantly fasts. She accepts food from her mother-in-law but gives it away to the poor. Thus, she also meets the ascetic requirements of fasting and voluntary poverty. In spite of the fact that Ulianiia lives in the world, she separates herself from it as best she can. In this connection it is interesting to note that Ulianiia, like other ascetics before her, has a distaste for formalized, ecclesiastical ritual. Although the author excuses her failure to regularly attend church services in a variety of ways, he nevertheless underscores it by mentioning that the Virgin herself appears to a priest and urges him to encourage Ulianiia to worship in church.

Just as Ulianiia undergoes a kind of separation-without-separating, so too does she achieve a type of initiation which is not an initiation in the strictest sense. Ulianiia is twice beset by demons, once when she is asleep and once when she is praying in church. Both times Nicholas the miracle worker, the saint to whom she is particularly devoted, appears to her and chases away the demons. The vision of St. Nicholas, which comes to Ulianiia just when she has shown herself to be more powerful than the devil, may be said to substitute for the vision of God, which comes to other ascetics at similar points in their careers. Ulianiia is also discovered to have the ability to work miracles. Like Prokhor, Polikarp's transformer of dross into epicurean delights, Ulianiia bakes bread from bitter grasses during a famine, and the bread is sweet and delicious. This shows that she has been singled out for God's special favor. Such a manifestation of divine choice during a time of general misery and suffering may represent a distant echo of apocalyptic themes.

The final phase of the ascetic-heroic pattern is the most difficult to apply to Ulianiia. Since she never really separates, there is little logic in speaking of a return. To the extent that she does enact a limited type of separation, however, she also enacts a limited return. On her deathbed Ulianiia calls for her loved ones and instructs them in the moral precepts which have guided her life. She also requests a priest and receives the last rites. She thereby makes her peace with the Church and returns to the mainstream of the religious community.

We see from this that Ulianiia's status as an ascetic is questionable. Although her behavior is ascetic, she fails to conform narrowly to the ascetic-heroic pattern defined earlier in this study. Moreover, her motivations towards the ascetic life are unclear. These difficulties undoubtedly arise from several causes: a growing shift away from solitary contemplation and towards ritual observance; a tendency for lives to incorporate material taken from folk genres; a perception of the need to jettison time-honored but predictable and worn devices in order to achieve new artistic value.

Just as the heroic pattern of the *Life of Ulianiia Osor'ina* corresponds in some respects to the lives of ascetic saints but differs in others, so too does its depiction of space, a point of particular interest in post-Kievan lives, bear a certain, if not full, resemblance to what we have seen in the lives of Sergii Radonezhskii and Kirill Belozerskii. The major turning points in Ulianiia's life are marked by journeys—her own or others'. When she is orphaned, she moves to her grandmother's village. When she marries, she moves to her husband's lands. She conceives the desire to enter a monastery while her husband is away on one of his frequent and protracted trips to Astrakhan, and she is admonished for her failure to attend church even though the cold is so severe that the ground cracks, an indication that, even at the age of sixty, Ulianiia can be expected to face the rigors of nature without suffering from them. From all of this, it is clear that Ulianiia is able to move across the expanses of nature at need and that nature has no power over her. Although the ability to overcome space is common to all northern ascetics, however, in the *Life of Ulianiia Osor'ina*, its logical connection to the course of the narrative is severed. Ulianiia's immunity to the constraints of space has nothing to do with her pressing need to separate from society. All her trips have as their goal well-known, previously settled areas, and none of them has any specific connection with either solitary contemplation or the vision of God.

We can conclude that certain broad principles of structuring and poetics, which are first formulated to describe the ascetic hero, continue to resound in the *Life of Ulianiia Osor'ina*. These principles are divorced from their philosophical and theological underpinnings, however, and are retained strictly out of loyalty to canonized forms. Unmotivated as these structures and devices are, they are unlikely to resonate in literature for long. They do, of course, persist in strictly religious works, but such nonliterary realizations of the ascetic are of no direct interest to this particular study.

THE DECLINE OF THE TYPE

Sergii Radonezhskii is the spiritual father of many famous anchorites and the initiator of a new wave of asceticism in Russian religious life, and it would be reasonable to assume that his *Life*, together with that of Kirill Belozerskii, should mark the beginning of a long and rich line of lives of northern ascetics, lives structurally similar to Sergii's. This, however, is not so. Although Sergii's example continues to inform the writings of religious thinkers, it generates no new saints' lives of outstanding literary merit. The *Life of Ulianiia Osor'ina* borrows certain ascetic structures but leaves them only ambiguously connected to doctrine. Why then does the ascetic become a figure of primarily religious interest, and what is the fate of the literature which portrays him?

In answering this, we must take into account, as we have done several times before, the close relationship between literature and religious thought. Subtle changes occur in the religious life of Russia at the time of the debates between Iosif Volotskii and Nil Sorskii. These changes affect the entire life of the nation and, of necessity, influence literature as well.

We know very few of the biographical facts of Nil Sorskii's life. His *Life* seems to have been lost soon after it was written. What we do know, however, is that he rejects the cenobitic way of life which has replaced northern anchoritism and leaves Kirill's monastery. After visiting Byzantium, he returns to Russia and strikes out on his own into the wilderness. His fame eventually spreads, and followers settle near him. Although he concerns himself with the practical questions of bringing some type of order to his small community, he nevertheless manages to maintain the integrity of the ascetic way.[46]

Nil stands in the spiritual tradition of Sergii Radonezhskii and Kirill Belozerskii. The main events of his career recapitulate similar events in the careers of his two great predecessors. Nil's name is closely associated with Russian Hesychasm, a medieval blossoming of the quest for personal contact with God. We may assume that the initiation phase of his *Life* must have described a moment or moments of just such contact. We may also posit that Nil's rejection of cenobitic monasticism and his subsequent flight into the wilderness must have oriented the work away from temporal and towards spatial descriptions.

Unfortunately, however, the fact is that the *Life* has disappeared. We can talk about Nil's spiritual heritage, but we find no immediate reflection of his life in belles-lettres. And his spiritual heritage, as has been mentioned, is not destined for recognition as the main driving force of Russian ecclesiastical life either. For reasons which fall outside the scope of the present study, the ritual purity and discipline associated with Iosif Volotskii superseded the tradition of contemplative prayer in many Russian monasteries. The deeply individual quest for the vision of God yields to a community-based system of charity and good works,[47] and in saints' lives, ascetic nonreturn yields to a canonical return and reintegration.

Iosif's victory is extremely important because of his close ties to the tsar. Iosif and his followers tend to gravitate towards the centers of imperial power, while Nil, because of his doctrine of nonpossession, more closely reflects the interests of the nobility. The adherence to ritual, characteristic of Iosif's monasteries, spreads into daily life as a direct result of the identification of monastic and secular interests. This ritualization of society, in turn, affects literature.[48] Saints' lives also reflect the new emphasis on ritual and, in so doing, become overburdened with formulae and *topoi*. They accordingly lose much of their freshness.[49] It is important to note that the formulae most frequently employed are ascetic ones: the hero is always a great faster; he never sleeps; he prays night and day.

One explanation for the ascetic hero's disappearance in literary works, then, is tied to the evolution of religious thought. The ascetic ideal is replaced by a social ideal, so fewer ascetics exist in real life. Concurrently, Muscovite lives of saints come to reflect the society which produces them: they are dry and unimaginative transformations of life into ritual; and they borrow the formulae and *topoi* of lives of ascetic saints without any regard for whether these are truly appropriate to the careers of their heroes. A saint may be described as an ascetic who fasts and mortifies his flesh, and yet no underlying motivation for his ascetic behavior will be supplied; or a saint may reject his ties to family or social groups but replace them with very similar ties to a monastic community instead. He too will be described as an ascetic, when in fact, his life is essentially nonascetic.

A second explanation for the demise of the ascetic is connected with the evolution of literature. The saints' life is the genre which generates ascetic heroes in Old Russian literature, and the genre itself enters a decline in the sixteenth century. Fewer high-quality lives are written, and therefore, fewer ascetics are portrayed. Lives either begin to resemble other genres—non-religious ones, to be sure—or they come to reflect religious needs to the exclusion of literary ones. It is Chizhevskii's contention that

> The sixteenth-century Lives of the Saints provide evidence of the genre's decline. They are still numerous; and revisions of older works are even more plentiful. But many of the legends are entirely divorced from tradition. On the one hand, there now emerge "apocryphal legends" in which folk-lore material is linked with the name of one saint or another; and on the other, there appears a series of revisions and new legends which because of lack of subject-matter become merely exercises in stylistics or replace facts by fabrications.[50]

We can synthesize a third, more general explanation of the disappearance of the ascetic on the basis of the two already given. Either religious or literary factors can be cited as leading to the ritualization of the saint's life, but regardless of which are preferred, the result is the same; the genre becomes too reliant on stock phrases and formulae. These phrases are borrowed primarily from works which describe ascetics. By the sixteenth century, the literature of the ascetic has existed for five hundred years on Russian soil. Although, as we have seen, its poetics evolves over time, its most characteristic structural feature, the special pattern of heroic non-return, has remained constant. Even though Old Russian genres remain viable for much longer periods of time than do modern ones, they, too, eventually yield to the law of literary change formulated by Tomashevskii. According to his formulation, the literary devices which distinguish one genre and one period from another begin their lives as fresh, original creations. With time they become canonized, and the genre connected with them becomes clearly demarcated from others. As yet more time passes, however, these same devices "outlive themselves," because literary art places a premium on originality.[51] The *topoi* and formulae which distinguish the life of the ascetic saint begin to outlive themselves in the sixteenth century. Lives continue to be written utilizing the now worn and tired phrases, but they have no place in the literary tradition; they belong exclusively to the history of Russian spirituality.

The question we must ultimately confront is whether the ascetic hero has left the literary tradition for good. The answer to this question depends in great part on how firmly the motivation towards asceticism is embedded in the Russian consciousness. If either the desire to pursue the vision of God or the tendency to see reality in apocalyptic terms is a recurring theme in the Russian intellectual makeup, then the ascetic hero should reemerge at a later point in time.[52] In this case, the Russian mind would be bound to return to a hero who expresses certain of its own most deeply felt urges. If, on the other hand, both of these motivations are generated by medieval conventions and beliefs rather than by specifically Russian considerations, then we may expect that the ascetic hero is truly dead to literature.

When we ask whether either of the two motivations towards ascetic behavior is central to Russian thought patterns, we are asking about cultural context. The criteria we have set up to analyze cultural context are expressed by three sets of relationships which the hero enters into: relationships between the hero and the supernatural, the hero and society, and the hero and himself. It will be remembered that these three relationships correspond to the initiation, separation, and return phases respectively. We did not discuss the question of cultural context and significant recurring patterns in our analysis of the Kievan period because there was insufficient material on which to base such a discussion. The existence of a handful of ascetic heroes at the dawn of the Russian literary tradition does not necessarily constitute a significant pattern, especially in light of the fact that we do not have the entire corpus of Kievan works extant. Now that we have seen that the ascetic hero continues to be portrayed into the sixteenth and, with certain modifications, the seventeenth centuries, however, we are justified in asking whether he does in fact exhibit certain traits which reflect cultural values.

We have seen that the ascetic hero begins his career by separating himself from his fellows, monks as well as laymen. The reason for this separation lies in his radical answer to the problem of his relationship to society. He is in search of his own personal salvation, and the good of others does not concern him. From Polikarp's emasculated hero Moisei to Nil Sorskii, the seer of mystical visions, the tradition of ascetic heroes includes those who strive to perfect themselves through mortification of their flesh. They search for different things—sometimes close, personal contact with their creator; sometimes assurance of their status as members of the chosen—but they proceed from the same premises—that a radical separation of the flesh from the spirit is necessary for the achievement of their goal. They are also bound by the conviction that perfection can be achieved in this life by those who will it. This conviction holds within itself the potential for asocial behavior. It implies that the individual can become perfect on his own, without the agency of society. It also implies that it is the strong individual who becomes perfect, and that those who fail to do so are weak and incapable of being helped. Given that these "weaklings" cannot be helped in any case, the ascetic is free to disregard them altogether.

In the next phase of his career, initiation, the hero comes face to face with his relationship to the supernatural. This relationship has been defined as the tension between the hero's freedom to live without sin and his inevitable subjection to its snares. The ascetic, as we know, stands firm in his belief that he can live free from sin. Only by remaining in a pure state can he expect either the divine vision or an assurance of his inclusion among the saved. If the urge towards asceticism truly does lie deeply buried in the Russian consciousness, it must be because there is a strong belief in both the possibility and the desirability of leading a perfect life.

The final phase of the heroic career is connected with the hero's relationship to himself. Is the hero portrayed as one who learns new truths and tries to apply them to his own life, that is, as man in the process of "becoming," or is he portrayed in a static fashion, as one who has always known the necessary truths, that is, as one who "is"? It is clear that, within the Russian context, the ascetic hero has known his own special truth since earliest childhood. He rarely plays with other children because there is nothing they can tell him that he does not already know. He has no need for deep introspective searching because his truth lies outside himself. Finally, he has no need to "return" because his truth cannot be conveyed to anyone else; each must find it on his own.

Thus, we find that the ascetic hero is engaged in a quest for perfection, a quest which he is convinced can be achieved. This quest rests on a strongly dualist pattern of thought; whenever the hero is confronted by the need to make a choice, he makes an extreme one. Although the most important choices he confronts are always ones which allow for compromise, the ascetic disdains such half-measures. He sees only two paths: the path to salvation and the path to damnation.

Vatro Murvar, in his study of messianism in Russia, finds that both the search for perfection and the reliance on dualist thought patterns are, in fact, important constants in Russian society. He sees Russia's reactions to a whole range of social and intellectual stimuli as indicative of her permanent eschatological mindset. In his view, Russian thinkers have always been marked by a dogmatic exclusiveness which often evolves into intolerance towards the ideas of others. They also tend to favor total rather than gradual solutions and a type of extremism, which may culminate in martyrdom, as a means to attain their goals. Although they may express a sense of guilt towards the masses (the "lost" in apocalyptic terms), they are totally isolated from these uninitiated and humble folk and are unable to save them.[53] If these tendencies to analyze reality as either all good or all bad, to feel that the individual is free to pursue and attain the good, and to pursue the good with a single-minded determination which excludes others from the pursuit do in fact underlie certain areas of Russian thought, then it is likely that they account for the ascetic hero's appeal to Russian readers. They also assure that the ascetic quest for perfection, in one form or another, will remain a theme in Russian art.

Of the two motivations to dualist, ascetic behavior, one, the pursuit of the vision of God, is inextricably bound to religious doctrines and traditions. Although it may hold a lasting significance for the Russian people, it is unlikely to be the exclusive motivating force in the creation of new literary works beyond the sixteenth century. By the seventeenth century, Russian thinkers have begun to manifest a pronounced tendency to separate various intellectual disciplines from each other, a tendency which spells the end of Russia's medieval age. History becomes a different branch of knowledge from theology, and theology can no longer be considered identical with literature. The search for direct communication with the divine properly belongs to the realm of religious experience throughout the course of the seventeenth and eighteenth centuries.

The belief in the imminence of apocalypse, however, has a

different fate. Although it too continues to find resonance in religious life, among Old Believers in particular, it also takes on political significance and eventually influences the genesis of Marxism as well as certain other utopian, totalitarian thought systems.[54] It continues to exercise a particular fascination for Russian thinkers long after its religious underpinnings have been relegated to the seminary. David M. Bethea notes this when he states that

> . . . Russia has tended to define itself by radically breaking, or at least *by seeing itself* as radically breaking, with an earlier period. This break is never, to be sure, as clean and final as the principals might imagine for the very reason that the earlier period which is supposed to be overcome is preserved willy-nilly in the cultural memory as a necessary opposition.[55]

What is important, then, is not the reality of an actual break but rather the perception that history should and does function through the mechanism of radical change.

We have seen that belief in the apocalypse is *an* important, although not necessarily *the* most important, motivating force in the creation of ascetic heroes in Old Russian literature. In the Kievan age we find the eschatology of Avraamii Smolenskii, and in the post-Kievan period we find much fainter suggestions of apocalyptic beliefs in the lives of Kirill Belozerskii and Ulianiia Osor'ina. Perhaps the apocalyptic episodes that we find in these works are merely echoes of medieval Russian society's widespread fascination with apocalypse. Be that as it may, concern with apocalypse begins to coexist with desire for the vision of God as a doctrine which influences the behavior of the literary hero. Once the question of contact with the divine becomes the province of religious thinkers, the belief in apocalypse takes its place as the primary motivation for ascetic behavior in works of Russian literature. This development, however, belongs to future chapters of this study.

Chapter 5

THE UNIDIMENSIONAL HERO IN
A MULTIDIMENSIONAL WORLD:
GOGOL, TOLSTOY, DOSTOEVSKY

REBIRTH OF THE TYPE

The nineteenth century sees a new birth of the ascetic hero in Russian literature. In this modern period we encounter him in short stories by both nineteenth- and twentieth-century writers as well as in a number of novels. And surprisingly, it is in large part in the work of such "classic" writers as Gogol, Tolstoy, and Dostoevsky that the ascetic first makes his comeback. Concurrently, and perhaps more predictably, the ascetic hero also secures for himself an ultimately more enduring place in the radically different literary tradition generated by Chernyshevsky, Gorky, and Gladkov.

It seems unlikely, on first consideration, that such a hero might appear in a work of modern literature at all. The novel, the vehicle *par excellence* for the nineteenth-century literary hero, has been defined as a "humane," "questing"[1] genre which seeks to duplicate reality in all its multifaceted complexity. It is "open-ended" in that it is grounded in the present,[2] a vantage point from which the hero is necessarily incapable of predicting his future. Its very concentration on the hero's development, his self-valuable progress, is incompatible with a character who knows everything from the outset and consequently fails to develop or change in any significant or unforeseen way. Moreover, although both the nineteenth-century Russian novel and the story often explore questions of religious belief, as indeed they explore many and varied questions of the profoundest import, they are nevertheless more purely literary forms, unlike the saint's life which combined and fused both literary and theological elements.

The nineteenth century was, by and large, an age of naturalistic art forms, forms seemingly incompatible with the creation of a unidimensional hero like the ascetic. Worringer has defined such ages as times in which "aesthetic enjoyment is objectified self-enjoyment. To enjoy aesthetically means to enjoy myself in a sensuous object diverse from myself, to empathize myself into it."[3] We need only think of Turgenev's justly famous descriptions of nature or of Tolstoy's meticulous portrayals of hunt scenes and ballrooms to be reminded that these writers, at least, often delighted in "sensuous objects" diverse from themselves.

It should be noted, however, that this delight was neither universally shared by Russian writers nor even consistently or rigorously preserved by its most notable exponents. We are able to gauge the extent to which the "golden age" of the Russian realistic novel was colored by a non-naturalistic dread of the observable universe when we attempt to forge more thoroughgoing correspondences between specific works of literature and Worringer's criteria for the creation of naturalistic art. Worringer tells us that

> amongst a people with such a predisposition [towards naturalistic art], this sensuous assurance, this complete confidence in the external world, will lead, in a religious respect, to a naive anthropomorphic pantheism or polytheism, and in respect of art to a happy world-revering naturalism. Neither in the former nor in the latter will any need for redemption be disclosed.[4]

A belief in the ordered harmony of the universe, which allows man to express an optimistic confidence in his own place in the cosmic order, is a hallmark of purely naturalistic art. And yet, the works of most major nineteenth-century Russian writers stop short of endorsing a complete confidence in the external world, and the question of the necessity of redemption must certainly be regarded as central to many of them. Beneath the surface harmony created in many of the novels of this period, Edward Wasiolek has discerned a deeper sense of unease.

> The Russian vision, as it is embodied in the novel, oscillates between the conviction that reality is design-haunted and the fear that there is no design, the belief that the world is continuity and the fear that it is rupture, the conviction that there is a place for everything and everyone and a place for nothing and no one.[5]

We detect a secret fear that things "do not fit."[6]

This is not to say that the period is best characterized by non-naturalistic art forms. We must, however, at least note tendencies on the parts of Gogol, Tolstoy, and Dostoevsky to incorporate non-naturalistic elements into the body of essentially naturalistic literary works. It is precisely this tendency which allows the ascetic to gain a tenuous foothold in works in which we would not normally expect to encounter him.

It is understandable, then, that the ascetic enjoys not more but also not less than a marginal existence in a number of works by the great nineteenth-century writers. The most important of these are Gogol's "The Portrait" ("Portret," 1835, 1842), Tolstoy's "Father Sergius" ("Otets Sergii," 1890–8), and Dostoevsky's *The Brothers Karamazov* (Brat'ia Karamazovy, 1880).[7]

When we posit the ascetic as a heroic type in these works, we assume, of course, that he continues to meet the criteria established for the category. He must follow a pattern of separation-initiation-nonreturn, and he must always opt for an extreme and individualistic resolution of both the tensions between his existence and those of others, as well as of the tension between his own need to stand firm in his convictions and his natural tendency to evolve as a result of life experience. His separation phase must be characterized by severe ascetic privations, voluntarily accepted, which serve to underscore his conviction that he stands apart from and above the rest of society. His initiation phase will include an experience of the transcendent, which will affirm his belief that he not only can, but has, reached a state of perfection. Finally, he will not return to the milieu he has separated from; having achieved a state of perfection, he will see no need to reimmerse himself in profane reality which can teach him nothing new.

One or another of the characters in each work selected here for study does, in fact, partially meet these criteria. It is noteworthy, however, that the ascetic, by virtue of appearing in a tradition not usually associated with unidimensional heroes, loses the privileged position he held in medieval saints' lives. In Gogol's and Dostoevsky's works the ascetic is, to varying degrees, a peripheral character, while in Tolstoy's he is harshly judged in a manner reminiscent of the *Patericon* tale of Isakii.

The ascetics in the works selected for discussion in this chapter are very much men engaged in a religious quest. Other authors like Chernyshevsky create ascetics in a more productive tradition— the political—but the nineteenth-century ascetic is fated to also enjoy a final moment as a religiously motivated hero. The saintly icon painter of Gogol's "Portrait," Tolstoy's Father Sergius, and Dostoevsky's deranged monk, Ferapont, are all in search of the kind of perfection which is brought by communion with a transcendent God. In each work, however, they are compared and contrasted, sometimes favorably sometimes unfavorably, with members of a society for whom their search has little validity. The religious ideal held by the ascetic is no longer one which is shared by an entire culture. The aura of an organic Christian community, which permeated Old Russia, has for the most part been dispelled even before the advent of the nineteenth century, leaving the religious ascetic more isolated from his society than ever.

In the nineteenth century it is particularly the educated classes of society, those producing Russia's great writers, that tend to be a step removed from the organic religious community of Old Russia. Although these writers more often than not direct their talents towards depicting the secular society in which they themselves move, however, they are also drawn to the original religious vision, sometimes idealizing, sometimes criticizing it. Their ascetic heroes are at one and the same time both products of the secular order into which they are born and throwbacks to a different age. As ascetics in a nonascetic world, they stand as uncomfortable reminders of the fact that something does indeed "not fit." They are truly alone in their grim and isolated reality.

The grimness and isolation of the nineteenth-century ascetic come as no real surprise. His medieval forefather was a product (even if an anomalous one) of the official, ecclesiastical culture of Old Russia, a culture which Mikhail Bakhtin has defined as dry, humorless, and ascetic. He was never to be found among the life-affirming, laughing creations of folk art.[8] Even though heroes like Sergius and Ferapont are created in a tradition which has only indirect links with the official culture of Old Russia, it can be easily argued that this culture served as an important model in their creation.[9] In any case, these two ascetics share little or nothing with the vibrant heroes of the medieval folk tradition.[10]

The sense of isolation which the ascetic heroes of Gogol, Tolstoy, and Dostoevsky convey cannot, however, be wholly attributed to their estrangement from the society of their day. It is, in other words, not entirely a social phenomenon. It also has a literary dimension. These heroes are misfits within the literary work. Their very presence calls forth a change in the controlling imagery of the story or novel in which they are found. Northrop Frye has discovered broadly applied patterns of imagery which he associates with the comic and the tragic visions of reality. Representative images for each vision are the following:

	Comic Vision	Tragic Vision
Human world:	community of friendship and love	tyranny, anarchy, isolated man
Animal world:	domesticated animals	beasts and birds of prey
Vegetable world:	garden	sinister forest
Mineral world:	city, temple, precious stone	desert, rock, ruin
Unformed world:	river	sea[11]

Scenes depicting the ascetic tend to be described with the aid of "tragic" imagery, while scenes in which other characters dominate are frequently, if not always, described through "comic" imagery. Thus, the shift in imagery which can occur when the ascetic is introduced becomes another device contributing to the atmosphere of estrangement and isolation generated by him.

We shall discuss this shift in imagery patterning in greater detail in connection with individual texts. We should note, however, that its presence creates a palpable unevenness in the texture of a work and is a characteristic mark of the intrusion of a unidimensional, geometrically simplified character into a universe of multidimensional complexity.

AVERTING APOCALYPSE: GOGOL'S VISION OF THE POWER OF ART

Gogol's "The Portrait" (1835, 1842) is chronologically the first of the works under study to be written, and in certain ways it is the closest to medieval models. A comparison of its two published versions, the original version of *Arabesques* (1835) and the reworked version for the 1842 collected works, suggests that perhaps even Gogol himself recognized that certain aspects of his first story constituted a sort of ill-digested duplication of medieval practice. Most probably, he came to the realization that the story's two parts quite simply would not come together as a satisfactory whole without a more convincing tie between the ascetic's endeavors in the second part of the work and those of the worldly characters in the first, and this was perhaps one of the factors which contributed to his decision to rewrite.

The 1835 version of "The Portrait" opens with a description of the second- and third-rate paintings for sale in a Petersburg shop. Chertkov, an aspiring young artist, is browsing about the shop and manages to find an unexpectedly fine portrait. Without really understanding what he is doing, he bids his entire month's living expenses on it. Once he has paid for the portrait, however, he looks more carefully at its eyes and is overcome by a sudden wave of terror. He drops his purchase and flees. Upon arriving home, Chertkov berates himself for spending so much money. The landlord threatens to have him evicted, and the young artist seems to have no alternative but to move out onto the streets. He is engaged in contemplating this precarious situation when he glances at his wall and finds, to his amazement, that the portrait he abandoned in the shop is now hanging there. Chertkov makes some perfunctory attempts to ascertain how the portrait has mysteriously appeared in his rooms but comes to no conclusion. He then, rather suddenly, decides to go to bed. He has a dream in which the figure in the portrait comes to life, leaves the picture frame, and suggests that Chertkov betray his art and paint wealthy and fashionable ladies. Chertkov awakens, acts on the advice given him, and becomes a wealthy, famous, and distinctly second-rate painter.

Some years after his "betrayal" of art, Chertkov is invited to view a painting done by one of the friends of his youth. The purity and depth of expression of this painting contrast markedly with the lack of talent evinced by Chertkov's own work. Chertkov is consumed with envy and determines to buy any and all new works by talented young painters and destroy them. After some time he begins to lapse into insanity. In his lucid moments he begs those near him to find the mysterious portrait he bought so long ago and remove it. The portrait cannot be found, and Chertkov dies.

The second part of the story begins at an auction. One of the bidders discovers the portrait which brought about Chertkov's downfall among the items to be sold. He explains to a curious audience that his father had painted this portrait fifty years previously. The man depicted in the portrait, a terrifying old pawnbroker, had pleaded on his deathbed that the artist paint him. He indicated that if a good portrait of him were to be made, half his former life would pass into it and he would not have to face the eternal torment decreed for him. The artist had only painted a portion of the portrait when he felt to his horror that the power of its fierce eyes was overcoming him. He ceased working immediately. The enraged pawnbroker cajoled and threatened him, but to no avail. The pawnbroker died, leaving his portrait with the artist. The portrait, however, exercised an evil influence over one and all, and the artist burned it.

Strangely enough, the painting's unclean spirit survived the burning, and the artist entered a monastery in order to escape it. There he adopted extremely severe ascetic practices and lived in great privation. He became famous, however, for a superb icon of the Virgin which he painted. Eventually, when the artist felt the approach of death, he called his son to him and told him that the Virgin had appeared in a vision and revealed that the pawnbroker was really a human embodiment of Antichrist. As long as his portrait existed, Antichrist would have power in the world. On the fiftieth anniversary of the pawnbroker's death, however, the portrait would crumble into dust and pass out of the world.

The auction with which the second part of the story begins takes place on the exact date set for the crumbling of the portrait. As the artist's son finishes speaking, the unclean work does in fact crumble before everyone's eyes.

Gogol's 1842 version of the story differs from the original in several important respects. In the later version the young artist of

the first half of the story, rechristened Chartkov, buys the mysterious portrait very cheaply and takes it home himself. It is only when
Chartkov finally settles into his rooms that the terrifying eyes in
the portrait seem to come alive. In this second version of the story,
Chartkov's dream is given in much greater detail. Questions concerning the aesthetic and moral value of art are also raised much
more prominently. Overall, considerably more emphasis is given
to the first half of the story vis-à-vis the second. Finally, and very
significantly, the story of the ascetic icon painter and his ill-omened
portrait is greatly changed.

In the later version of the story, the pawnbroker, seemingly
in good health, comes to the artist's house and requests that a portrait
be made of him. The artist, who has been searching some time for
a model of the devil's face for an icon he is painting, readily agrees
to his request. As in the earlier variant of the story, he is overcome
with terror midway through his work and flees. The pawnbroker
sends him the portrait and dies. The artist, sensing that the portrait has an evil effect on him, gives it to a friend, who in turn gives
it to someone else. Misfortunes continue to plague the artist, and
he enters a monastery. Here he is asked to paint the central icon
for the church but refuses, saying that he is as yet unworthy. He
sets off for a wild and deserted place where he lives in great poverty. He eventually returns to his monastery and paints an icon of
the birth of Christ. His son, who in this version of the story is also
an artist, arrives to visit him, and they discuss the moral qualities
of art at some length. Finally, the artist-monk tells his son about
the portrait he once painted and asks him to find and destroy it.
The son, who is telling this tale to a crowd at an auction, turns and
finds to his great dismay that the portrait has vanished.

The divergences in plot line just mentioned give rise to a difference in focus in Gogol's second variant of "The Portrait." The
1842 story concentrates much more clearly than does the 1835 on
the moral and spiritual dimensions of art.[12] Considerably more of
this story is given over to discussions of esthetics and the mission
of true art. In keeping with the emphasis on art and the artist's
responsibility towards society, both Chartkov and the icon painter
are artists and, more importantly, decision makers. Each of them
actively brings evil onto himself and others by perverting his high
calling. Chartkov buys the unclean portrait and brings it into his
rooms of his own free will, so that the dream in which the pawnbroker convinces him to abandon true art is, in a certain sense, of

his own making. The icon painter willingly creates the portrait which causes so much evil in order to have a model for another work. The central theme of art and the artist is not our primary focus here, however, so we shall forego analysis of the 1842 version of the story, which concentrates most strongly on art, in favor of the 1835, which deals more specifically with such religious concerns as are germane to our study of the ascetic hero.[13]

The 1835 story lifts much of the responsibility for the outbreak of evil in the world from its two artist-heroes by describing the portrait of the horrible pawnbroker as mysteriously appearing in Chertkov's rooms on its own and by explaining the icon painter's decision to paint it in the first place as an act of pity towards the pawnbroker. The icon painter even burns his creation in a vain attempt to undo its power. The acting force in this story is not art but rather evil, which seems to be free to spread throughout society regardless of humans' attempts to block it. The nature of evil is very simply spelled out; it is the power of Antichrist, who will bring "great torment to those who remain true to Christ."[14] The ascetic icon painter of this story enters a monastery and cuts himself off from his family and friends not in a spirit of atonement for evil done but rather in order to stay, however briefly, the imminent apocalypse. His asceticism arises out of a perceived need to take sides in an impending struggle.

The apocalyptic message present in "The Portrait" has been noted by others. Donald Fanger calls the story an "allegorical fable, rendered in terms of apocalyptic earnestness," and Konstantin Mochul'skii asserts that the story is Gogol's first systematic formulation of an eschatological world view.[15] Although these two assessments seem to apply most obviously to the second half of the story, they also find resonance in the first half. The icon painter is unquestionably an ascetic and a believer in apocalypse, but a similar path might be predicted at the beginning of the story for Chertkov as well. There are numerous signs that Chertkov begins his career in the story as an ascetic. Simon Karlinsky has noted, for example, that each of the heroes of Gogol's Petersburg stories seeks comfort from a woman or a thinly disguised substitute for one. Chertkov is the only exception.[16] Furthermore, at the beginning of "The Portrait," we find Chertkov living in utmost poverty and want, not because he is forced to, but voluntarily, because he is pursuing a great quest. And although he later amasses considerable wealth from his painting, he rarely uses it to gratify his personal wants and desires.

Chertkov does indeed indulge in a new and elegant set of clothes and fashionable rooms, but he seems to derive very little pleasure from them. Rather, he buys them so as to succeed in a world he has mistakenly interpreted as the world of great art.

Chertkov's initial behavior, then, is such as might permit us to tentatively parallel him with ascetic heroes. His characterization also encourages us to do this. He, like so many of Gogol's heroes, is static and unidimensional. Once he embarks on his career as a successful society painter, he neither learns nor changes.[17] He lives for only one thing—to be a renowned artist. His goal is a false one; this we learn through comparing his fate with that of the icon painter, who dies peacefully, secure in the knowledge that evil, exemplified by the pawnbroker's portrait, will also die from the world. Chertkov abandons the ascetic way under the influence of the evil portrait and loses his salvation. He has unwittingly chosen the wrong side in the cosmic struggle between good and evil; he has bought and kept the portrait, which is to say, he has accepted Antichrist, and he dies in great torment.

If we are to understand how it is that Chertkov comes to make the wrong choice, we must look to those who choose correctly. The friend of Chertkov's youth, the wonderful artist whose work brings Chertkov to realize his own error, is described as someone who "wrenched himself away from his friends, his family, his accustomed pastimes and . . . suffered poverty, degradation, even hunger. . . ." (p. 260). And the icon painter, who comes close to making the same mistake as Chertkov, also abandons the pleasures and pains of the world to suffer poverty, degradation, and hunger. By twice pointing to a solution adopted by characters who have succeeded where Chertkov has not, Gogol asks us to accept this solution, the ascetic one, as the only possible means towards redemption.

We have said before that the ascetic path is a grim and isolated one and that it imposes its own tragic view of the world on a work which is structured around it. "The Portrait" is the only one of Gogol's works which advocates the ascetic way, and it is one of the few which almost totally eschew humor. From start to finish, there are few, if any, comic moments. Although the limited imagery present in the first half of the story is comic (in Frye's definition of the term), that of the second half, which is meant to point the way towards redemption, is tragic. The artist-monk, for example, is the quintessential isolated man, and he lives in a "remote monastery, in the midst of a pale and desiccated nature" (p. 279). The only animals are crows, circling ominously overhead. These images, which are consonant with the tragic worldview, are intended to supersede those of the first half of the story, just as the icon painter's morality supersedes Chertkov's.

In "The Portrait" Gogol compares the view of art and society held by the educated classes of his day with that held by a religious community grounded in the beliefs of Old Russia. He shows how even a young man of talent and ambition like Chertkov is lured from the ascetic path by the temptations of the complex, multidimensional world around him. When the hero succumbs to evil, he not only brings about his own fall but also releases evil into an unsuspecting world. In the 1835 version of the story, however, Gogol holds out the hope that evil may, for a time, be vanquished. If one holy man perseveres in a strict, ascetic life, he may avert the inevitable moment of catastrophic upheaval a little longer.

THE ASCETIC UNMASKED: TOLSTOY'S "FATHER SERGIUS"

A very different view of asceticism emerges in "Father Sergius" and *The Brothers Karamazov*. For all the many and much-touted differences between Tolstoy and Dostoevsky, the two agree on one thing at least; asceticism is no way to achieve the quest for human perfection.

Both the question of asceticism and man's quest for perfection are central to Tolstoy's "Father Sergius." Although one critic has gone so far as to conclude that Tolstoy himself was an ascetic,[18] however, even the most cursory reading of "Father Sergius" refutes this idea. On the basis of this particular text it would be absolutely impossible to link the achievement of perfection with asceticism, which is repeatedly condemned as self-serving and morally bankrupt.

Tolstoy finds an appropriate vehicle for his criticism of asceticism in the figure of his hero, Father Sergius. Sergius, like the *Patericon* hermits, lives much of his long life in a lonely cave. He suffers a great moral fall, however, and through it comes to see his asceticism as a mere exercise in pride and self-admiration. He concludes that as an ascetic "I lived for people under the pretext of living for God, while she [his cousin Pashen'ka] lives for God, all the time assuming that she lives for people."[19] For Sergius, it turns out that the great thing is to live for others, never worrying whether one's actions find favor in the eyes of God (p.409).

Sergius begins his career in the story as Prince Stepan Kasatskii, a young cadet who is vigorously seeking advancement in St. Petersburg society. His carefully laid plans turn to dust, however, when he discovers that his beautiful and much-loved fiancée was once the mistress of Nicholas I. Kasatskii cannot free himself from the feeling of humiliation and ridiculousness which he attaches to being used as a cover for the sins of others, and he enters a monastery as Father Sergius. His first years pass quickly and easily, but then he is transferred to another monastery, where he conceives an immediate dislike for the worldly abbot. Sergius regains his sense of equanimity when he again moves—this time to a solitary cave dug by a pious hermit. During his years in the cave, Sergius achieves a reputation for great holiness. Amidst all the trappings of tragic imagery—a lonely forest, deep and isolating snow—he is visited by a beautiful woman. Tormented by desire, he chops off one of his fingers and succeeds in quelling his passion. When this becomes known, it brings him great renown. His many healings of the sick contribute even more to his reputation. Just when the danger of becoming a true celebrity begins to loom over him, however, Sergius succumbs to the devil's machinations and seduces a young woman. In despair, he flees his wilderness cave and makes his way to his cousin Pashen'ka, whom he has seen in a dream.[20] From Pashen'ka he learns the right way to achieve perfection and embarks on a life of lonely wanderings. He is arrested and sent to Siberia where he "works in gardens, teaches children and cares for the sick" (p. 411).

Sergius moves from one way of life to another, constantly seeking a perfection which evades him.[21] When he reaches his penultimate stage, during which he willingly cultivates his reputation by undertaking to heal the sick, he begins to sense that the best part of his life is already past. He looks back to the time when he chopped off his finger as to a highpoint, a time when, without realizing it, he truly achieved perfection. This vision of perfection-through-asceticism belongs to Sergius's prefall experience of life, however. His discovery of Pashen'ka's answers to life's dilemmas shows him that in his earlier life he missed the mark altogether. Asceticism, he learns, is but a variation on the theme of vanity and ambition.

Although it has been shown that the most likely hagiographical subtexts for "Father Sergius" are the Life of Saint James and the Life of Sergii Radonezhskii,[22] Tolstoy's story, as a work featuring an ascetic hero, also reminds us of the Patericon tale of Isakii, the Cave-dweller. The general outlines of both stories are identical: a wealthy man gives his fortune to a monastery and goes off to live in a cave; he falls to temptation just as he begins to feel a certain sense of smug satisfaction about his way of life; and he goes on to lead a new life in which he humbles himself to the extreme by rigorously submitting to others. This is to say that in each story the ascetic pattern of separation-initiation-nonreturn is enacted once in its entirety and then is followed by a different, nonascetic pattern which culminates in return. In this second pattern, Isakii becomes a *iurodivyi*, and Sergius, by feigning to be much simpler than he really is, avails himself of a modern variation on the traditional theme of folly for Christ's sake.[23]

Tolstoy, then, reverses the sequence of actions which characterizes the ascetic hero's career in Gogol's "Portrait." In "Father Sergius" the static, unbending hero comes to reject the world of ascetic unidimensionality and enters into the multidimensional world of change and complexity. He mixes with others and finds alternative paths to salvation by helping them solve their daily problems. By finally recognizing that seemingly trivial problems have a dignity and importance of their own, he also comes to the humility which has evaded him throughout his life. Thus, in his own idiosyncratic way, he begins to learn and grow.[24] When he admits that the path he originally chose was a false one, he repudiates his allegiance to the extreme solution accepted by Gogol's hero and immerses himself in the world of profane experience.

We must be careful to note that life experience alone does not lead to perfection in "Father Sergius." Of all the characters in the story, only three actually reach out to God. Only Sergius and the world-weary society woman for whom he cuts off his finger repent their lifelong misdoings, while Pashen'ka is portrayed as never having done anything requiring repentance. The other characters, all of whom are judged at one time or another by Sergius to be morally fallen, continue to be portrayed as such even after the hero himself changes. In other words, a man must show an active will towards the good if he is to achieve anything in this life, and very few have such a will. This notwithstanding, however, it is hard to escape the paradoxical conclusion that a thorough knowledge of and involvement in the everyday world of sinful pleasures and woes is a prerequisite for eventual spiritual transcendence. Pashen'ka, who inspires Sergius by her example, has always lived in this world, and Sergius must return to it in order to find the true path to salvation.

What is most important is *how* one lives in the world. Sergius, in his new life, witnesses the daily turmoils of the world without actually initiating them himself: "If he was able to help people with advice, or by reading for them, or by reconciling disputants, he never saw their gratitude, because he would leave. And gradually God began to be visible in him" (p. 410). Thus, he professes a rather equivocal affirmation of the material world, which, up to a certain point, allows him to remain separate from it. Here is a different variation on the incorporation of unidimensionality and multidimensionality into one work: the hero himself is an uneasy mixture of both simplicity and complexity.

ASCETIC FAILURE: DOSTOEVSKY'S FERAPONT

The Brothers Karamazov is the final work chosen for attention in this chapter, and it presents certain special problems. In neither of the other works selected, for instance, is the ascetic character of such seemingly secondary importance. Ferapont, Dostoevsky's crazy ascetic monk, has so little to do with the actual unraveling of the story line of the novel that it would be tempting to leave him out of this discussion altogether. He certainly cannot be called a "hero" in the fullest sense of the word. Nevertheless, Dostoevsky clearly wanted him in the novel, so he must hold some significance. In the first pages of the notebooks for *The Brothers Karamazov*, we come across the following:

> There were also monks in the monastery who were enemies of the Elder, but there weren't many of them—They kept quiet, suppressing their hate, even though they were important people. One was an ascetic, another somewhat simpleminded, but the majority were on his side.[25]

Very early Dostoevsky made plans to incorporate an ascetic into his novel, and very early he conceived him in dialogue with a more positive and, at the same time, versatile character, Zosima.

Although Ferapont, of all the ascetics discussed in this chapter, occupies the least significant place in the narrative in which he is found, he is, by virtue of his total isolation and emptiness, a most fitting representative of the type. His isolation is manifested in a number of ways. He enters the novel, for example, in a chapter called "Father Ferapont," a title which invites us to assume that the segment will deal primarily with him and his ascetic beliefs.

The chapter begins, however, with a lesson delivered by the Elder Zosima to the monks who support him. Zosima talks to the brethren about the holy life and explains his belief that each man is responsible for the sins of every other. Next we hear of a miracle which has come to pass through his mediation. It is only after we have been presented with the opportunity of reacquainting ourselves with the beliefs professed by Ferapont's adversary, the Elder, that we meet Ferapont himself. The "Ferapont" chapter also ends with Zosima, who sends Alesha out into the nonascetic world of profane and sinful turmoil. By so demonstratively relegating asceticism to the background of the chapter, as indeed of the novel as a whole, Dostoevsky serves notice that Ferapont and his like share the world with other, very different seekers after perfection. And within the context of *The Brothers Karamazov*, perfection, if it is to be found at all, is ultimately to be found among the nonascetics.[26]

There can be no question that Ferapont is a true ascetic. Although the information that we are given regarding him is rather scant, we are able, nevertheless, to quickly fix upon characteristics typical of an ascetic living in a cenobitic community. Ferapont has withdrawn to the most isolated cell in the monastery, where he lives in almost total silence, rarely willing to share his visions and insights with others. He subsists on bread and water alone, and although he receives communion regularly, he does so in his cell, thereby avoiding the necessity of attending mass. He favors dirty, tattered clothing, and wears thirty-pound chains. Rumors circulate in the monastery that Ferapont is in direct communion with the Holy Spirit,[27] serving as confirmation of the fact that he seeks to establish direct contact with the divine.

Other more subtle circumstances identify Ferapont less with ascetic triumph than with its failure. It is stressed several times, for example, that his cell is located well beyond the apiary. Bees are, of course, emblematic of social, community-oriented life, and Ferapont rejects his community when he chooses to live beyond their pale. Since it is the community, represented by Zosima, which helps and inspires Alesha, the character who is widely considered the novel's hero, Ferapont's choice is presumably a wrong one.

It is also significant that Ferapont is able to see devils. This actually means that devils present themselves to him, as to a man they still hope to win power over; in truth he himself has no power over them. With true ascetic initiation, it will be remembered, temptations by the devil cease because there is no longer any hope of their success. Ferapont's ability to see devils suggests that he has achieved a grotesque parody of self-perfection; he has attained communion with the forces of evil rather than with God.

Of course another, more central character in the novel also sees devils—Ivan Karamazov. Ivan, like Ferapont, is much more self-reliant and isolated than the characters with whom he is most clearly in dialogue, his brothers. Like Ferapont, he tries to give the appearance of having no needs, no desires. Compared with Dmitrii, for example, he never makes demands. Compared with Alesha, however, he also never gives of himself. His intense inner life can find no outlet until the devil offers himself as interlocutor. Ivan is not an ascetic, at least not in the sense used here, and his encounter with the devil is a much more significant one than Ferapont's. The message that comes from it is central to Dostoevsky's meaning, while Ferapont's encounter is only peripheral. Ivan, then, is the multidimensional character whose demonic drama Ferapont prefigures and debases.

These two characters' association-through-debasement is seen in other places in the novel as well, for example in the pupil/mentor relationships both men establish in the novel. Ivan acts as teacher to Smerdiakov, who trivializes his ideas, just as Ferapont poses as spiritual guide to a narrow-minded visiting monk. The difference is that the visiting monk hardly deforms Ferapont's ideas more than the master does himself. Thus, the network of associations and interconnections in *The Brothers Karamazov* which places Alesha in communion with Zosima also places Ivan in communion with a monk, Ferapont. Although each of the two brothers is placed in some kind of relationship with a monk, however, there is no exact parallel between Alesha and Zosima and Ivan and Ferapont. While Alesha's emulation of Zosima is conscious, simple, and sincere, Ivan does not even know Ferapont. He certainly has no idea that he is the more significant member in a pairing in which Ferapont acts almost as a caricature.

Ferapont, viewed in this light, takes on a rather different meaning. We realize that through him Dostoevsky is not so much making a statement about asceticism as illuminating Ivan from another angle. The side of Ivan's character which comes in for the most criticism is his inability to give. This is what both links him with Ferapont and sets him apart from Alesha. Alesha's willingness to give of himself allows him to become a true disciple of Zosima, while Ivan's isolation has the potential for degenerating into Ferapont's ascetic madness.

I suggested earlier that Ferapont is ultimately very representative of the ascetics analyzed in this chapter. This is so not because the significance of asceticism is greater for this work than
for others, but rather because Ferapont's quest, like Ivan Karamazov's,
so clearly ends in madness and failure. Failure to achieve a quest
is a thread which runs throughout this chapter. It may be realized
to varying degrees, but it is, nonetheless, found in each work. In
Gogol, for instance, the true ascetic succeeds, while Chertkov, an
aspiring ascetic, does not. In "Father Sergius," failure is complete.
It touches not only the hero but also the very nature of his quest.
The Brothers Karamazov depicts ascetic failure even more forcefully.
Although the hero and his quest are both unmasked by Tolstoy,
Dostoevsky goes further by denying the ascetic's very status as more
than a caricature.

MUTATIONS OF HAGIOGRAPHICAL CANONS

It remains to explain this failure of the ascetic quest. Since in
the next chapter we will discover at least one piece of nineteenth-
century literature, *What Is to Be Done?*, in which an ascetic will be
said to "succeed," we would not be quite correct in suggesting that
the literature of the times was thoroughly hostile to any and all
ascetics. [28] Rather, an explanation for the failure of the ascetic quest
must lie with the specific works in question.

In Gogol, Tolstoy, and Dostoevsky we see only one realization of the reborn ascetic tradition. In the medieval period the ascetic was the hero of a religious quest, and in these nineteenth-century
works he continued to be engaged in a very similar search. Although
the seventeenth and eighteenth centuries, which separate the modern
ascetic from his medieval prototype, frequently witnessed a sun-
dering of theology and literature, the nineteenth sometimes saw a
new synthesis of them—admittedly in a form which was much more
literary than theological. This synthesis, a powerful factor in the
creation of nineteenth-century literary ascetic heroes, leads us back
in time to older ascetic patterns. We do not, however, need to look
to it for a comprehensive explanation of the ascetic heroes of the
revolutionary tradition.

Clearly the "classic" nineteenth-century writers knew their
medieval religious traditions. Both their childhood and their adult
readings point to this fact,[29] and many of them made pilgrimages

to great monastic centers where medieval manuscripts still survived. Gogol's saintly icon painter follows the path of strict restraint advocated in ascetic lives. He is chosen to show the way to true sanctity. At the same time, the failed painter Chertkov starts on the same path but comes imperceptibly to live for a secular vision of art and to, thereby, create a false and misguided hagiography. This suggests that only by close adherence to hagiographical conventions— that is, by re-creating in modern life the medieval synthesis of art and religious belief—can evil be eradicated. By juxtaposing a false hagiography to a true one, Gogol vindicates hagiography and announces its continuing relevance for modern life.

Margaret Ziolkowski has very correctly suggested that Tolstoy used hagiographic patterns in a very different way. He created what she calls "anti-hagiography."[30] As another reader of "Father Sergius" points out, Tolstoy, the perpetual iconoclast, wanted to investigate the nature of "true" spirituality, a concept he opposed to conventional notions of spirituality exemplified in saints' lives.[31] Older hagiographical motifs were combined to create a new tale which denied the message of the original lives.

In his treatment of Ferapont, Dostoevsky does something similar, although not quite identical. He, too, strongly disapproves of his ascetic monk, but with an important difference. He does not allow Ferapont to create a new vision of spirituality. The ascetic path is so far removed from true spirituality that the hero who follows it is permanently denied salvation. Instead, salvation is granted to Zosima, a character whose career departs from the norms of the saints' life to a much lesser degree.[32] Accordingly, both anti-hagiography (Ferapont) and a less radical "neo-hagiography" (Zosima) are present in the text.

Alastair Fowler has described a pattern of literary growth and evolution which is quite pertinent to our discussion of these classic writers' use of medieval models. Fowler looks at literature as a system of signs which, like all other systems of communication, relies on senders and receivers of messages. In order for communication to be successful, both sender and receiver must interpret the majority of the signs in which any given message is encoded in one and the same way. An important point in this theory is that literature differs from other forms of communication primarily insofar as it is marked by a much greater redundancy of signs. In other words, literature communicates its "message" in many ways.

According to Fowler, literary forms as well as extraliterary reality change with the passage of time. Owing to such changes, later readers are unable to interpret many of the signs in a given work in the exact way the author originally intended. Therefore, the "message" is no longer understood as clearly as it probably was when the work was first written. Literature's high degree of redundancy, however, guarantees that something of the original "message" continues to be conveyed to new readers even after the form has partially "outlived" itself, that is, has ceased generating new works.

Older forms which have lost some of their meaning over time may sometimes be adapted and made to convey a completely new "message," however. When and if this occurs, it is because the form has reached a secondary stage of utilization. In this stage authors consciously base their own work on earlier, primary works. They may vary their themes or purposes, but major features, including formal structure, remain true to the original. A yet more developed, tertiary stage may also be reached. Here the original form is re-worked in a radically new way, and certain of its most basic features may disappear. Typical examples of such a tertiary stage might be burlesque or satire.[33]

It seems highly likely to me that the works discussed in this chapter belong to a tertiary stage in the development of the ascetic type. Although each text uses hagiographical models in its own way, creating false hagiography, anti-hagiography, and neo-hagiography, they share certain broad similarities. Put more simply, "The Portrait," "Father Sergius," and *The Brothers Karamazov* reflect, but in no way completely duplicate, aspects of the poetics of medieval saints' lives. Moreover, they are, to varying degrees, *consciously* conceived by their authors as reflections of older works. Their idiosyncratic pattern of heroic actions mirrors the pattern found in medieval prototypes, a fact which justifies grouping both the medieval and the modern ascetics in the same heroic category.

Other facets of the poetics of the modern works are radically different from earlier hagiographic models, however. The medieval penchant for reducing literary movement to just one or the other of its constituent parts, time or space, for instance, does not apply to them. The older tendency to restrict the story line to the actions of one single character, the ascetic, is also much less pronounced. Most importantly, the overarching structure of the saint's life is exploded in these works. The ascetic portion of Gogol's story, like the *Life of Ulianiia Osor'ina*, is narrated by the saint's son, but the standard *topoi* of the life are missing. The saint's only miracle is, paradoxically enough, the creation of a moment of opportunity for Antichrist. And as Tolstoy's Sergius fades into the anonymity of humble wanderings, he leaves neither disciple nor spiritual tradition behind. The saint's new life is open-ended, ongoing, and unwitnessed. The very possibility of narrating it is, accordingly, denied. The fate of Dostoevsky's ascetic merges with Ivan's, which is also left open-ended and unwitnessed.These modern works, then, fail to mirror their medieval models in truly significant ways. This could not, of course, be otherwise, given that the naturalistic urge in art exercises an overarching, if not wholly consistent influence on them. Their loyalty to naturalistic conventions dictates a more complex, multidimensional type of art.[34]

We can say, therefore, that certain nineteenth-century works reflect a conscious decision to play with art, to adapt an inherited form to prevailing circumstances. In many ways these works themselves "succeed." Their ascetic heroes, however, do not and cannot. Their motivations and aspirations are invariably viewed from the perspective of nineteenth-century experience. They are simplistic, unidimensional characters living in a world which has become used to posing complex questions and seeking equally complex answers. The sign system in which they were once encoded has become obscure both to other characters in the same work and, more often than not, to modern readers. The incorporation of a unidimensional hero into a naturalistic work of literature is ultimately a difficult and only partially feasible undertaking. The ascetic is inherently a misfit in such works, and very little can be done to make him fit.

Chapter 6

VISIONS OF THE PERFECT
SOCIETY

REVOLUTIONARY APOCALYPTICISM AND
NON-NATURALISTIC ART

In the last chapter we noted the difficulties an author encounters when he attempts to reconcile a unidimensional ascetic hero with the "humane," "open-ended" novelistic form or, for that matter, with the classic short story. We also noted changes both in the typology of the hero and in the imagery of the literary work which accompany such an attempt. It is now appropriate to turn to a rather different group of novels depicting the ascetic hero, novels in which the hero's quest is grounded in social ideology rather than religion. The creation of a revolutionary ascetic coincides with the earliest stirrings of a new movement towards non-naturalistic art forms, and this accounts for the fact that many of the difficulties attendant on reconciling two dissimilar views of reality will be considerably less pronounced in the works to be discussed.

Although it was previously suggested that the ascetic hero is ultimately a misfit in the multidimensional complexity of the novel, it might well be argued that the works to be discussed in this chapter, Chernyshevsky's *What Is to Be Done?* (*Chto delat'?*, 1864), Gorky's

Mother (*Mat'*, 1907), and Gladkov's *Cement* (*Tsement*, 1925), are neither "humane," "open-ended," nor, for that matter, multidimensional. In her study of the Soviet novel, Katerina Clark asserts, for example, that

> the Soviet novel performs a totally different function from the one the novel usually performs in the West, and this difference in function has given rise to a different kind of text. The differences extend right across the board—in the type of plot that is used, in mode of characterization, point of view, etc.[1]

This novel is formulaic and didactic and is written according to canonical exemplars.[2] Although Clark bases her findings on novels written after the first Soviet Writers' Congress, they certainly apply in great part as well to the three above-mentioned novels, each of which has been routinely cited by Soviet literary authorities as one of the exemplars on which the Soviet novelistic tradition is founded.

It is not my intention to investigate how well either the Soviet novel or its exemplary predecessors conform to the naturalistic novelistic tradition of the nineteenth century. The ambiguous position of these novels in the tradition has already been much discussed and analyzed. I would, however, like to point out that many of the qualities (or flaws, depending on one's point of view) which are inherent in the Soviet novel, that is, didacticism, optimism, and an ideological engagement which exacerbates the tension between the poetic and communicative functions of literary art, are precisely those which would facilitate the depiction of the ascetic hero. I do not suggest that they necessarily *dictate* the presence of such a hero, but merely note that they allow for it. If actual concrete occurrences of the ascetic type are to be fully explained, one more ingredient is essential—a proper extraliterary motivation towards asceticism.

Of the two motivations towards asceticism which were operative in Old Russian literature, one, the pursuit of the vision of God, is less frequently encountered in Russian nineteenth- and twentieth-century literature. Presumably heroes like Sergius and Ferapont are still moved by it, but for the most part, the combination of this theme with an ascetic hero gradually becomes the province of religious literature rather than of belles-lettres. In any case, depiction of asceticism as a strictly religious phenomenon is hardly likely in a novel coming out of either the utilitarian or the Soviet traditions.[3]

Apocalyptic expectations, however, offer a much more fruitful field of investigation. Although belief in a millennial Second Coming
is associated in its earliest stages of development with religious
doctrines, Judaic and Christian, the basic theoretical assumptions
which make belief in a millennial kingdom possible—the convictions that history has meaning and that there is a controlling force
behind history—are not, in and of themselves, religious. As David
Bethea points out,

> It has long been maintained that as the idea of history as divinely
> inspired human activity with an imminent conclusion from
> without gave way to the idea of history as secular progress
> with an immanent conclusion here on earth the historical "plot"
> was constantly modified to include an ever wider and disparate
> reality.[4]

The religious believer defines the controlling force behind history
as God, but the social thinker, and the post-Hegelian thinker in
particular, is equally within his rights to define it as social necessity.[5]

The history of pre-Hegelian millenarian movements has been
traced and analyzed by Cohn.[6] It is a history marked by the intermingling and confusion of religious doctrines with social protest.
This intermediate stage of chiliastic development does not concern
us here, however. As Cohn has pointed out, socioreligious millenarian
uprisings occur in times of great social stress and upheaval, primarily in periods when an agricultural order is giving way to an
industrial one.[7] Such a change does not really begin to take place
in Russia until the nineteenth century, by which time social thinkers have largely replaced theology with philosophy. The movements
which Cohn describes are also initiated, in large part, by the illiterate masses. Accordingly, they leave little in the way of belletristic
documentation.[8]

Nineteenth-century traditions, however, are often colored by
conceptions of history having meaning and direction. Armed with
the potent mechanism of Hegel's dialectic, tempered by Feuerbach's
materialism, for example, the nineteenth-century Russian revolutionary, frequently the product of a church-school and a religious
family, becomes enamored of the new, and yet essentially familiar
idea of inevitable salvation through history.[9] A revolutionary thinker
like Chernyshevsky, hampered by well-known tsarist prohibitions

against publishing political material, not only dreams millennial dreams but also commits them to paper in the most expedient way possible, in the guise of belles-lettres. His dreams, couched as literature, are filled with shining visions of the future, a future in which all mankind will enjoy unparalleled freedom and bliss. For Chernyshevsky, however, the imperfect present also continues to exist. He attempts to see beyond its harsh realities and finds hope in the few strong individuals who are willing to sacrifice material comforts in order to bring about social upheaval and the reign of the chosen. Enter the ascetic hero.[10]

When Marxism is introduced to Russia, social thought acquires an even more millenarian variant. Marxist thought, much more stridently than Hegelian, insists that progress towards the future is inevitable, that this progress will be realized through a great conflict which will determine who are the saved and who the lost, and that the nature of the millennial kingdom can be known even before its advent. In orthodox Marxism, history is closed; it will find its culmination in the achievement of the communist kingdom.[11]

Marx, of course, was strongly influenced by Ludwig Feuerbach, a figure who is also crucial for an understanding of the Russian followers of Left-Hegelianism. Feuerbach, who, in opposition to Hegel, derives spirit from matter, argues in *Das Wesen der Religion* for a new philosophy based on anthropology and physiology. His popularity in Russia guaranteed that at least some millenarian thinkers would interpret the approaching final stage as an anthropocentric, material kingdom.

Lenin's adaptation of both Feuerbach and Marx to Russian conditions reinforces, among other things, the concept of the strong, ascetic individual. Although this concept also appears to have been anticipated by Engels, ("... in order to concentrate as a class, the lower strata of society must begin with stripping themselves of everything that could reconcile them to the existing order of society. They must renounce all pleasures which would make their subdued position in the least tolerable. ...."),[12] Lenin, by his own personal example, gives it more precision. The ascetic must now not only deprive himself of all pleasures; he must also be a man apart. He is no longer one of a mass of like-minded fighters. He is now the *leader* of the humble masses, who guides them, against their will if need be, towards a goal which their ignorance keeps them from clearly seeing.

The Leninist correction to Engel's picture of the ascetic revolutionary has interesting ramifications. Although the Marxian dialectic has as its stated goal the improvement of all mankind, or the perfection of society as a whole, the Leninist variant is willing to sacrifice the desires of mankind, insofar as it is made up of the ignorant masses, for the vision of a few strong individuals. We come face to face with the paradoxical proposition that the ascetic leader, who nominally acts in the name of the people, must not, in fact, consult with the people; rather he must act according to his own vision, which is formed by apocalyptic hopes for the advent of a new transcendent kingdom.[13]

Thus, the engagement with eschatological teachings first evidenced by Avraamii Smolenskii resurfaces in Russian intellectual life. As early as the medieval period, it begins to subtly evolve a political variant. The original vision of Moscow as the Third Rome substitutes national salvation for Avraamii's vision of personal salvation. Although medieval rhetoric remains ecclesiastical, salvation nevertheless begins to be connected more and more frequently with Russia's national destinies. Russia is identified with the earthly representation of the heavenly kingdom. And although much of the intellectual speculation of the eighteenth and early nineteenth centuries revolves around the more practical question of Russia's rank among the foremost European powers, issues of the internal life of the country gradually begin to gain the upper hand as the nineteenth century wanes. A pressing problem—Russia's unevenly balanced social structure—absorbs the attention of the minds of the day, and many of the proposed solutions have a strongly millennial coloration. Many Russian thinkers fall into a time-honored pattern of seeking an extreme and immediate solution, one which will be guaranteed of success. They opt for a radical upheaval of society, in which the working classes, the "saved," will stand forth and condemn the gentry, the "lost." When Marxist theory is grafted onto previously existing revolutionary fervor, the guarantee of success is in place. Once again Russians dream of the establishment of the heavenly kingdom on earth—only this time it is connected neither with the Church nor with the concept of an individual nation state, but rather, with the rule of a chosen class. Paradoxically, however, Russians come to realize that this class is unprepared for its destined role, and they substitute ascetic leaders in its place.

The potential danger of the ascetic solution to Russia's social problems is recognized by certain thinkers. When each of the writers of the *Landmarks* group (*Vekhi*, 1909) subjects the *intelligentsia* to his powerful analysis, he comes to a conclusion which remains remarkably consistent throughout the collection of essays—that the Russian *intelligent* cultivates the eschatological dream of establishing a "City of God" or "Kingdom of Justice" very much in the same way as the religious ascetic. The *intelligent* approach to establishing this kingdom, however, is seen to be fated to deliver unexpected and negative results. As Sergei Bulgakov reasons,

> The very essence of heroism presupposes a passive object for its activity, the nation being saved or mankind; whereas the hero—individual or collective—is always thought of in the singular. If there turn out to be several heroes and heroic methods, rivalry and dissension are inevitable, for several "dictatorships" at one time is impossible. As a prevailing attitude, heroism is not a unifying principle but a divisive one . . .[14]

And Semen Frank suggests that the ascetic revolutionary is

> intoxicated with the ideal of the radical and universal realization of people's happiness; and in the light of this ideal, one person's simple aid to another, the simple easing of each day's troubles and worries not only pales and loses its moral attractiveness, it even seems a harmful waste of energy and time on petty and useless cares, a betrayal of all mankind and its eternal salvation for the sake of just a few nearby individuals.[15]

Although cultivating the ascetic solution is seen to be fraught with potential far-reaching social and political consequences, however, the *Landmarks* message is not heeded.

How is the evolving millennial dream reflected in *literature*, and how, more specifically, does it begin to generate ascetic heroes again? We must be careful not to jump directly from social thought into the literary work. Although art is sometimes considered a mere mirror of man's social concerns, although Russian art, in particular, is often cited as being a very accurate mirror, although authors like Chernyshevsky beg their readership to view art as a mirror, we must nevertheless argue that art has its own concerns and evolves along its own paths.[16] This is borne out by the fact that, although millennial patterns recur throughout Russian history, they fail to generate a significant number of ascetic heroes until the second half of the nineteenth century. Why is this? What intermingling of literary and extraliterary factors explains the reemergence of a strictly unidimensional ascetic hero and assures us that his reemergence will take place precisely in nineteenth-century Russia?

We have determined that the classic ascetic is primarily a manifestation of non-naturalistic art, and we have examined why he fails as a heroic type in the great tradition of the realistic novel. His very simplicity and linearity allow him to appear, at best, as a caricature or a secondary character in such works. He fails to reflect the delight in complexity which is characteristic of works which celebrate the here and now. Although the millennial theories which generated ascetic heroes like Avraamii continue to inform Russian social thought, their radical simplicity has no place in the world of naturalistic art.

It seems fairly evident that the end of the nineteenth century marks a shift towards a more consistently non-naturalistic trend in art in much of Europe, as well as in Russia. Worringer explains earlier periods of non-naturalistic creation as products either of a primitive view of the world which fears complexity or of a spiritual view which comprehends and yet rejects complexity. He gives no explanation for the resurgence of non-naturalistic art in Europe in the modern period.

A likely explanation is that modern nineteenth- and twentieth-century man suffers from a plight which, however much it reverses that of primitive man, is nevertheless equally productive of the non-naturalistic urge. Modern man is far from needing an explanation of the world's intricacies. He is inundated at every turn by myriad explanations, scientific and nonscientific. It is most probable that man's oversaturation with complexity creates a reaction in the form of a compelling need to flee into a simpler world, a reaction which ushers in a new age of non-naturalistic simplicity.

Although we can posit that the ascetic hero will perhaps reappear when there is a return to non-naturalistic art forms, we must explore the question of why his reemergence should take place precisely in nineteenth-century *Russia*. Furthermore, Susan Ruben Suleiman points out multiple realizations of unidimensional character types in simplistic, non-naturalistic nineteenth-century fiction.[17] Again, why the *ascetic* hero? We must search for answers in the heroic tradition which immediately precedes the reinstatement of the ascetic pattern.

The hero of most classic realistic novels is complex and dynamic. This complex hero begins to dissolve at the end of the nineteenth century, however, and ". . . [his] elements are dispersed in one of two directions, either backward into the substratum of myth (from which the human heroic form originally emerged) or forward, as it were, into the multiple ambiguities of the narrator who celebrates the hero's achievements."[18] Given nineteenth-century Russia's attachment to dualist, millennial social doctrines, it is reasonable to expect that representations of some of those heroes who move "backward into myth" will be based on the medieval pattern of dualist ascetics. For nineteenth-century authors like Chernyshevsky, it is not necessarily important whether their medieval prototype is motivated by a desire to see God or by a desire to be numbered among the "saved." The religious shading of the hero's motivations will be dropped in any case, and only his most essential characteristics—a simplistic view of reality as either all black or all white, a megalomaniacal reliance on his own powers, a belief in the ultimate reality of his own salvation—will be retained. Thus, the medieval ascetic emerges as an ideal candidate for the hero of a simplified, socially engaged fiction.

This simplified fiction is very much a recognizable branch of the larger tree of Russian literature. It has organic links with all the preceding stages of literary history. Clark points out its structural affinities with works of both the medieval period and the nineteenth century,[19] while A. Sinyavsky connects its thematics, its undisguised sense of political purposefulness, with the eighteenth century.[20] Most important, however, is the question of how this simplified, purposeful fiction evolves into its own tradition, beginning with works by nineteenth-century social critics and culminating in full-blown Socialist Realism.

Some critics have viewed works of literature written in the tradition which eventually evolves into Socialist Realism as a regrettable departure from the high standards of literary art achieved in the nineteenth century. Mirsky, for instance, divides *fin-de-siècle* literature into two schools, the Symbolist and the New Realist, and clearly finds the Symbolist the better and more innovative.

> But the main issue between the two schools has nothing to do with the talents of the two parties—it is a matter of cultural level: the Gorky-Andreev school are the successors of the old *intelligentsia* who had lost much of the ethical education of the old Radicals and acquired nothing in return beyond a 'craving void' of pessimism and unbelief. The Sym-

bolists were the pioneers of a new culture which, though one-sided and imperfect, infinitely widened and enriched the Russian mind and made the *intelligentsia* at once more European and more national.[21]

Trotsky, writing from a very different perspective, seems, strangely enough, to concur in this opinion. Writing on the impossibility of "creating" a proletarian culture, he states that "our epoch is not yet an epoch of new culture, but only the entrance to it. We must, first of all, take possession, politically, of the most important elements of the old culture, to such an extent, at least, as to be able to pave the way for a new culture."[22]

The argument that the old art must be assimilated by the working class and must function as a basis for the new art to come seems to lie at the heart of most pronouncements on the relationship between Socialist Realism and the nineteenth century. The problem confronting Soviet literary theorists is the extent to which the old tradition must be reflected by the new. Mirsky implies that the new tradition consciously aspires to take over the old *in toto* but fails for want of inspiration. The official Soviet view is, as might be expected, somewhat different. It asserts that "works of bourgeois literature were centered on the fate of an individual pursuing egotistic aims in defiance of society. In Soviet literature the life of an individual is inseparable from that of the social collective, and he can succeed only if his actions are stimulated by socialist ideals."[23] In other words, the old literature is based on the individual, while the new celebrates the collective.

Does this argument not miss the point, however? Implicit in it is the assumption that socially engaged art, beginning with works by the nineteenth-century social critics and progressing to Socialist Realism, can be judged by the same standards as works by the great nineteenth-century realists. We have already ascertained that the late nineteenth and early twentieth centuries mark the turn from naturalistic to non-naturalistic styles in art. We can posit that Symbolism and Mirsky's "New Realism" are related, if formally different, indicators of this turn. While one reflects man's frustration with the excessive ordering of his universe, the other reflects his sense that it is perhaps not yet ordered enough. In any case, the art produced by these two schools shrinks away from concrete depictions of reality in all its complexity.[24] Symbolism rejects the concreteness of reality, while Gorky and his followers reject its complexity. The fact that literature in the tradition of Gorky has so often been called "realistic" camouflages its complex nature. As will be seen subsequently, many works of Socialist Realism include elements of romanticism. Neither Symbolism nor Socialist Realism is "realistic" in the strictest sense of the word, and neither should be judged by the criteria of realism.

In her study of Soviet literature, Clark uses Bakhtin's distinction between the epic and the novel. The epic focuses on actions which occur in an "absolute past," a period which is in no way related to present, profane reality. Its hero is externalized. He "sees and knows in himself only the things that others see and know in him. Everything that another person—the author—is able to say about him he can say about himself, and vice versa."[25] The novel deals with contemporary reality and its interconnections with the past and the future. No segment of time is foreign or unrelated to the present. The hero is internalized in that his actions and desires are found to be in conflict with his abilities and possibilities.

Assuming that we, like Clark, substitute the millennial future kingdom for the absolute past of the epic, do we not discover a literary form which more closely approximates works like Gorky's *Mother* than does the novel? And are we not then required to shift our analysis away from the relationships between this kind of literature and the literature of Russia's "golden age" and towards analogies with Russia's other "epic" period, the medieval? We are forced to realize that not only similarities in socioreligious thought patterns but also similarities in basic literary structuring devices tie works of medieval authors to those of Marxist and utilitarian writers.

This realization brings us back to our original subject of inquiry, the ascetic hero. The pervasiveness of millenarian thought patterns, while an essential precondition for his creation, does not by itself lead to his depiction in literature. Although he is regularly portrayed in religious works, he will rejoin the literary tradition, if at all, only in an age which cultivates non-naturalistic art forms.

CHERNYSHEVSKY'S "MOVER OF MOVERS"

Extraliterary factors, in the form of dualist, millenarian social teachings, and literary factors, in the form of a full turn towards a non-naturalistic art form, the epic, are successfully joined together for the first time since the medieval period in Chernyshevsky's novel, *What Is to Be Done?* This much-celebrated and much-disparaged work is also the vehicle for the reentry of a simplistic ascetic hero into Russia's literary tradition.

Although Chernyshevsky's novel is often cited as a precursor of the Socialist Realist novel, we must exercise caution in making an unqualified identification between it and those works of high Socialist Realism which come after it and further develop the depiction of the ascetic hero. As Clark has shown, Soviet novelists have created their own pedigrees by finding direct literary ancestors, like Chernyshevsky, where others might see only distant relatives.[26] Thus, Chernyshevsky is no Socialist Realist, nor is his novel a premature representative of the Soviet tradition.[27] There are, nevertheless, numerous points of similarity between Chernyshevsky's work and later, twentieth-century works which cannot be denied. And the very fact that Soviet critics might find much of interest in Chernyshevsky indicates that connections do exist. Chernyshevsky is but one of the first in a long line of authors who reject many of the conventions of the classic nineteenth-century novel in favor of a simplified, didactic fiction. We will find in him the earliest stages in the development of this fiction, as well as in the development of the ascetic hero.

The history of the composition of *What Is to Be Done?* is well known. Regardless of whether we agree with Georg Lukács's assessment that Chernyshevsky came to write a novel only because no other avenue of activity was open to him,[28] or with Francis B. Randall's opinion that he willingly cultivated the form,[29] we must concede that Chernyshevsky's task was very difficult. Prison conditions robbed him both of the possibility of seeking the critical opinion of others and of the time to draft and redraft at length. *What Is to Be Done?* can thus be said to be an extreme example of the novel which reflects only its author's own views.[30] As we shall see, this sets it apart from twentieth-century novels which are extensively rewritten to more accurately reflect others' interpretations of the canon.

Where in this classic work of revolutionary fiction do we find the ascetic hero? For that matter, where do we find the hero at all? Critics continue to disagree on so basic a question as that of who the novel's hero truly is. Some propose Vera Pavlovna and suggest that her liberation from society's anti-feminist tyranny is meant as a metaphor for Russia's inevitable liberation from tsarist rule.

Others suggest the "new man," by which they understand a collective hero consisting of those traits held in common by Dmitrii
Sergeevich Lopukhov, Aleksandr Matveevich Kirsanov, Vera Pavlovna,
and Katerina Vasil'evna. Yet others propose Rakhmetov, "the rigorist,"
whose actions are, however, ancillary to the main relationships worked
out in the novel.[31]

All of these characters do suggest themselves as candidates
for the role, but none of them combines to a necessary degree the
quality of self-assertiveness with a position of centrality in the structural
design of the plot. Rather than searching for a single hero, then, it
might be wiser to view the major characters as Chernyshevsky seems
to have wanted them to be viewed, which is to say, in comparison
with each other.

One group of characters—Vera Pavlovna's mother, her wealthy
suitor, his mother—falls into the traditional category of villains. None
of these characters plays any significant role in the novel, however. Another group consists of the "new men," the "good, strong,
honest, and capable" few (p. 14), who are as yet a minority within
society. These are the Kirsanovs, the Lopukhovs, and their likes.
The final group has but one member—Rakhmetov. He stands apart
from the others by virtue of being "the flower of the best in humanity; the mover of movers; the salt of the salt of the earth" (p.
284). Chernyshevsky states his intention to compare and contrast
Rakhmetov and the others very clearly.

> If I were not to show the figure of Rakhmetov, the majority
> of readers would miss the mark regarding the main characters
> in my story. I'll make a bet that up until the final segments of
> this chapter, Vera Pavlovna, Kirsanov, and Lopukhov seemed
> to the majority of my audience to be the heroes, beings of a
> superior nature, perhaps even idealized characters. . . . No,
> my friends, . . . they do not stand too high, but rather you
> stand too low. (p. 308)

There are those who claim that the three groups are neither
mutually exclusive nor closed.[32] Chernyshevsky himself seems to
imply this when he states that the second group, the strong, decent individuals, is growing day by day. Presumably it is fed by
converts from the first group, the low natures. Chernyshevsky even
allows himself to digress on the subject of Vera Pavlovna's mother,
suggesting that she might have been different were it not for the
evil social system into which she was born.

In fact, Chernyshevsky wavers on this question. As an avowed materialist and follower of Feuerbach, he seems to give credence to a determinist position according to which environment conditions man's actions. As N.G.O. Pereira points out, Vera Pavlovna's second dream, in which the health of crops is tied directly to the quality of the soil which produces them, implies that no progress in human affairs is possible. At the same time, however, Chernyshevsky also defends the proposition that on rare occasions poor soil produces good plants (that is, that corrupt social conditions do, from time to time, produce "new men").[33] William F. Woehrlin notes that although Chernyshevsky never worked out a systematic theory of determinism, he nevertheless tried to formulate an ethic consistent with materialism.[34] The tension in Chernyshevsky between determinism and progress, in turn, raises the question of just how consistently he espoused a materialist philosophy.[35]

In spite of his hopes for mankind's regeneration, however, Chernyshevsky fails to supply a convincing example of how low natures can ascend to the level of the decent. Vera Pavlovna's friend Julie, the mistress of a wealthy social rake, never rises above her physical desires, even though she understands that they are low. Nasten'ka Kriukova, a seamstress in Vera Pavlovna's model sewing cooperative, appears at first to have made the transition to a higher level of existence. She has abandoned a life of prostitution and become virtuous. She is suffering, however, from consumption, which she has contracted owing to her earlier dissolute behavior. Her tenure among the new men is quickly and inexorably cut short by a death which is the preordained consequence of a low life. Within the actual text of *What Is to Be Done?*, there is no overt instance of a permanent change in a low individual's status.

Even less susceptible to penetration is the exclusive group consisting of the "salt of the salt of the earth." In comparing Rakhmetov with decent, strong men, Chernyshevsky instructs his reader that "superior natures, which are not to be expropriated by the likes of you and me, my poor friend, superior natures are not like these" (p. 308). Vera Pavlovna and her like marvel at men such as Rakhmetov but can never aspire to their heights.[36]

Of what do the heights attained by men like Rakhmetov consist? Chernyshevsky, hindered most certainly by the censor, gives a very sketchy picture of the life of an extraordinary man. Rakhmetov's goals are never openly stated. His methods for achieving them, however, are specified in detail. Rakhmetov has given away his fortune and adopted a very singular way of life. We are told that, although he is fond of elegance, he dresses shabbily and sleeps on the floor. He allows himself meat only in order to maintain his physical strength and denies himself most other foods. He has vowed to do without women, although he is much attracted to them. He spends no more time with his fellows than is absolutely necessary. Finally, as the ultimate test of his resolve, he forces himself to lie on a bed of nails all night.

It should be fairly clear that Rakhmetov has *voluntarily* chosen to exile himself from society and its pleasures and that he has adopted ascetic practices as a means of doing so. He has not completely severed his physical links to society, as did the medieval ascetic, but he has cut himself off from it in more subtle ways.[37] His physical presence in St. Petersburg's intellectual circles is analogous to the Kievan ascetic's physical presence within the monastery's walls. Just as the medieval ascetic removed himself from both secular and ecclesiastical society, so too does Rakhmetov remove himself from both the wealthy society he was born to and progressive intellectual circles formed by men like Lopukhov and Kirsanov.

A more metaphysical separation—separation of the spirit from the body also takes place. Rakhmetov's own words attest to it: "'Yes, pity me, you're right, pity me: why even I am not an abstract idea but, rather, a man who would like to live. But this is nothing, however, and it will pass.' And it did pass" (p. 281). Thus, Rakhmetov intentionally crushes all his feelings and emotions in order to refine himself into an essence of pure spirit and will.

Why are such sacrifices necessary? What goal does Rakhmetov pursue? Chernyshevsky gives us the answer quite overtly—perfection. The author tells us that Rakhmetov's only remaining weakness is his addiction to tobacco. Because of this one minor tie to the world of physical pleasures, Rakhmetov's opponents are within their rights to say, "So you see, *perfection* is impossible" (p. 272, emphasis mine). Such reproaches cause Rakhmetov to redouble his efforts to break this one final tie to the material world.

What kind of perfection does Rakhmetov pursue, societal or individual? Although Chernyshevsky devotes all his energies to contrasting realistic depictions of the life of the masses with idealized ones, he never succeeds in uniting the theme of the improvement of society with the activities of its great mover, Rakhmetov. As we have seen, the masses are incapable of rising to the level of the Kirsanovs and Lopukhovs, much less to the lofty heights of the

Rakhmetovs, and although we can assume that Rakhmetov's secret activities are aimed at improving the lot of these masses, he never overtly undertakes anything remotely connected with this task. The most salient details of Rakhmetov's life are all indicative of his efforts to improve himself, and only himself.

The excuses for Chernyshevsky's failure to expand on Rakhmetov's intentions are legion and, for the most part, correct. Nevertheless, the author must be expected to give some clue as to his hero's motivations if the work is to convey any meaning at all to its readers. I propose that Chernyshevsky gives us just such a clue in a little-commented-on passage which introduces the one segment of the novel which is dedicated entirely to Rakhmetov. In this segment Rakhmetov comes to hearten Vera Pavlovna with the news that Lopukhov is not really dead, but finding her engaged in various important matters, he retires to the library to read. He rejects any number of interesting and important books in favor of just one— Newton's *Observations on the Prophecies of Daniel and the Apocalypse of St. John*. This book alone merits Rakhmetov's highest praise: "It is a book worth studying" (p. 265).

Rakhmetov explains that the *Observations* draw his attention because they reflect the growing insanity of their semisenile author.[38] Rahkmetov intends to study the union in one single man of two phenomena which are usually kept separate one from another, sanity and insanity, or in other words, the rational and the irrational. This question interests Rakhmetov precisely because it closely concerns his own activities. He is, in his own mind, the ideal embodiment of rationality, while society, as it exists, is a picture of irrationality. I would suggest that his life's goal is, in fact, to effect a union of the two, in which his rationality will transform society's irrationality.

How is this seemingly impossible task to be achieved? Through apocalypse. Chernyshevsky could have chosen works by any number of authors in their waning years to illustrate his point that sanity and insanity can be reconciled with each other. His choice of a work which seeks to interpret Old and New Testament apocalypses and which suggests that much of the original ecclesiastical terminology of apocalypse can be replaced with equivalent historical terms, therefore, cannot be completely arbitrary.[39] He sees the coming transformation of society as an apocalyptic one, one which is as inexorable as it is desirable, and he further sees it as one which will be heralded by a strong, ascetic individual, a leader who is capable of seeing a truth no one else can.

Rakhmetov, then, like the Kievan ascetic, is involved in a quest which is anathema to institutionalized society. His moment of initiation—the moment when he is found worthy to be numbered among the saved[40]—cannot, therefore, be named. Just as Avraamii Smolenskii has a vision of the future which seems higher to him than the institutionalized Church's, so too does Rakhmetov have a vision which is higher than the government's. To describe it in detail would be to risk the wrath of the censor, the nineteenth-century equivalent of ecclesiastical censure.

Rakhmetov, like all true ascetics, separates himself from society, is initiated into a great truth, and fails to return to the society which sent him forth. He disappears not only from the scrutiny of his author, Chernyshevsky, who drops him in order to return to the fate of the new men, but also from the intellectual circles among which he is known. He leaves Russia altogether on a mysterious mission of his own devising. He takes care to put all his personal affairs in order, thus making it clear that he will never return. Katerina Clark has suggested that Rakhmetov's nonreturn should be viewed as a sign that *What Is to Be Done?* is, in fact, still an open-ended, "novelistic" novel. By this she means that the narrative is still free to take unexpected turns.[41] I prefer, however, to interpret his disappearance as an action, predictable within the context of his heroic career, which allows him to join the ranks of the ascetic heroes—heroes of a non-novelistic, non-open-ended fiction.

We have established that one of the heroes of *What Is to Be Done?* meets the criteria for definition as an ascetic: he follows a pattern of separation-initiation-nonreturn; and he opts for extreme solutions to complex problems. He rejects the existence of a tension between himself and society by unilaterally declaring his own superiority to all others; he rejects his own subjection to social necessity (Chernyshevsky's equivalent of the supernatural) by refusing to remain a member of the privileged, aristocratic family into which he was born (the equivalent of Feodosii Pecherskii's rejection of his family); and he rejects any tendency in himself to fall victim to the complexities of life and thus to alter his already completed and perfected nature (as for instance, when he refuses the love of a noble and "decent" woman to whom he is greatly attracted, an action which recalls Moisei's rejection of physical love in the KCP).

Are the other major characters with whom Rakhmetov is to be compared and contrasted also ascetics? The answer to this question is a very definite "no." These other "heroes," like the cenobitic monks of Kievan literature, remove themselves from the low and ignorant masses only to build a better, more ideal society among themselves. They do not, therefore, endure a complete and radical separation from society. Like cenobites, they engage in moderate asceticisms— Vera Pavlovna's celebrated celibacy in her first marriage, all the characters' scorn for large sums of money and luxuries—but these ascetic acts are important primarily because of their significance as models of behavior for others to follow. They are never extreme, and they are never intended either to produce results by themselves or to change the nature of the characters. Finally, these heroes create their own self-contained social institutions, like Vera Pavlovna's sewing shop, Kirsanov's medical practice, and the shared living accommodations of the Lopukhovs and the Kirsanovs, in order to create a model in the here and now of the beautiful society which will come into being with the advent of the millennial kingdom. This reminds us of Feodosii's ordering of the monastic life by means of the Studite *Rule*. Therefore, like the cenobites, the Kirsanovs and Lopukhovs strive for aesthetic perfection. Each, by performing his own task well and efficiently, contributes to the smooth functioning of the greater societal unit (sewing shop, etc.), and the unit itself becomes, in turn, an "icon" of the ideal society. The new men "return" to society in the sense that their actions are directed towards providing concrete and practical examples of how to bring about the "salvation" or transformation of society as a whole.[42]

What Is to Be Done? presents us with two different types of heroes. We have, on the one hand, the proud, aloof ascetic and, on the other, the social reformer, who is personally involved in society's woes. This contrast between two types of heroes parallels a contrast between two types of writing. The greater number of chapters, which are concerned with the new men, are novelistic. For all its saccharine didacticism, its kitsch, What Is to Be Done? still manages to present heroes who learn and grow. Its action progresses in a clichéd manner, but it is not yet totally predictable. Melodramatic incidents like Vera Pavlovna's rejection of Lopukhov and his feigned "suicide" and eventual return to St. Petersburg may be contrived, but they are, nevertheless, legitimate devices for retarding and complicating the narrative. The major events of the story line are firmly fixed in the present and refer only obliquely to a beautiful but unreal future.

The chapters which deal with Rakhmetov, however, are different. His life story belongs to the past, and to a very obscure and unreal past at that. Its details are pieced together primarily from rumor. His present is completely ignored, but his future is bright, if somewhat shrouded and mysterious.[43] It is very unlikely that Rakhmetov will change. He already possesses a rigidly observed set of living habits and has, by the author's own admission, completed his self-imposed course of reading. The future holds no new truths for him. No confusions or distractions interfere with the development of his affairs. *What Is to Be Done?* mixes two styles, the naturalistic or novelistic and the non-naturalistic or epic. It is a transitional work which contains both multidimensional and unidimensional heroes.

What Is to Be Done? opposes two different orders, the transcendent order of the millennial kingdom and the profane order of everyday reality. As a result, the novel wavers between two different concepts of time. On the one hand, we have the static atemporality of the mythic future. The future will be an age of reconciliation when the reign of the saved will be firmly consolidated. There will be no conflict and, therefore, no change. Time, understood as progress and change, will cease to exist. This is the world to which Rakhmetov belongs. On the other hand, we have the profane temporality of everyday life. Characters are born and die, traumas are experienced and surmounted, and social experiments win or lose in value and significance. Life is in flux, and time is dynamic. Occasionally the world of dynamic temporality is even allowed to intrude on the static world of atemporality. Rakhmetov, for example, is forcibly drawn away from his apocalyptic concerns to comfort Vera Pavlovna. The small comings and goings of everyday people are considered important enough to interrupt the greater affairs of the movers and shakers.

The result of the interplay between the temporal and atemporal in *What Is to Be Done?* is an uneasy suspension of the work between the worlds of naturalistic and non-naturalistic art. Dynamism belongs to the world of fiction. It is a recognition of the constant evolution of the here and now. In Frank Kermode's terminology, fictions are the "agents of change." Atemporality is the hallmark of myth, which tries to make sense of a lost order of time, or, in this case, of a golden age yet to come. Myths are thus "agents of stability."[44] *What Is to Be Done?* is part myth, part fiction; part epic, part novel; part non-naturalistic, part naturalistic; and finally, part ascetic, part worldly. Regardless of the terminology chosen, the result is the same; a mixture of generically incompatible elements.

These features of *What Is to Be Done?* remind us of the literature of Kievan ascetics. Elements of dynamism compete with elements of stasis; profane concerns clash with eternal visions; the hero
chooses a path, but the author, reader, and other characters are drawn
to propose an alternative one. This is not to disregard the differences between modern and medieval literature. The modern audience is used to viewing time from a dynamic perspective, to finding
disparities in point of view. The medieval reader views art from
the opposite perspective, taking atemporality as the literary norm
and unanimity as the accepted practice. Nevertheless, both *What
Is to Be Done?* and works featuring medieval ascetics achieve similar effects. They startle their readers by introducing unexpected,
intrusive elements. The Kievan work achieves its effect by introducing a strongly novelistic element, temporality. *What Is to Be Done?*
surprises us by introducing an epic element, atemporality. Although
medieval and nineteenth-century readers' and authors' expectations
are based on opposing understandings of literary convention, they
are equally disrupted by the mixture of two different temporal orders.

What Is to Be Done? also shares another feature with works
about Kievan ascetics—its approach to space. Kievan ascetic literature,
it will be recalled, neglects space. It either fails to mention the hero's
surroundings or specifies them as tightly bound and cramped (caves,
monastic cells). Nature plays no part in this literature. Nature is
also conspicuously absent from *What Is to Be Done?* Again, the heroes
live in modest rooms, not houses or palaces. Like Avraamii, who
moves from monastery to monastery, Lopukhov moves back and
forth between St. Petersburg, Moscow, Riazan', and Western Europe, but his movements are merely a pretext for advancing the
plot. There is no description of his travels, no feeling that he is actually
moving from one place to another, experiencing a new space, seeing new sights.[45]

In her discussion of the literary chronotope in the Stalinist novel,
Katerina Clark notes that

> . . . ordinary characters and events represent the present-day
> time of the novel, and extraordinary ones simultaneously bear
> the imprint of the two Great Times of Stalinist culture, the earlier
> heroic era of Lenin's time, and the future time of communism.[46]

On first consideration this split between two orders of time/space
looks very similar to the one which pertains in *What Is to Be Done?*

Clark further suggests, however, that the function of the positive hero in Socialist Realist novels is to mediate between the two time orders portrayed. Initially he is the "most promising" of the characters who represent present time, but by the end of the novel he makes a "great leap" into heroic future time.[47] This is not the case with Rakhmetov. Although he does, on rare occasions, mix with the "new men," he is portrayed from the outset as being far superior to them. He has already made his "great leap" and acts as an inspirational leader rather than a mediator. We can speculate that if mediation is to be achieved, it will most likely be achieved by one of the characters who represents the present order, that is, by Vera Pavlovna, Kirsanov, or Lopukhov.

By the same token, *What Is to Be Done?* also differs from earlier, medieval works in its use of chronotope. We have said that ascetic works of the earliest period, like Soviet novels, were organized around an alternation in temporal orders, more particularly, an alternation between adventure and everyday time. These works concentrated on the development of the hero, a man living in adventure time. Everyday time was "seamy," the realm of sexuality and violence. Furthermore, throughout the work, contact with everyday time was accidental. In *What Is to Be Done?* the major focus is shifted onto those characters who represent everyday time, and everyday time itself is seen as having both positive and negative sides. Contact between representatives of the two temporal orders is consciously sought out. And if reconciliation between the two orders was unthinkable in the earlier works, it is the overarching goal of *What Is to Be Done?*

Although the world as it is portrayed in *What Is to Be Done?* is torn by dichotomies and splits between what is and what is to come, the hope is expressed that all such breaches will somehow be healed. Such reconciliation lies, as yet, outside the world depicted in the novel, however. The novel itself, like earlier works, depicts a static ascetic, working to establish a future millennial kingdom.

We can say in conclusion that Chernyshevsky reintroduces the ascetic hero into a work which is essentially non-naturalistic for the first time in two centuries. His ascetic, while ostensibly working to heal all breaches, nevertheless champions a radical, dualist[48] way of life as a means of entering the ranks of a small group of chosen "movers," who will be the leaders of the "strong and decent" members of society. The ascetic answers the need for a simple, uncomplicated hero who will respond to the challenges of a revolutionary era, a hero who will be on the side of the good when the inevitable end of the present, evil order comes.

GORKY'S "MAN OF IRON"

It is easy to see how a man like Chernyshevsky, son of an Orthodox priest and graduate of a Church school, could become familiar with hagiographical patterns of characterization. Even during his years as a student, he "led an ascetic life. . . . He determined . . . not to know a woman until he was married."[49] At the university he "merely learnt . . . how to extend his study of Russian medieval documents, which had already begun to enthrall him at Saratov . . . ."[50] A man like Gorky, however, had fewer opportunities for serious study of medieval patterns. His formal education was scant. Although he absorbed a good deal of Orthodox tradition in the pious atmosphere of his grandparents' house, he never benefited from consistent and thorough training in Church doctrines.

Religion and its effects on the people clearly fascinated him, however, as is evidenced by his period of involvement in "god-building" (bogostroitel'stvo). This philosophy, which taught that God did not yet exist but could be created through the collective efforts of humanity, appealed strongly to Gorky during the prewar years when he was engaged, among other things, in creating his novel *Mother*.[51] It has been said that Gorky's *Confession* is the work which most overtly reflects his interest in the god-building movement,[52] but many traces of it can also be found in *Mother*. In fact, Gorky remained attached to ideas reminiscent of god-building as late as the first Soviet Writers' Congress, long after the time when such ideas had begun to be disparaged in official circles.[53]

The quest to create God through one's own efforts and in one's own image is a new evolution in the centuries-old quest to "see" God, to become a part of the essence of God. The understanding of God held by the god-builders is very different from that of Christian believers, but the basic idea that one can become part of a superhuman entity is shared by both.

Another feature of Gorky's work which is pertinent to a discussion of *Mother* is his attachment to romanticism. Although no very clear consensus has been reached regarding the definition of his type of romanticism, it is generally agreed that he is a romantic or, perhaps, a "revolutionary romantic." Gorky divided romanticism into a passive, individualistic type and an active, social type. He defines these types in the following way:

> Individualistic romanticism arose from the striving of a personality, which sensed its isolation in the world, to convince itself of its powers, of its independence from history, of the individual's possibility of controlling life. Social romanticism [arose] from the personality's consciousness of its connection to the world, from its consciousness of the immortality of those ideas which are fundamental."[54]

He himself was a practitioner of social romanticism.

Although Gorky's own formulation of romanticism gives us very little concrete information from which to predict the shape of a work written according to its precepts, it is clear enough to allow us to wreak a certain amount of chronological violence and include Gorky in the group of postrevolutionary writers of whose works it has been said that they "demonstrated one characteristic very graphically: they reflected not certain concrete signs of the times, not realistic heroes, but rather romantic dreams and a belief in the shining future."[55] This further specification of romanticism, with its emphasis on the author's approach towards portrayal of time, is obviously significant to the present study. We must now ask to what extent *Mother*, Gorky's only work featuring an ascetic hero, reflects god-building, the twentieth-century substitute for the quest for the vision of God, and to what extent it is romantic and disregards the realistic, novelistic conception of time.

Mother, like *What Is to Be Done?*, is difficult to analyze because there is a good deal of ambiguity regarding the identity of its hero.[56] Most critics identify the hero as Pavel Vlasov, but a significant minority opts for Nilovna, the mother of the title. Although Nilovna gradually changes her way of thinking and brings it more into line with her son's, she never really relinquishes certain of her own most deeply held beliefs, among which is a belief in a transcendent, loving God.[57] Moreover, the differences of opinion which separate Nilovna and Pavel are not the only differences manifested in the novel. Other important characters voice beliefs which do not always accord with either Pavel's or Nilovna's. All these characters are nevertheless conceived of as positive, morally upright men and women. This makes it difficult, within the context of the novel, to decide where Gorky really stands on certain issues.

In light of the difficulty of ascertaining who is *the* hero, it would be best to adopt the same method of analysis used in connection with *What Is to Be Done?*, namely, to compare the two most important characters, Nilovna and Pavel. Pavel is unquestionably the simpler, less interesting character, while at the same time the greater ascetic, so he will be looked at first.

Gorky's Pavel is "pale and colorless, he is neither portrayed as outwardly dynamic [plastisch], nor is attention devoted to his emotional or psychic experiences; he is an ascetic, a revolutionary who is totally true to his principles."[58] Although Gorky alludes to a brief period in Pavel's youth when he drank and carried on like the other young men of his neighborhood, this allusion is perfunctory, and the descriptions of the drunken Pavel are inconsistent with the ascetic Pavel we see for the remainder of the work. We can compare this uncharacteristic phase of his career with the period in Sergii Radonezhskii's life when he is unable to read or write. Just as Sergii's weakness is miraculously removed by an angel, so too is Pavel's through contact with representatives of the revolutionary movement.

After Pavel's brief bout with drunkenness, he becomes "simpler" (p. 160). His new-found simplicity takes the form of abstention from alcohol, disregard for the material benefits that a good worker like himself could gain by cooperating with the management of his factory, and a determination to remain celibate. The mother herself offers Pavel vodka on several occasions, and a beautiful, well-educated revolutionary falls in love with him, but Pavel remains so firm in his convictions that his "monastic severity" (p. 178) begins to trouble his mother. All of this is symptomatic of a more sweeping change which his mother cannot at first comprehend. Pavel is "floating off to the edge of the dark current of life, stubbornly and with concentration" (p. 159). He is, in other words, purposely separating himself from society.

He not only separates himself from the toiling masses, however. He also removes himself to a certain extent from the revolutionaries whose ranks he has joined. He proves much stronger than his friend Andrei, for instance, who dreams of marriage. Pavel insists that after marriage, life becomes "life for the sake of a piece of bread, for the sake of the children, for the sake of an apartment; you're no longer there for the cause" (p. 179). Andrei tells Pavel's mother that, even among the revolutionaries, Pavel must be considered a "man of iron" (p. 213). When one man is needed to carry the banner during a workers' demonstration, when one man is needed to make a stirring speech at a group trial, Pavel is always chosen. He is a leader, a power unto himself.

Again, as we did in the case of Rakhmetov, we must ask ourselves what makes Pavel willing to accept so many sacrifices. Although he is a revolutionary and is engaged in creating a new life from which one and all will benefit, Pavel is never said to be a lover of humanity. In his mother's words, he is arrested because he "is seeking the truth" (p. 199). It is significant that he is not arrested for seeking justice for the people. His "truth" is further defined as "a fairy tale about a future holiday for everyone on earth," (p. 220) but when it comes to actually dealing with individual representatives of those on earth, Pavel is conspicuously reluctant. In a discussion with Andrei, also a revolutionary who is working for the establishment of the future "holiday," Pavel makes it clear that he, for instance, "didn't like the peasants, although the Ukrainian [Andrei] stuck up for them . . . " (p. 233).

Pavel's moment of initiation involves the assurance that he is indeed the chosen leader in the revolutionary struggle to come. At first this much-desired assurance is tantalizingly dangled in front of him only to be taken away. Pavel tries to organize a strike at his factory because the management is unfairly exacting a tax on the workers. The boss addresses the workers, however, and they decide to go back to work. Pavel mourns openly to his mother: "I'm young and weak, that's what! They didn't believe me, they didn't follow my truth, which means that I wasn't able to express it! I'm unhappy; I'm offended for myself!" (p. 198) This reminds us of Avraamii's early and only partially successful attempts to assume spiritual leadership in Smolensk. When Pavel is arrested for the second time, he makes a ringing public speech, in which he denies the civil court's jurisdiction over him and promises the advent of a bright, new day. His performance is so much more impressive than the other defendants' that he becomes the *de facto* leader of the revolutionary group. This public triumph corresponds to the moment of Avraamii's triumph—the moment when his prayers for rain are heeded and he is recognized as a spiritual leader.

Nonreturn is another hallmark of Pavel's career. He is offered the possibility of escape from prison, and an attempt is actually made to free him. He sends someone else out in his place, however, preferring to remain in prison and face the inevitable sentence of hard labor in Siberia. As the novel closes, Pavel is still in the hands of the authorities, and it is unlikely that he will ever again be a useful member of society for any extensive period of time. His nonreturn is paradoxical; Pavel is a revolutionary, committed to the downfall of the old order and the creation of the new. He is needed as an active member in society for the good of his cause. He knowingly chooses a path which keeps him from his appointed task, however, and this is consonant with the fact that he does not really like working with the people.

There is no particular inner logic to Pavel's choice. I would argue that this lack of logic stems from the fact that Pavel is a representative of a particular character type, the ascetic hero, not a unique literary creation. He makes his choices in the same way that other ascetics have made them before him and not according to the logical needs of the particular literary work in which he is found.

Pavel is an example of the ascetic hero who is striving to bring about a millennial kingdom in which he will be the leader of the chosen. Nilovna, on the other hand, is neither a fully realized ascetic nor a believer in the millennial kingdom. She might be considered an ascetic in the making, however. She is totally engrossed in survival, in keeping her body intact even at the expense of her spirit, until her husband dies and Pavel's cause begins to interest her. When she is freed from her husband's tyranny, she begins to give up many of the beliefs she once held. She comes to see that socialists are not all bad, that the factory management is not a divinely ordained authority, and that there are causes which are more important than a full stomach. She never completely adopts Pavel's creed, however. Although she adores her son and is always anxious that no one offend him, her own beliefs are closer to those held by Rybin, the god-builder.

Rybin makes a declaration of his creed when he tells Nilovna that "god created man in his image and likeness, which means that he is like man, if man is like him! And we are not in the image of god, but are like wild animals. In church they show us a bugbear. . . . We have to transform god, mother, to purify him!" (p. 190). At first Nilovna is frightened by Rybin's sacrilege and repelled by his single-minded hatred of the ruling classes. In time, however, she comes to accept his message about God, even if she continues to reject his fanaticism. After she has witnessed the brutal murder of Rybin, Nilovna declares, "About god, I don't know, but I do believe in Christ. . . . And I believe in his words, love thy neighbor, as thyself . . ."(p. 350). Nilovna believes in Christ, the manifestation of the Christian God most obviously like man. She believes specifically in those teachings which concern love of man, not love of God. It is significant that in the last moments before she too is killed for her beliefs, Nilovna sees not her son, but rather the battered face of Rybin.

Nilovna's belief in God is a circumscribed one. She believes in the God of mercy but not the threatening God of justice. Pavel offends her by suggesting that God must be dispensed with but mollifies her by explaining that he is talking "not about the good and merciful god in whom you believe, but about the one with whom the priests threaten us, as if with a stick, about the god in whose name they want to force everyone to subjugate himself to the evil will of the few . . ." (p. 190). This suggests a division of the divine being into a good essence and an evil one, a belief held by the Bogomils of old. Nilovna is willing to suffer martyrdom in order to have a part in the creation of this God of goodness and mercy, who is, in fact, only an extension of herself. Thus, as she moves towards an ascetic way of life, she does so for a completely different reason from her son. She never becomes fully ascetic, however, because her God is so deeply human that he requires no separation from others.

Much of what has been said about *What Is to Be Done?* can also be said about *Mother*. Two different types of hero are presented, an ascetic hero and a heroine who is morally superior to the other characters, who bears certain ascetic traits, but who is nevertheless not an ascetic.[59] These two different heroes figure in different sections of the novel—very rarely are Pavel and his mother presented together. The sections of the novel which deal with Pavel are mythic in that they proceed as rapidly as possible towards an end which is foreordained.[60] The sections which deal with Nilovna may not be particularly sophisticated in their meanderings, but they are nevertheless more interesting and complex. They show Nilovna's gradual evolution from an unthinking, purposeless drudge to a politically conscious activist.

The parts of the novel devoted to Pavel and his vision are static. They focus on an unchanging ideal order. The means necessary for achieving this order are unimportant to Pavel. The minutiae of his daily life, of his revolutionary activities are missing in *Mother*. For Pavel, only the vision itself matters. The sections of *Mother* which are devoted to Nilovna have a different focus. Here the final end—

the regeneration of man and the creation of a God in man's new image—is a social one. The quest for the vision of God no longer pertains to the individual. It takes in society as a whole. More importantly, this final end is, in and of itself, of only secondary importance. The actual details of Nilovna's quest are the important thing for Gorky. If Pavel's daily activities remain a question mark, Nilovna's are portrayed with care. What she eats, where she sleeps, how her activities mesh with those of others—these are the things we read about Nilovna.

In *Mother* we once again find a work which is generically mixed; epic features coexist with novelistic ones. The generally low repute the novel enjoys with critics, including Gorky himself, attests to the fact that the two types of literature cannot be satisfactorily fused in modern literature. Connoisseurs of the realistic novel find Pavel wooden and unnatural. They rightly see him as representing a step backwards, towards an older type of hero. Followers of the conventions of Socialist Realism, however, are quick to see that, even though the novel presents a distressing variety of points of view, Pavel's views can be made to seem the most important. By reducing the complexity of the novel to the simplicity of Pavel's heroic career, they can create a worthy predecessor for their own unidimensional works.

Much of what jars in *Mother* can be attributed to Gorky's romanticism. His attraction towards "those ideas which are fundamental," towards the "shining future," explains his overemphasis on static, ideal images. The novel fails to move forward towards an artistically satisfying conclusion because its true goal, the millennial kingdom, has not been achieved. Nilovna's career is marked by closure, but Pavel's is not. Such a career can never come to its proper culmination as long as the struggle continues.

GLADKOV'S DASHA CHUMALOVA

This same struggle is picked up in a different setting by Fedor Gladkov's famous novel, *Cement*. *Cement* is about the post–civil war reconstruction movement, about the efforts of a few dedicated individuals to build the "shining future," which, revolution notwithstanding, has failed to materialize on its own. The novel, like *What Is to Be Done?* and *Mother*, assumes the eventual advent of an age of joy and plentitude. History will inevitably reward those who are on the right side even if it needs a little help from its champions, the proletariat.

Cement is a novel which has undergone extensive revision. The question of its writing and rewriting is complex and must be briefly touched upon because of its relevance to the present study. Gladkov made extensive changes affecting both the content and the style of the work over the course of three decades.[61] Therefore, the conscious choice of a version for analysis is crucial.

Of primary interest to this discussion is the image of Dasha, the novel's heroine. In the first versions of the novel, Dasha is described as "sleeping with many Bolshevik guerrillas during the Civil War— pro bono publico, so to speak. In the later editions Dasha sacrifices many things for the revolutionary cause, but her chastity is not one of them."[62] As Dasha is my candidate for the ascetic hero in this novel, and as promiscuous behavior is incompatible with asceticism, the choice of a text is clearly a major issue.

The first version of Cement which totally deletes Dasha's promiscuity is the 1933 edition. Considering the lateness of this and all other "ascetic" variants, there is some justification in grouping the novel together with other works of the thirties, such as Time Forward! and How the Steel Was Tempered.[63] The later versions of the novel remain true in so many important features to the original edition, however, that I choose to analyze it here, along with What Is to Be Done? and Mother. My major consideration in making this choice is the fact that Gladkov continues to structure his revised texts around the tensions in Dasha's relationship with her husband, Gleb.[64]

Gladkov compares and contrasts Dasha, the ascetic heroine, with Gleb as well as with a host of other nonascetic characters in a way which is quite similar to Chernyshevsky's and Gorky's treatments of Rakhmetov and Pavel Vlasov. There is a shared conception of the ascetic as a character who has reached perfection and of the other positive characters as decent, worthy individuals who also have a role to play in reforming their corrupt society. In all three works, the ascetic is presumed to stand much higher than his fellows, to busy himself with much more urgent tasks than they, but all three works fail, to a similar degree, to give a convincing picture of the ascetic's concrete activities. The nonascetics are the ones who actually perform the pressing tasks at hand. To the extent that the three novels concentrate on the daily activities of nonascetic characters who are heroic in their own way, who are continually searching for answers to life's questions, and who, therefore, continue to learn and grow throughout their careers, they are still very novelistic and literary. To the extent that they portray the static, perfected ascetic, they are epic and mythic. These novels remind us again of those Kievan works which derive most of their narrative interest from the actions of their nonascetic characters. I, therefore, group them together and separate them from more typical works of the 1930s whose epic qualities almost completely eclipse their novelistic ones.

There are, however, important differences between *Cement* and *What Is to Be Done?* and *Mother*. In *Cement*, Dasha is meant to function as an example to others, and there is hope that, with time, her fellows will also reach her heights. Many of them come very close. Polia and Gleb, in particular, are candidates for eventual ascetic perfection. Polia, like Dasha, has renounced family happiness, material goods, and physical pleasure. The only thing that holds her back from ascetic fortitude is her inability to master her emotions. She rebels against NEP and the return of physical pleasures with inappropriate outbursts of indignation and venom. Although she has set herself apart from the way of life enjoyed by her fellows, she is unable to make the final separation of her spiritual essence from her emotions.

Gleb is able, in most situations, to do what Polia cannot—keep his emotions at bay. He is unable to separate himself from Dasha and his daughter Nurka, however, and he is tormented by both physical and emotional needs. He cannot forget the domestic happiness he once enjoyed. When Gleb is guilty of emotional outbursts, it is because of jealousy and sexual desire.

Dasha, however, is a true ascetic.[65] Although she once lived in harmony with Gleb and shared his joys and sorrows, she now tears herself away from him and Nurka. She claims that she still loves them both, but she grieves only briefly and unconvincingly when Nurka dies. Her rejection of her own sexuality is, in the later versions of the novel, complete. Even in the first version, where she is quite promiscuous, her behavior cannot be taken at face value. Promiscuity is a metaphor for her liberation from domestic ties, not for any new-found enjoyment of physical sensation.

Most important, Dasha rejects involvement in daily life. If the children's homes have neither food nor firewood today, they will have both tomorrow. The fact that children are dying right now for want of basic necessities does not enter into Dasha's calculations. If the cement factory is not in operation now, it will be tomorrow. The actual mechanics of putting it into operation are left to Gleb and others, of course. Dasha is busy from morning until late into the night, but it is impossible to say what she does. We know that she reads, writes reports, and serves on committees; but what does this really mean? Why does she read, to whom does she write reports, what do her committees achieve? The answers to these questions are vague and indefinite.

Dasha's life is essentially eventless. We see her take a brief and dangerous trip to a rebellious mountain village, but other than this, all her experiences belong to the past. Her last major experience of the turmoil of life is her incarceration by the Whites at the time of Gleb's three-year absence. She is arrested on suspicion of aiding the Soviets and is forced to watch her comrades being tortured and killed. In the midst of this horror Nurka comes to her in a dream but then vanishes, ". . . as if she were an image out of an extinguished dream" (p. 150). Dasha is raped by the Whites and then, miraculously, released. After this, "she was home only at night. The room became shabby, and the corners became overgrown with cobwebs and dust. The flowers on the windowsill faded and dried up"(p. 152). She has effected her transformation into an ascetic. She drops her daughter, neglects her home, and lets her emotions dry up like her potted flowers. As she ceases to be affected by daily events, she rises above the ebb and flow of time into an atemporal existence.

What is interesting about the final emotional experience in Dasha's life is that so much of its imagery resembles imagery used in medieval literature. An important perception, the relative insignificance of domestic happiness, is couched in the form of a dream or vision, and the only concrete period of time mentioned is Gleb's three-year absence. We have noted before that the number three is heavily laden with symbolic significance. Dasha, like Christ, is taken off to her execution with two others, but, like Christ, she triumphs over the ordeal and returns to a world she promises to transform. Thus, in this consciously Soviet novel, a pivotal scene is described in symbolic images whose ultimate derivation is religious.

We may presume that Gladkov deliberately set out to create a mythic heroine whose acts are emblematic. As the set phrases and situations which could identify crucial scenes in a Soviet myth had not yet been codified, Gladkov made use of Christian imagery. Gladkov was familiar with Christian imagery from his childhood, in which "the mysticism of an Old-Believer milieu with its apocrypha and religious fantasy had a great influence on my soul. Singing women, ancient verses and songs, asceticism, reading the Scriptures awoke a love for music and literary fictions." And M. Pakhomova states that Gladkov had definitely read the Psalms, Prologue tales, and Chet'i-Minei by the age of fourteen.[66]

If Dasha's "resurrection" marks her initiation into a new life, it also spells the end of her old one. Dasha never returns either to her flowerpots or to her emotional attachments. She eventually settles in Polia's room and leaves her husband altogether. Like all the ascetics I have dealt with, she is unable to effect a change in others. Her detachment from the things of this world bars her from helping Gleb to overcome his jealousy or Polia to quell her emotions.

Dasha's ascetic heights, however, are not completely inaccessible. Various characters experience transcendent moments when they are able to put aside the constraints imposed by time and see a vision of the shining future.[67] Gleb, for instance, also undergoes an ordeal for three years and returns home amidst suggestions that he has been resurrected ("What devil dragged you out of the other world?" [p. 13]; "Gleb Chumalov . . . Our Gleb! . . . Dead and now alive. . ." [p. 24]). Although he is never able to fully overcome the charms of living in the profane world of ordinary humans, he does overcome them on significant occasions. During the celebration of the recommissioning of the cement plant, for example, Gleb transcends his ties to Dasha, as he muses, "Dasha . . . She no longer exists: she has drowned in the crowds, and she won't be found again. All of that is so far away and so unnecessary" (p. 272). He has risen above his daily passions under the influence of the vision which also captivates Dasha. "We are building socialism, comrades, and our own proletarian culture. Onward to victory, comrades!" (p. 278).

Polia also shows signs of pulling out of her emotional crisis and resuming the struggle to envision the new life. She admits that Dasha's path is the correct one and goes to a sanatorium in search of the calmness of spirit which will enable her to be like her friend. She is like those medieval monks who seek the advice of more perfected ascetics in quelling their passions.

Although the gap between the ascetic and the nonascetic is closed ever so slightly, it still remains. Secondary characters like Savchuk and Motia remain attached to the pleasures of life—children, work, food. The average worker has no desire to be like Dasha Chumalova or even like Gleb, for that matter. Such characters are, nevertheless, conceived of as good, decent human beings, who have an important role to play in building the future.

Cement, then, recognizes many acceptable paths towards the ultimate goal. If Dasha's way is somehow higher and more admirable than others, it is, nevertheless, not the only one possible. Other characters are free to choose their own paths without hindering the cause. Although the desirability of the ultimate goal is never questioned, each character is free to pursue it in his or her own way.

THE REVOLUTIONARY ASCETIC AND THE POETICS OF RESISTANCE

Each of the three works analyzed here has included an ascetic among its characters. The ascetic can never reasonably claim to be *the* hero, who eclipses all others, but he is always recognized as standing higher than his fellows. He always has the clearest vision of the goal towards which all the positive characters strive, and he always lives more for the future and less for the present than they. He is admired by one and all, but few are willing to live as he does.

The relationship of the three novels to each other is complex. Gorky obviously knew Chernyshevsky's novel, just as Gladkov knew both Chernyshevsky's and Gorky's. Thus, each of the earlier works could be said to have influenced the later ones to a certain extent. Each of the three novels is independent from the others, however. Gorky set out to describe a different milieu and, in part, a different class from Chernyshevsky; Gladkov, in turn, is known to have disagreed with Gorky's outlook on the proletariat. To posit each work as a model for the succeeding one is to oversimplify the situation.

Certain factors come into play which may explain why these three works share both ascetic heroes and the mixed novelistic-epic structure which results from juxtaposing ascetics with nonascetics. Each of the novels in question chooses the life of an urban factory or shop as its basic subject over a village, agricultural one. Most novels which describe factory workers are rigorously "proletarian."[68] The novel of the ascetic hero, however, tends towards romanticism. The literature of "industrial romanticism"[69] takes an intrinsically unheroic subject and tries to invest it with heroic stature and interest. It does so by moving its focus away from the daily grind of manual labor towards the vision of a bright new day. In order to retain its credibility as a literature of the working class, however, it must continue to depict some aspects of actual labor. Such literature combines characters who perform the tasks assigned to the proletariat with characters who dream the millennial dreams dear to the hearts of the Russian *intelligentsia*.

Another factor which helps to explain the mixture of incompatible elements in these novels is the strong tendency of Marxist literature to reject depiction of the particular in favor of the general. While many novels of the early Soviet period continue to focus on man's fragmented, senseless existence, Marxist novels strive to create a harmonious, meaningful universe.[70] Chernyshevsky, Gorky, and Gladkov all create works which lean markedly towards generalization.[71] None of them, however, is willing to underplay the particular. They are still too much under the sway of the nineteenth-century novelistic tradition to dispense completely with the fine points and contradictions of real life. Their novels, therefore, contrast the lives and adventures of harmonious, superhuman heroes with those of normal, doubt-ridden mortals.

The reemergence of the ascetic hero in the late nineteenth century is totally consistent with the evolution of Russian literature. It can be explained by the convergence of various factors, among which are the abiding Russian fascination with millenarian doctrines, the onset of a new period of non-naturalistic art, the turn towards romanticism in an effort to make the proletarian theme truly heroic, and, finally, the religious training received by each of the authors, which acquainted them with an ideal hero who would be suitable for a semimythic type of literature.

I would argue that the secular, revolutionary ascetic is very similar to his religious predecessor. He actually does little, within the confines of the novel, to promote the welfare of his fellows, although they seem unaware of this. His disregard for society's claims is complete. He regularly challenges necessity, be it societal, historical, or physical, and always emerges victorious. He learns a great truth early on and never departs from it. He neither adds to it nor subtracts from it. He easily and singlehandedly resolves all the tensions which normally torment the multidimensional hero.

I find that the inclusion of an ascetic hero in the works of literature analyzed in this chapter has a similar effect to the inclusion of an ascetic in Kievan literature. In both periods the ascetic is viewed as someone new and unexpected. At first he is suspect, and his aims and goals cannot be discussed in detail. He issues a challenge to the beliefs held by society's institutions and calls for allegiance to a different, transcendent order. He is always juxtaposed to other characters who either do not share his goal or cannot follow his path, and there is always some small room for doubt as to whether he is right. There is a difference between him and his medieval prototypes, however, in that the nineteenth-century radical ascetic foresees a time when the rift between him and his fellow men will be closed. Nevertheless, the work which includes an ascetic hero challenges the reader to decide for himself and to take a black or white stand for or against the ascetic's goals and methods.

These works *are* much closer to medieval prototypes than are the more naturalistic works of Gogol, Turgenev, Tolstoy, and Dostoevsky. Their unrealistic poetics of time and space and their straightforward, unironical call to the ascetic quest are very reminiscent of the saints' lives we have analyzed. This brings us back to Alastair Fowler's theory of literary evolution. It will be recalled that Fowler suggests the existence of a secondary stage in the utilization of literary forms in which themes or purposes may diverge from primary models (that is, social ideals replace the original religious ones) while original formal structures (treatment of time and space, in this context) remain largely intact. Surely Chernyshevsky, Gorky, and Gladkov work on this secondary level. It is, however, noteworthy that Gorky and Gladkov create their works later than those authors who work with tertiary forms of the tradition. This failure of the literary form to follow chronological constraints on its evolution must be explained as the result of its being used in both naturalistic and non-naturalistic ages. The all-encompassing differences in poetics imposed by these two radically different views of life are major enough to upset the normal order of literary development.

If we look beyond these earliest realizations of secondary literary development, we discover that the ascetic hero continues to be a productive type in Soviet literature throughout the early thirties. Although he himself does not differ from his late nineteenth- and early twentieth-century brothers, however, the work in which he is found does. The ascetic remains as the ideal embodiment of the "mover of movers," but the role of the little man who performs the actual "moving" gradually diminishes. With the fading of the little man and his daily concerns comes a shift away from depiction of the here and now and towards glorification of the magnificent future with which the ascetic concerns himself.[72] The ascetic of the thirties is free to deny the fetters of time and space imposed on him by association with the masses. He becomes, in truth, the hero of a new mythology.

Chapter 7

RACING AGAINST TIME:
ASCETICS OF THE THIRTIES

THE FADING AND REVIVAL OF THE REVOLUTIONARY
ASCETIC: OPPOSING VIEWS

The coming of peace after the Revolution and Civil War marks
a new stage in the development of Russian millenarian thought.
If Chernyshevsky and Gorky assume that an era of unprecedented
freedom will be ushered in with the victory of the proletariat, if
Gladkov sees the dawning of a bright new day after the defeat of
the last pockets of counterrevolution, those who follow them are
forced to grapple with harder realities. Society's problems have
not yet been completely solved, and a materialist basis of life has
not yet been established. Serious work lies ahead for society's movers.

For a time, of course, writers enjoy a certain amount of freedom in interpreting the task of building the new society. They can
express reservations as to measures adopted by the government,
and they can portray characters who voice varied and conflicting
views. They can even poke fun at the character types which are
fast calcifying into exemplars of revolutionary behavior.

In 1923 Mikhail Slonimsky's short story "The Emery Machine,"

("Mashina Emeri") appears. Its cast of characters includes Liutyi, an artist with decadent tendencies, Frania, the object of Liutyi's affections, and Oleinikov, a dedicated builder of communism. Slonimsky deliberately casts Oleinikov as the standard unidimensional ascetic, but he portrays his other characters as multidimensional. Unlike Gorky and Gladkov, however, Slonimsky does not identify his own interests with those of Oleinikov. Instead, he presents his ascetic as a somewhat ridiculous fanatic; Oleinikov tries to bully Liutyi into painting a mural which entirely ignores the present while glorifying the future, and he marries to discharge a debt of honor to a friend but refuses to consummate his marriage. Frania, his frustrated bride, quickly manages to break him, however, and he agrees to live according to the accepted norms of middle-class behavior.

In "The Emery Machine," Slonimsky recognizes the ascetic as one of the clichéd character types used in portraying the revolutionary. He takes a humorous but critical view of Oleinikov and refuses to grant him any kind of initiation or transcendent experience. Although the decadent artist Liutyi perishes while Oleinikov marries Frania, this cannot be construed as a victory for the ascetic hero. Oleinikov is transformed by his marriage and drops his ascetic ways. His dedication to the communist cause is greatly reduced. This suggests that asceticism is perhaps no more than a superficial incognito which is adopted only as long as it is convenient. Slonimsky implies that the ascetic hero will fade as life settles back into its regular rhythms.

Boris Pilnyak also portrays the passing of the ascetic hero. He, unlike Slonimsky, shows a great deal of sympathy for his doomed hero. In *Mahogany* (*Krasnoe derevo*, 1929) he traces the rise and fall of Ivan Ozhogov, an ascetic visionary turned alcoholic. Ozhogov glorifies the year 1919, when the realities of the present were of little value and dreams of the future were all-important. In the NEP period, however, Russian society becomes increasingly concerned with making accommodations with the present. Ivan is expelled from the Communist party because he refuses to compromise his ideals. Ivan's fellow citizens, stranded in a stagnating provincial town, are out of touch even with the present, and they slowly lapse into a way of life characteristic of pre-Petrine Muscovy. In *Mahogany*, Pilnyak contrasts three types of heroes and three ways of life with each other. Ivan, the mad ascetic, is a mythic hero who lives for the future; his brother Iakov and his family and neighbors are the sensual villains of a mythic past; and the brothers Bezdetyi, who come from bustling, commercial Moscow to deal in mahogany antiques, are typical products of the complex and often hypocritical present. Pilnyak clearly sympathizes with Ozhogov. He describes him as a victim of society's duplicity, a man who is cast off because his idealism no longer suits the tenor of the times. He is rejected by society, and the mahogany dealers, who have neither ideals nor morals, become respected and successful citizens. The mahogany dealers are the representatives of an unperfected society which no longer even reaches towards perfection, but they, nevertheless, replace the idealistic ascetic in society's esteem.

Mahogany is not the only work in which Pilnyak portrays an ascetic. Mahogany was rejected by the Soviet censorship, and Pilnyak was severely criticized for allowing its publication in Berlin. He tried to make amends by expanding and substantially revising it. He titled the resulting novel The Volga Falls to the Caspian Sea (Volga vpadaet v Kaspiiskoe more, 1930).

The Volga Falls to the Caspian Sea also describes a provincial town and includes many of the same characters as Mahogany. In the later work, however, the town is the site of a massive industrial project. Its pre-Petrine denizens play strictly secondary roles, and Ivan Ozhogov is now more a mad wanderer, a modern fool for Christ's sake, than an ascetic. A new cast of ascetics is introduced, however. Pimen Poletika, the designer of the project, is very much an ascetic. Although he was once married, he now lives alone. He shuns the company of other engineers, lives very frugally, and dreams ceaselessly of the transformation of society. Like most other ascetics, he himself is not involved in the actual work of transformation. His daughter Liubov' also has ascetic characteristics. She too lives frugally and is adamant in rejecting the advances of men who are attracted to her. She too dreams of the transformation of society. The engineer Sadykov, while a secondary character, is somewhat of an ascetic as well.

Although Pilnyak's ascetics are among his central characters, and although he paints them very positively, he is still not able to convince himself that asceticism is the standard by which the future Soviet society will live. As the novel closes, Poletika is reconciled with his wife, and Liubov' and Sadykov fall in love with each other. Each character is poised on the threshold of a new and different life in which ascetic restraint will no longer be necessary. If Pilnyak seems to suggest in Mahogany that the ascetic's ideals are doomed, then he concludes in *The Volga Falls to the Caspian Sea* that they must be tempered and softened.

Certain writers of the twenties, then, accept the ascetic as a legitimate heroic type. They suggest that his heyday has come and gone, however. They take the relatively free and prosperous life of the twenties as a sign that society's upheavals are over and that millenarian dreams are no longer relevant.

Other writers are not as sure that the ascetic can be so easily laid to rest, however. In the late twenties the government begins to reassert strong control over most aspects of Soviet life, and literature is also reined in. The heroes of the revolution can no longer be taken lightly or be relegated to history with impunity. They must be incorporated into the very fiber of Soviet literature. Zhdanov himself calls for the creation of a type of literature which seems to beg for an ascetic hero.

> We say that socialist realism is the basic method of Soviet *belles lettres* and literary criticism, and this presupposes that revolutionary romanticism should enter into literary creation as a component part, for the whole life of our Party, the whole life of the working class and its struggle consist in a combination of the most stern and sober practical work with a supreme spirit of heroic deeds and magnificent future prospects. . . . Soviet literature should be able to portray our heroes; it should be able to glimpse our tomorrow.[1]

Zhdanov's formulations call on authors to bring together many of the same elements that we have already discussed as fundamental for the creation of ascetic heroes: romanticism, with its emphasis on extraordinary flights of heroism; the theme of labor; and the theme of the transformation of society. In the late twenties and thirties, it also becomes increasingly evident that rigorously naturalistic art is unacceptable, as are those types of non-naturalistic art which can be branded "formalist." The combination of a millenarian theme with a mythic, non-novelistic literary form is made almost mandatory.

At the same time, a phenomenon which Richard Stites refers to as "sexual Thermidor" sets in. As early as 1920, Lenin speaks out against the sexual excesses which marked much of the revolutionary and civil war period. In 1923 an attack on Aleksandra Kollotai for her alleged support of free love presages an era marked by new restrictions on divorce and abortion laws. Legislation concerning marriage stresses a stabile, productive family unit over equality and independence in sexual matters. Self-control becomes a byword.[2] Under these circumstances ascetic heroes are bound to emerge.

KATAEV: NARROWING THE GAP BETWEEN NARRATOR AND HERO

Valentin Kataev's *Time Forward!* (*Vremia vpered!*, 1932) marks a turning point in the transformation of the naturalistic novel into the non-naturalistic epic as well as a similar turning point in Kataev's own career. It has been said that Kataev's fiction of the 1920s should be divided into two very different types, lyrical and satirical.[3] Work along both of these lines was suspended, however, after the May 1930 publication of a virulent attack on Kataev by Mashbits-Verov. The critic lambasted Kataev for being out of step with the times. Kataev's earlier work, both lyrical and satiric, had typically portrayed an "acceptance of life as it is. . . ."[4] and had featured a hero who lived "completely and selfishly."[5] This, of course, was inappropriate by the early 1930s.

In *Time Forward!*, Kataev, who had once written verse on religious themes,[6] portrays his first active "mover and shaker," a hero who manifestly refuses to accept life as he finds it. This hero is also one of the very few twentieth-century ascetics who appeals to readers as an interesting and even amusing literary creation.

David Margulies is the chief engineer of a vital construction sector at the Magnitostroi project. He is responsible for helping to create an industrial giant which will enable the Soviet Union to compete with, and even overtake, the West in steel production. The novel depicts a twenty-four-hour period in which Margulies's workers set a world's record for the tempos of their labor. Although the workers actually set the new record, Margulies, the ascetic, is given credit for it. It is his vision, controversial and much disputed, which guides his workers and wins the day.

We can immediately recognize the ascetic hero in the figure of Margulies. All the outward signs are there. Margulies goes through the entire twenty-four-hour period without eating anything more substantial than some candied watermelon peel, and Kataev points out this self-deprivation rather insistently. He repeatedly mentions Margulies's attempts to find food. Each attempt fails for a different reason: sometimes Margulies has no money; sometimes he has to rush off somewhere; and on several occasions, the restaurant is closed.[7] In any case, Margulies's work, rather than being hampered by his hunger, seems to be enhanced by it. Margulies not only makes do without food, he also dispenses with the attentions of women. He admits that he was once married, and he playfully responds to Shura's affection, but there can be no question of a relationship between him and a woman. He leaves that aspect of life behind him when he arrives at the site. Finally, Margulies, like other ascetics before him, dresses badly. Kataev mentions several times that his jacket is soiled and too big for him. He also notes that his hero fails to bathe in the morning.

All these outward manifestations of asceticism serve to label Margulies as one who stands apart from his fellows, that is, as one who is separate. Margulies even lives separately. The brigade leader, Ishchenko, has no more than a partitioned-off area in the workers' barracks. Margulies, however, lives in a private room in the site hotel. He is also separated from his fellows by his education. While Ishchenko can barely come to grips with arithmetic, Margulies is a university-trained engineer. Finally, Margulies is a Jew whose father is killed in a pogrom. This is one more factor which sets him apart.

The religious ascetic experiences not only a separation from society but also a metaphysical separation—his spirit is freed from the bonds of his body. Interestingly enough, Margulies also undergoes a metaphysical separation. While he is waiting for his telephone connection with Moscow to be completed, he has a vision of a sunny summer morning. A diver ascends the ladder of the high dive and effortlessly glides through the air into the water. He merges with the water and becomes one with it, losing all sense of himself. I would suggest that this vision is one which allows Margulies to recall and relive similar moments of transcendence in his own past. Unfortunately, Kataev fails to tie this moment to Margulies's life at the construction site and leaves the reader confused as to its meaning and significance.[8]

Margulies also experiences initiation. This comes with the awareness that his calculations and surmises are correct and that he can, in fact, hope to establish a new world's record without endangering the quality of his work. His sister Katia has dictated an article over the telephone to him which confirms his hopes. When we next see him, he is transformed.

Margulies was unrecognizable. Where did his listlessness, his indecisiveness, his lisping disappear to? He was gay, sociable, light and precise in his movements, albeit a bit restrained (p. 271).[9]

It is clear that Kataev wants to highlight Margulies's new state. On the one hand, he is "unrecognizable." On the other, he is neither indecisive nor listless. Strangely enough, however, he has never been described as being either of these things, and his lightness and precision of movement are actually alluded to more than once earlier in the novel. Kataev wants to indicate the transforming moment of initiation and does so by describing a change in his hero. He is tied, however, by the conventions of asceticism to a static, ready-formed hero who cannot change.

Kataev seems to vacillate between openly following the conventions of ascetic characterization and concealing his hero's asceticism. He emphasizes superficial manifestations of asceticism, but obscures deeper ones. We can only speculate as to why this is so. We know that The Embezzlers (Rastratchiki, 1927) does not display the epic features found in the literature of the ascetic. We know that his post-Stalinist work is written to a different convention. Last but not least, we also know that writers were pressured in the early thirties into choosing industrial themes and glorifying the economic transformation of society. Perhaps Kataev, a consummate compromiser and survivor, feels some embarrassment at "betraying" novelistic art, at writing a novel so alien in form and content to his other work.[10] This might explain why he hesitates at some points in his characterization. It would also explain his attempts to soften his ascetic by adding elements of humor and eccentricity.

The circumstances under which Time Forward! was written had an unquestionable influence on the content and structure of the novel. Kataev was, in a sense, forced to write a novel like Time Forward! in order to survive both as an artist and as a man. The novel is, to a great extent, an objective cataloging of impressions taken from life—it results from Kataev's study of an actual construction site. The genesis of the novel sets it apart from other works we have discussed.

Gorky's and Gladkov's novels, for instance, are also based on historical figures, events, and themes. Although they draw from their author's experiences of real life, however, they maintain their status as fictions. Their authors clearly sympathize with their ascetic heroes, but they maintain a semblance of critical distance from them, which creates at least the illusion that other characters also have their own legitimate voices. In *Time Forward!* this is not so. Kataev, for example, couches his novel in the form of an almost raw chronicle of experienced events. He reproduces an authentic newspaper article verbatim and continually quotes Stalin to the effect that Russia must be part of Europe, not Asia. More importantly, he closes *Time Forward!* with a letter in which he identifies himself and his correspondent as two of the novel's minor characters. In the novel, both of these characters take a firm stand in favor of Margulies and his vision of life. Accordingly, Kataev himself becomes a supporter of Margulies, and this closes the gap between author and hero. Even if disguising fiction as fact is a consciously assumed literary device, it nevertheless yields the same result, a narrowing of point of view.

Another feature which results from the author's need to write a politically acceptable work is the division of characters into heroes and villains. The heroes are those who support Margulies, while the villains are those who fight him. The majority of the workers at the construction site are positive heroes. Some of them are less politically literate than others, but all of them are struggling towards the same goal. A number of characters are villains. They include a kulak's son, an engineer with roots in the bourgeoisie, and foreign specialists and visitors who are unhappy victims of their capitalist mentality. In a few cases the reader is temporarily uncertain as to how to categorize a character, but by the end of the novel, he knows exactly who the heroes and who the villains are. *Time Forward!* is the first modern work we have looked at since the northern saints' lives in which all is either black or white. Gray areas have disappeared.

It is quite reasonable to suggest that Kataev is very close to medieval conventions with *Time Forward!* Both Kataev's novel and the northern lives go to extreme lengths to restrict point of view. Characters must declare that they are either for or against the hero's way. The author, too, abandons his critical distance and makes his choice. The reader has no alternative but to agree with the others.

The novel's most central concern is stated in its very title, *Time Forward!*[11] Time and man's relationship to it are the threads which tie the novel's episodes together. Kataev fulminates against the traditional understanding of time. He totally rejects the notion, which underlies most of modern literature, that time must be viewed subjectively. For Kataev, time cannot be understood to pass sometimes slowly, sometimes quickly. This view of time is held only by Saenko, one of the villains, not by the novel's heroes. For the heroes, time is a quantifiable entity. It always passes at the same rate, and this rate can be easily determined by a clock. Man's most important task is to regulate his labor, so that it too will move along at a steady rate. He must pace himself, so as never to stray from the clock. This is time as it is understood by science (or by the cenobitic monk, for that matter).

Margulies, however, has yet another view of time. He accepts the fact that most men are tied to a clock, but he challenges himself to break this restraint and establish a new relationship between man and time. Margulies himself is always ahead of time. Although he regularly sets his alarm clock, for example, he always wakes up before it goes off. ("Margulies couldn't trust such a valuable thing as time to such an essentially simple mechanism as a clock" [p. 131]). He never wears a watch, because he can gauge time perfectly without one. While waiting to talk with Moscow, he muses on the fact that the construction site is two hours ahead of Moscow. He compares Moscow, which is still tearing down cathedrals and other remnants of the past, with the site, which holds within itself a tremendous potential for the future. In his mind, the construction site exists in a different order of time from Moscow. Margulies takes the simple scientific expedient of time zones and transforms it into an almost mystical concept. The rest of the world moves along according to the recognizable standard of the clock, but his small enclave has escaped the clock's constraints. It is ahead.

In *Time Forward!* time is sometimes tied to space and sometimes freed from it. Space is alluded to almost as frequently as time. Often it is monumental and static. Space is the dimension best suited to describing the new construction, for example. Kataev never misses an opportunity to point out how massive the project is. The project, however, is itself dwarfed by the magnitude of the steppe, and the steppe, in turn, shrinks in comparison with the expanse of the Soviet Union. In descriptive passages, space often exists independently of time.

Margulies, however, is able to yoke time and space together. This is the ultimate heroic achievement. Without time, space is barren and unproductive. The massive reaches of wilderness can know neither change nor development until they become subject to time. Margulies unites time and space and then conquers them in a variety of ways.

In his efforts to save time, he moves across the vast territory of the construction much more easily than the other heroes, for example. While Ishchenko suffers from want of transportation and Olia wastes valuable time searching all over for members of the brigade, Margulies seems to move as if by power of miracle. When he discovers that his path is blocked by barbed wire, he reaches for a post and leaps over the barrier. This would seem rather unexceptional were it not for the fact that Smetana, a Komsomol member, has to crawl under the same wire and tears his shirt. Later in the day, he is faced by the same obstacle. This time he tries to imitate Margulies, but he jumps badly and loses time picking up all the things he has dropped. Only Margulies has the power to move about easily.

Margulies also forces time and space to work for him when he speaks over the telephone. The telephone allows him to travel over broad reaches of space without losing time. It gives him information (the latest newspaper article) which would otherwise take too much time to arrive. At the beginning of Margulies' conversation with Moscow, Kataev notes, "as soon as he put the special receiver to his ear, space spoke in place of arrested time" (p. 195). At the end of the conversation, he says that "as soon as he had closed the door to the booth, liberated time moved, rustled, and gushed, in place of arrested space" (p. 199). The importance of controlling time and space is underscored by the fact that this central scene, in which Margulies makes time and space work for him, is connected to the telephone, and through it, to the moment of his vision of metaphysical separation. The telephone, conquering time and space, also provides Margulies with the information which marks his initiation.[12]

So we see that the ascetic hero masters both time and space. Like Sergii Radonezhskii and Kirill Belozerskii, he covers great distances without difficulty. He takes undifferentiated, untamed space and creates something new and lasting. At the same time, he refuses to be bound by the fetters of time. He lives for the future, for the creation of a better society, and since he is already so much an inhabitant of this new life, he is able to ignore profane time.

With *Time Forward!* the literature of the ascetic hero becomes ever more mythic. Characters are divided into heroes and villains, the constraints of time and space melt away, and multidimensionality fades. Kataev completes the transformation of the naturalistic novel into the non-naturalistic epic which was begun by Chernyshevsky.

We can explain this development in two ways. First, we can cite literary factors. The change seen in Kataev's novel seems to correspond to the natural direction of evolution in the literature of the ascetic hero. *Time Forward!* is remarkably close to fourteenth- and fifteenth-century lives of ascetics in its treatment of point of view and time and space. We have seen that once the ascetic's goals are recognized and accepted by society, he becomes an admired and emulated figure. Although his heights remain unobtainable, his heroics are applauded by all. This substantially alters the author's treatment of point of view. For Chernyshevsky and Gorky, revolution and social transformation were dangerous and punishable offenses, while for Gladkov's contemporaries, the wisdom of re-commissioning the cement factory was also questionable. For Kataev, however, there can be no question as to the desirability and even necessity of developing an industrial basis for the future paradise. And once the validity of the future kingdom is universally conceded, profane conceptions of time will recede entirely. The sufferings of profane time pall in comparison with the pleasures of the Golden Age. We can see that changes in Kataev's treatment of various basic elements of composition parallel changes that are also evident in later medieval literature. Kataev develops certain themes and techniques inherited from Chernyshevsky and others in the same way that Epifanii develops what he receives from Simon and Efrem.

A second factor which helps to explain the evolution of literature into myth is societal. By the 1930s, the pressures put on authors to depict society in rosy hues were formidable. Gorky recommended the drive for industrialization as a theme, and authors heeded his advice. Gorky did not address the question of *how* to turn industrialization into literature, however, and many authors erred by failing to transform reality through their own artistic vision. *Time Forward!* does tend to remind us of a documentary, and as Kermode cautions, "fictions can degenerate into myths whenever they are not consciously held to be fictive."[13]

OSTROVSKY: THE TRIUMPH OF CLICHÉ

Kataev's novel can still lay claim to the title of fiction, even in the face of its documentary nature, because it is marked by a certain "concordance between beginning, middle and end."[14] Unfortunately, this cannot be said of *How the Steel Was Tempered*, the work to which we must now turn. *How the Steel Was Tempered* recounts the adventures of Pavel Korchagin, a Civil War hero and Komsomol activist. Korchagin is, however, identical in all respects with Nikolai Ostrovsky, the novel's author. Ostrovsky never attempts to hide this fact, and the novel's very first readers were already well aware of it.[15] Because *How the Steel Was Tempered* is so unabashedly autobiographical and because Ostrovsky is so utterly lacking in literary talent,[16] there is no discernable narrative strategy at work in the novel. Material is presented in a disorganized and unprocessed fashion, and any sense of closure is completely lacking.[17] Oddly enough, however, the very fact that *How the Steel Was Tempered* is a raw, unmediated autobiography seems to account for its extraordinary popularity.[18] The novel's admirers, deeply affected by Ostrovsky's much-publicized sufferings and premature death, celebrate Korchagin's single-minded determination to leave his mark on society.[19] They see in Korchagin the ultimate hero, the doer of great deeds, the undaunted revolutionary.

Pavel Korchagin, like Pavel Vlasov before him, is a great ascetic. The reader gets his first inkling of this in the opening scene of the novel, when Pavel is expelled from a Church school. Pavel has thrown tobacco in the priest's dough, and this is the ostensible reason for expelling him. Pavel, reflecting on the matter, realizes that this is not the real reason, however. He remembers how he sat in a more advanced class one day and heard a scientific, non-biblical explanation of the creation of the world. When he questioned the priest about it, the priest punished him severely. From that time on, Pavel was unwelcome in his regular class. The prank with the tobacco was merely the formal occasion of his expulsion.

In this episode, the episode which Ostrovsky consciously chooses as the introduction to his hero's career, we already have the first stage of Pavel's separation from society. Further incidents, such as Pavel's unhappiness and eventual dismissal from his first job, his arrest and seclusion in prison, and, most obviously, his ultimate paralysis and blindness, which permanently remove him from the activities of daily life, merely serve to confirm and support our first vision of the hero as a man who rejects his society. Although, on the face of it, the school has rejected Pavel, it is really the other way around. Pavel, by insisting on his right to his own truth, sets himself at variance with his fellows.

The outward signs of Pavel's asceticism are predictable. Although he is a very attractive young man, he dresses badly and is generally unkempt. On one occasion he cleans himself up in order to impress a wealthy young girl, but he quickly rejects both her and his neat garments. This girl is neither the first nor the last to try to lay claim to Pavel's heart. A village hussy flirts with him; a girl in prison, who is faced with imminent rape, offers herself to him; and a communist activist tries to woo him. Pavel resolutely rejects them all. He tells his mother that he plans to stay away from women until every last member of the bourgeoisie is wiped off the face of the earth.

Pavel also voluntarily courts starvation. We hear many times of the hunger prevailing among the populace, but this affects each member of society equally. Pavel, however, actually rejects food even when it is available. He walks out on his brother's dinner invitation because his brother has married a peasant. He leaves a party where food and drink are being offered because his friends are flirting with girls. He forbids peasants to sell their home-grown produce.

The most impressive manifestation of Pavel's asceticism, however, is his voluntary acceptance of suffering. He works in the frost without proper boots or jacket and spends a week working in a freezing river, even though he has already noticed the first signs of the degenerative condition which will eventually paralyze him.

When we come to the question of motivation, the question of why Pavel Korchagin engages in such relentlessly ascetic behavior, however, we run into trouble. Although Pavel tells his mother that he will remain an ascetic until such time as the entire world is transformed according to his own vision, his actions are not calculated to bring this about. In fact, the exact opposite is true. Korchagin's asceticism leads to the complete destruction of his body, the tool he relies upon in his struggle. Although he is still able to write, we know that this activity, too, will cease with his inevitable death. Thus, Korchagin actually destroys himself through asceticism rather than asserting his unique vision.[20]

And what exactly is his vision, and how is it connected with his ascetic way of life? The connection is difficult to find. We have seen in *Time Forward!* that Margulies's asceticism does not, in and of itself, have any concrete effect on the task of transforming society. It does, however, play a role in creating his vision, which, in turn, inspires the work of society's actual transformers. Pavel Korchagin starts out with his own vaguely apprehended vision, but he relinquishes it in favor of the prepackaged vision supplied to him by the Party. Whereas Margulies's vision is clearly his own and is disputed by a significant percentage of Party members, Korchagin's is safe and unexceptional. In those cases where discord arises between Korchagin and his fellows, his fellows are found to be Trotskyites or members of the Workers' Opposition, that is, villains. What is important here is not that Korchagin's views are always correct, or that they accord well with the author's own, but rather that they are not really the product of his ascetic vision.

Where there is no inherent connection between the means adopted by the hero to effect separation and the goal which he pursues, there can be no initiation. In *How the Steel Was Tempered*, there is no single moment when the hero is transformed, when he transcends life's pettiness and glimpses its ultimate meaning. Korchagin moves from task to task with no overall sense of completion. Life is one unending chain of tasks, and there is no conviction that they will ever be swept away and replaced by a beautiful new society. Although Pavel looks forward to the victory of the working class, he has no clear picture of what this will mean.

This suggests that Ostrovsky does not completely understand the typology of the ascetic hero. His hero has all the superficial marks of an ascetic but is missing the inner motivation. He is a man of tremendous will, and his will is bent towards transforming the world, but there is no indication that he has come to his own understanding of what transformation entails and of what meaning it has for him. Although his body forsakes him, and he becomes, in essence, a man of pure spirit, we do not understand this spirit.[21] Korchagin remains separated from his fellows to a significant degree but does not experience moments of divine transcendence.

Although Ostrovsky fails to properly comprehend the ascetic as a heroic type, he does appreciate most of the literary conventions which are associated with him. He realizes that, in an age when society applauds the hero's goals, its members must also accept his methods. No character, other than a rank villain, ever seriously challenges Korchagin's way. All admire him, even if no one emulates him. Ostrovsky, of course, also applauds his exploits. The lack of critical distance between author and hero already noticed in *Time Forward!* has been taken to its ultimate limit in *How the Steel Was Tempered*. No author could be closer to his hero than is Ostrovsky to Korchagin.

Ostrovsky also appreciates that the ascetic's physical restraint and accompanying spiritual superiority give him a special power over time and space. Pavel Korchagin, every bit as much as David Margulies, is engaged in a race with time. True, Margulies has a clear understanding of the task he must complete before time runs out, while Korchagin only struggles to extend the span of time left to him as a productive worker. Nonetheless, Korchagin battles with time and gains mastery over it. Although he is told that blindness and paralysis will "force him from the ranks," he triumphs over adversity by entering a field in which movement and sight are not necessary. By becoming an author, Korchagin stretches his productive life beyond the limits set by time. He continues to work even though his time has run out. And Korchagin, no less than Margulies, sets records for the tempos of his work. As a brigade leader on a rush railroad construction project, Korchagin drives his workers to un-heard-of limits. The supervisor of the project admits that, techni-cally speaking, the job cannot be done in the time allotted, but Korchagin exerts his iron will, and the work is completed.

In those moments when Margulies triumphs over profane time, he experiences what we might call "the eternal." We recall his sensation of merging with the water and losing all sense of his own individuality. This does not happen to Pavel Korchagin. Again, we can explain this as a result of Ostrovsky's failure to comprehend some of the subtleties implicit in the heroic typology. Ostrovsky does show some faint signs that he realizes that big things are expected of his hero, though. On any number of occasions, Korchagin risks his life.

Three times, in particular, he comes very close to losing it. The first time he is arrested by the Whites for helping a Bolshevik to escape from prison, and the prison authorities loudly proclaim their intention to execute him for his role in the escape. Through a to-tally unexpected, not to mention unlikely accident, Pavel is freed. Later, he is seriously wounded in battle, and the doctors despair of saving him. Miraculously, his will to live pulls him through. Finally, Korchagin falls ill with typhus, and his friends actually hear that he has died. In truth, he has survived and returns to the ranks yet a third time. Three times the reader expects that Korchagin will die, and three times the hero defeats these expectations and triumphs. We see faint echoes of two things here. First, we have the number three, with all its mythic and religious significance. Second, we have the imagery of death and resurrection repeated over and over. It is difficult to say whether Ostrovsky is conscious of the religious resonance of this imagery, but even if he is not, he is definitely aware that his hero has battled with the temporal limitations imposed on life by death and has triumphed.

Korchagin also emerges victorious from his battle with space. Many of the characters we encounter in *How the Steel Was Tempered* have never even left their own native villages. Pavel Korchagin, however, ranges across the entire Soviet Union with no seeming difficulty. He spends significant periods of time in such places as Kiev, Moscow, and the Crimea. Even when he is totally incapacitated, he manages to travel easily.

Clearly space is a dimension which exerts a certain resistance. We see Korchagin, for instance, at a military exercise. His legs are already beginning to bother him, but he is told that he may not participate in the exercise on horseback. Undaunted, he completes the exercise on foot, covering vast distances, and he emerges none the worse for his experience. Even in his crippled state, Korchagin has the power to defeat the constraints imposed by space.

In her discussion of Stalinist literature, Katerina Clark notes that its distinctive chronotope is "represented in the novel in terms of place rather than of time."[22] Korchagin, the ultimate Stalinist hero, mediates between the novel's two orders, "Great Time" and the everyday. The concrete realization of his mediation is his triumph over space.

THE WANING OF THE ASCETIC

We see that *Time Forward!* and *How the Steel Was Tempered* share many compositional elements with each other as well as with the lives of northern saints. Both have an ascetic hero, both forego diversity of point of view in favor of a close, non-novelistic relationship between author and hero, and both revolve around the hero's race against the constraints imposed by time and, to a certain degree, space. Both seem, like the works discussed in the previous chapter, to represent a secondary stage of the ascetic-heroic form. In this respect they differ from *What Is to Be Done?*, *Mother*, and *Cement* in two ways: they seem to borrow much less critically certain elements manifest in the chronotope of their medieval prototypes ("adventure" time combined with "everyday" space, cf. pp. 148-50 above); and they reflect northern lives rather than Kievan ones.

There are marked differences between the *Time Forward!* and *How the Steel Was Tempered*, however. *How the Steel Was Tempered* has taken unanimity of point of view and developed it beyond the bounds proper to literature. Not even in pure myth does an author identify himself so closely with his hero. Ostrovsky also presents us with a hero who is sadly lacking in motivation. Because he is unable to formulate his own vision, he can experience no real initiation. This violates not only ascetic typology but also heroic typology in general. All heroes must undergo some type of initiation; initiation is the basic structuring device of the literary work. Finally, since Ostrovsky's hero is deprived of his own personal vision, his triumph over time and space leads to nothing. Although building a spur of railroad track in the middle of winter and writing a novel when blind and paralyzed are certainly impressive accomplishments, Ostrovsky never shows us how these feats tie in to the greater task of transforming society. While the threads of Margulies's triumphs are carefully woven into the fabric of the greater theme of creating Europe and repudiating Asia, Korchagin's seem to have strictly ephemeral significance. They answer to the needs of the day but not to those of the greater overall plan.

We can judge Ostrovsky's treatment of the ascetic hero to be a purely individual failure. We can account for it by noting his lack of talent and his ignorance of literary technique. It is interesting, however, that with the publication of *How the Steel Was Tempered*, the ascetic again disappears from Russian literature. Although heroism is still at a premium, although point of view remains restricted, although non-novelistic literature continues to flourish, the ascetic falls from favor. Dasha Chumalova of *Cement*, for example, makes a brief reappearance in Gladkov's novel *Energy*, but the reader senses that she no longer holds any heroic potential within her. Other characters in the novel have already found different and *better* paths to follow. Dasha's asceticism is dry and unproductive. Given that the literary climate remains favorable to the creation of unidimensional ascetic heroes, why do these heroes fail to materialize?

I would suggest that although literary factors continue to favor the creation of ascetic heroes throughout the late thirties and the forties, extraliterary ones do not. We remember that the question of ascetic motivation lies outside literature, in the sphere of religious and social thought. Two doctrines have been identified which supply the necessary motivation for the creation of ascetic heroes in Russian literature—the belief that the individual can "see" God in this life and the belief that this world is about to come to an end and that a new and better world will replace it. Both of these doctrines assume that certain select individuals are superior to the rest of mankind, and both rest on the belief that a radical separation of the body and soul, of matter and spirit, is possible and even desirable.

In her seminal work *In Stalin's Time*, Vera Dunham suggests that a change in Russia's social climate took place in the thirties. It may be that this change explains the demise of the ascetic hero. Dunham holds that, even in the most repressive years of Stalin's rule, there was a kind of working relationship established between the regime and the people. She characterizes this relationship as one of "accommodation." The "people" were originally defined as the proletariat, but gradually the workers came to be displaced by the middle class. As the proletariat was phased out of the accommodation relationship, the values associated with it—"selflessness, devotion to the party, asceticism, quixotic courage"[23]—were also phased out, and middle-class needs and desires replaced them.

> No hero could now claim leadership if he denied private needs. It was no longer his business to be concerned about society as a whole and still less to be dogmatic about it. In every way, moderation was emerging as a supreme value.[24]

It is easy to see how "the prosperous life became the end of a noble pursuit, while the ascetic came to be seen as leading to divorce from the people and, worse, to sectarianism."[25]

In an era in which philistine longings for common pleasures dominate, there is little room for a hero who stands above the crowd and denies material values in favor of elusive spiritual ones. Although the ascetic hero still fits into late thirties and forties novels *structurally*, the doctrines associated with him fail to capture the imagination of the reading public. He finally becomes the anachronism that Slonimsky had earlier branded him. Even an individual literary work like Gladkov's *Energy* can no longer breathe life into the dead type. The ascetic needs to be based in the broad context of society's myths. As Lévi-Strauss puts it:

> But some [elements of myths] at least acquire a certain solidity through being integrated into a series, whose terms can be accorded some degree of credibility because of their overall coherence. . . . each myth taken separately exists as the limited

application of a pattern, which is gradually revealed by the relations of reciprocal intelligibility discerned between several myths.[26]

In other words, in mythic literature, the individual work must find resonance in other, similar works. The Dasha of *Energy* has no like-minded contemporaries in Russian literature against whom she can define herself. The isolated hero can no longer claim to belong to a "type."

CONCLUSION

We have seen how the ascetic hero of the 1930s, like his medieval counterpart of the fifteenth century, gains society's recognition and uses it to strengthen himself. He triumphs over time and space and is poised on the verge of creating a magnificent new reality which will prove once and for all the power of his vision to friend and foe alike. We have seen the reading public grow disenchanted with the ascetic's vision, which can never quite be grasped, and which always costs so much pain, and we have watched it turn, instead, to the physical pleasures and spiritual compromises of profane life. Does this new rejection of the ascetic mark the end of his career in Russian literature?

It both does and does not. In a certain sense, middle-class values force the ascetic hero "underground," into the world of dissident literature, in the same way that they force Ozhogov, Pilnyak's ascetic, into a drunken, asocial existence. If the majority of the reading public wants heroes who remind it of itself, this is what it gets. A significant minority still remembers the "heroic" heroes of early Soviet literature, however, and studies them with a mixture of nostalgia and aversion.

Pasternak, for example, pays homage to the ascetic hero in *Doctor Zhivago*, in the figure of Antipov-Strel'nikov. Strel'nikov is a perfect ascetic; even his given name, Pavel, reveals ties to the great tradition of revolutionary ascetics, a tradition which includes both Pavel Vlasov and Pavel Korchagin. Strel'nikov voluntarily gives up a comfortable domestic existence in order to aid the Revolution in its struggle against the old order. Although he burns with desire to see his wife and child, he resists all temptation to do so. Like Margulies and Korchagin before him, he seems invested with magical powers which enable him to traverse the width and breadth of Russia effortlessly. His armored train, which regularly appears with no warning, is a symbol of his ability to move at will. In contrast to Strel'nikov, the multidimensional Zhivago is endlessly tormented by his inability to get from one place to another.

Strel'nikov is not the hero of *Doctor Zhivago*, however, a fact which sets him apart from other Soviet ascetics treated here. Furthermore, Pasternak does not identify himself with him and does not allow him to usurp the central position occupied by his weak-willed protagonist, Iurii Zhivago.

Strel'nikov and Zhivago meet face to face only twice, but these two occasions allow us to see the differences between them. The first meeting takes place aboard the armored train. Zhivago has been mistaken for a White officer and brought to Strel'nikov for interrogation. He makes known his identity, and Strel'nikov agrees to release him. He warns him, however, that there is no place for him in the new world which he, Strel'nikov, is creating.

> Now is the time for the Last Judgment, my good man, for creatures from the Apocalypse bearing swords, for winged animals, but not for totally sympathetic and loyal doctors.[1]

Strel'nikov is at the height of his power, and it seems very likely that his judgment of the doctor is a correct one.

The ascetic and the doctor meet again, however, and by this time it is clear that the ascetic's way is doomed. Zhivago has said farewell to Lara but is still living in the house in Varykino. Strel'nikov arrives unexpectedly, and the two talk at length. Strel'nikov has fallen from favor and is being pursued by government forces. He does not live to see his apocalypse; he commits an untimely suicide, having fallen victim to his own premature attempts to hasten the advent of the new age.

Pasternak utilizes the *topoi* of ascetic characterization very consciously and leaves us with no doubt that he means Strel'nikov to be considered an ascetic. He makes him a secondary character, however, and deprives him of his force by allowing a very different character, Zhivago, to triumph in the end. It is Zhivago whose artistic heritage survives, and Zhivago whose spirit corresponds most closely to Russia's. Strel'nikov vanishes, and no trace of his ideal remains.

It is, nevertheless, interesting that Pasternak chooses to portray an ascetic at all. Strel'nikov is a sympathetic, if fanatic, character. He does not gain the upper hand, but he is great in defeat. This suggests that although Pasternak does not endorse the ascetic way, he sees a certain nobility in it. He connects it with much that is good, even if it is misguided.

Solzhenitsyn also shows an interest in the ascetic hero. In *The First Circle* many characters have ascetic traits. None of them is a complete ascetic, however. His most interesting semiascetic is, perhaps, Nerzhin, the hero (if there can be said to be one hero) of the novel. Gleb Nerzhin, like other ascetics, is a man of strong will. We see him turn down the prison chief's offer of eventual freedom in exchange for work on an unpalatable project. We also watch him reject the intimacy offered to him by Simochka, a security agent. He stands on his own integrity and willingly separates himself from the pleasures and compromises offered by the representatives of the profane order.

Gleb, however, is still in search of motivation. He behaves as he does out of an innate sense of right and wrong. Although he develops very little in the course of the novel in comparison with a character like Rubin, he does discover certain truths which were previously hidden from him. In fact, he views his entire imprisonment as a learning experience. This indicates that Nerzhin, unlike the orthodox ascetic, is neither fully formed nor unidimensional. He is not a perfect ascetic.

Lev Rubin, another of the novel's heroes, does know a great "truth." His truth is the truth of the Soviet ascetics who came before him. He ardently believes in the Party's message and in the coming transformation of society. What he does not realize, however, is that he himself is subtly changing. His years of prison experience have subtly influenced his way of thinking. He already refuses to cooperate with the authorities in matters which he considers immoral, which reflects the fact that he has begun to recognize a complex mixture of "the moral" and "the immoral" in a doctrine which is essentially monolithic. Rubin, furthermore, is not an ascetic. He is lax in his personal habits and takes advantage of whatever comforts come his way.

Were Solzhenitsyn to combine Nerzhin's way of life with Rubin's sense of direction, a perfect ascetic would result. He clearly does not mean to, however. Rubin and Nerzhin are close friends and work together day in and day out. There is ample opportunity to bring their ascetic characteristics together, but this is not done.

Solzhenitsyn shows us that, in a world which is filled with evil, the literary hero must be a more complex man, a man who is able to judge matters on his own, without recourse to prepackaged doctrines. Like Pasternak, however, he is attracted to the ascetic, and he pays his own type of homage to him by incorporating his traits into many of his prisoner-heroes in *The First Circle*.

Thus, although the ascetic hero disappears from the mainstream of Russian literature in the early thirties, he continues to appear in various guises in the sixties and seventies. I find it interesting that it is precisely in dissident literature that he is portrayed. Obviously, in this period the "accommodation" between the regime and the middle class posited by Dunham continues to hold. Both Pasternak's and Solzhenitsyn's ascetics jar the middle-class reader. These heroes reject middle-class values and search for their own way. There is, as yet, no place for them in the mainstream of Soviet literature. Are these heroes not, however, the harbingers of yet another "heretical" quest to find a truth which is denied by the establishment? Do they not perhaps presage the beginning of yet another cycle in the ascetic pattern?

Our study of the Russian tradition of the ascetic hero has shown that at the onset of an ascetic cycle, heroes appear whose values are alien to those of other characters in the same literary work. They profess beliefs which are startling and new. These beliefs are in one way or another revolutionary. The ascetic either advocates religious doctrines which threaten the values of the established, institutionalized Church, or he professes philosophical beliefs which threaten to destroy the established institutions of society. The ascetic's most deeply held beliefs are so radical that there can be no question of reconciling them with the beliefs that prevail in society. As a result, he takes a radically polarized view of life.

The literary record, then, could be said to bear out a suggestion made by Sergei Bulgakov to the effect that ascetic heroism is "much more suited to the storms of history than to its calms, which debilitate heroes."[2] The Christianization of Kievan Rus', the creation of a new Muscovite state and its expansion to the North, the struggle for the overthrow and repudiation of the age-old tsarist order—all these are certainly examples of "historical storm." And the ferment awakened in Soviet and post-Soviet society today could well be indicative of yet another such historical storm, another opportunity for the rebirth of an ascetic heroism faintly preserved by Pasternak and Solzhenitsyn.

The ferment in contemporary Soviet society extends to many spheres—cultural, political, social, and economic. Counterculture groups, which first began to emerge in the Brezhnev era, have now established a visible presence on the streets. Some of them, following the Soviet "hippie" movement, advocate asceticism as a form of protest against the existing social order.[3] Religious groups, much freer than at any time since the beginning of Soviet power, are involved in recovering lost spiritual traditions. (It remains to be seen, of course, which traditions will be emphasized and how much of the population will be receptive to the Church's teachings.) Even the government itself has sounded calls for ascetic restraint. Economic shortages incurred as a result of attempts to shift from what Berdyaev once termed a system of "distribution and equalization" to a system of "production and creation"[4] have left the government no choice but to appeal to the people to exercise ascetic heroism. Ironically, the flaws of an economic system favored by *fin-de-siécle* prophets of asceticism can now be effectively combated only by this very same asceticism.

Concurrently, however, many Russians are also rediscovering the voices of moderation within their own tradition. As Boris Shragin explains in his introduction to the English version of *Landmarks*, this collection of essays is now regarded by many Russians as providing a remarkable explanation for much of recent Russian history.[5] The *Landmarks* authors strongly cautioned against the ascetic values held by the *intelligentsia* of their day. They suggested that ascetic triumph would lead to a government every bit as remote from its people as the tsar's, to the demise of cultural values, and to a general weakening of intellectual values in Russia.

We cannot know yet whether a wave of either real-life or literary ascetic heroes will emerge in resistance to more moderate thinkers who support judgments like those made in *Landmarks*, yet the Russian tradition predisposes us to think that they will. We also cannot predict with complete conviction whether the rediscovery of the avant-garde's achievements of the early twentieth century will provoke a return to a non-naturalistic aesthetic which favors the creation of ascetics.

Developments in contemporary literature suggest, however, that the ascetic hero may be making a comeback.[6] In Olesia Nikolaeva's recently published novella (*Invalid detstva, Iunost'* [1990]), the young hero, Aleksandr, is a monk. Aleksandr's deepest desire is to achieve a great spiritual victory, and his first attempt to do so is realized through a period of wandering with hippie bands, whose self-defined asceticism has already been noted. When this path to purification fails, Aleksandr enters a monastery and settles into a dank cell in a filthy basement. His mother, whose philistine behavior has driven the boy to embrace these ascetic forms of antisocial protest, cannot face losing her only son to an antimaterialistic and incomprehensible way of life, and she arrives at the monastery to take him home. The monastic elder encourages Aleksandr to leave, telling him that his mother needs him near her and that he must bear the cross decreed for him.

The characters in this novella are arranged in a sort of hierarchy reminiscent of the one created in What Is to Be Done? Aleksandr's mother, a self-deluded social butterfly who will probably never find moral redemption, is on the lowest moral level. The monks and elders of Aleksandr's monastery, men who understand the world and its corruptions and feel a mission to heal it, are like Chernyshevsky's new men, Kirsanov and Lopukhov. While they admit that society is fallen, these monks nevertheless move in it and feel a responsibility towards it. Aleksandr is a completely different type of character, one who refuses compromise. He cannot adapt himself to his elder's spirit of moderation and leaves the monastery unreconciled and rebellious. Out of an excess of spiritual pride, typical of the ascetic, he rejects the elder's wisdom. At the novella's close, the reader is left with the strong suspicion that Aleksandr's ascetic rebellion will not be quelled.

Another recent novel, Anatolii Kim's Father Forest (Otets-les, Novyi mir [1989]) provides a more complex and provocative view of asceticism. The novel has three heroes, Nikolai, Stepan, and Gleb Turaev, the father, son, and grandson of a once noble family. Each of these men rejects the vision of society shared by his contemporaries and flees to the deep, undisturbed forest, overcome by the "all-encompassing torment of matter,"[7] and hoping to be healed of the split between his outer, physical life and his inner, spiritual one. All three Turaevs attempt to heal the split in their natures through more conventional means, but to no avail. Unlike earlier ascetics, they look to romantic love, and when that fails, to family life. They marry, have children, make acquaintances. They continue to be plagued by an aching sense of separation from those they should be closest to, however, and are incapable of bridging the gap. As fathers, they never truly know their sons, as husbands, they never know their wives. The fact that a pervading sense of disharmony is passed from generation to generation suggests that the Turaevs cannot be integrated into a social community. Separation, imposed by the expanse of the forest, is their fate.

Father Forest is structured in such a way that its heroes' voices blend and merge into one another, and the reader is often temporarily unsure who is speaking and who is being described. This technique leaves the reader with the vision of a composite hero, one whose sensations and experiences are always identical regardless of the generation he belongs to. Accordingly, distinctions imposed by time seem to blur and disappear as the novel progresses. The only constant in the narrative is the presence of an ascetic in the vast, timeless forest. The resulting fusion of atemporality with spatial freedom is very different from the aesthetic of naturalistic time and restricted space utilized in Nikolaeva's novella and is suggestive, rather, of the poetics governing the second phase of an ascetic cycle.

The many differences between the two works notwithstanding, the shared feature of an ascetic hero is tremendously important. It would be hard to deny that the type is right now being revitalized. Nikolaeva's and Kim's ascetics are heroes in quest of a way out of the venality of everyday life. As the tensions and strains in Soviet society increase, and as solutions to problems become increasing complex, more such heroes, searching for a simple, heroic answer, will undoubtedly emerge. As yet, it is too early to say whether new works featuring the ascetic will more closely resemble Nikolaeva's, the poetics of which link it to the beginning of an ascetic cycle, or Kim's, which more clearly reflects a later phase. In either case, however, it is surely one of the great ironies of fate that the values their ascetic heroes condemn as commonly held, banal, and deadening are precisely those which were once championed by another generation of revolutionary ascetics as new, forbidden, and redemptive. Each ascetic vision of salvation seems fated to be transformed into a later ascetic generation's vision of damnation. As a direct consequence of realizing his mission, the Russian ascetic inevitably sows the seeds for the emergence of a new generation of ascetics which, in turn, pursues its new and yet strangely familiar quest.

NOTES

INTRODUCTION

1. D. Likhachev, *Chelovek v literature drevnei Rusi* (Moscow, 1970), p. 3.

2. L. Ginzburg, *O literaturnom geroe* (Leningrad, 1979), p. 18.

3. Joseph Campbell, *The Hero with a Thousand Faces* (Princeton: Princeton University Press, 1968), p. 30.

4. Jeffrey M. Perl, *The Tradition of Return. The Implicit History of Modern Literature* (Princeton: Princeton University Press, 1984), p. 19.

5. Ibid., pp. 17–18.

6. For a discussion of the significance of history for the course of action in the Soviet novel, see Katerina Clark, *The Soviet Novel: History as Ritual* (London and Chicago: University of Chicago Press, 1981), pp. 40–41.

7. Northrop Frye, *Fables of Identity: Studies in Poetic Mythology* (New York: Harcourt, Brace and World, 1963), p. 19.

8. This is one of three major criteria used by Hanning in his discussion of the evolution of the concept of the individual in the literature of the Western Middle Ages. (Robert W. Hanning, *The Individual in Twelfth–Century Romance* [New Haven and London: Yale University Press, 1977], p. 12).

9. John G. Cawelti, *Adventure, Mystery, and Romance: Formula Stories as Art and Popular Culture* (Chicago: University of Chicago Press, 1976), pp. 5–6.

192 Notes to Introduction

10. Ibid., pp. 10–14.

11. Wilhelm Worringer, *Abstraction and Empathy: A Contribution to the Psychology of Style*, trans. Michael Bullock (Cleveland and New York: World Publishing Co., 1967), p. 17.

12. Ibid., p. 16.

13. Ibid., pp. 34–35.

14. Ibid., pp. 38–39.

15. Lessing's view of literature as an art form which unfolds in time has been modified somewhat in the twentieth century. See, for instance, Joseph Frank's essay "Spatial Form in Modern Literature," *Sewanee Review* 53 (1945), pp. 221–40, 433–56, 643–53, in which the process through which the reader comes to understand certain works of modern literature is compared with the process of viewing graphic art.

16. Victor Brombert, "The Idea of the Hero," in *The Hero in Literature*, ed. Victor Brombert (Greenwich, Conn.: Fawcett Publications, 1969), pp. 12–13.

17. Susan Rubin Suleiman, for instance, has investigated a number of different unidimensional heroic types which have flourished in modern European literature. See her *Authoritarian Fictions: The Ideological Novel as Literary Genre* (New York: Columbia University Press, 1983).

CHAPTER 1

1. Although historians are turning an ever–increasing amount of attention towards the influence of steppe nomad groups on medieval Russian cultural life (see, for instance Charles J. Halperin, *Russia and the Golden Horde: The Mongol Impact on Medieval Russian History* [Bloomington: Indiana University Press, 1987] as well as the work of Omeljan Pritsak), it has not been shown that the nomads served as a conduit for Eastern ascetic traditions (Indian, for example). As Likhachev has pointed out, there is no written record of this type of cultural contact between Russia and the East. "Here, above all, we must note the total absence of translations from Asiatic languages. Old Russia knew translations from the Greek, Latin, and ancient Hebrew; she knew works written in Bulgaria, Macedonia, and Serbia; knew translations from Czech, German, and Polish; but she did not know even a single translation from Turkish, Tatar, or the languages of Central Asia and the Caucasus." (*Poetika drevnerusskoi literatury* [Moscow, 1979], p. 11). It is also unlikely that there was a well-developed indigenous tradition of asceticism inherited from pagan times. B. Rybakov has undertaken an exhaustive study of paganism in Old Russia and has

discovered no rites or practices which would point in the direction of asceticism. (*Iazychestvo drevnei Rusi* [Moscow, 1987]).

2. Peter Brown, *The Making of Late Antiquity* (Cambridge, Mass., and London: Harvard University Press, 1978), p. 12.

3. Ibid., p. 85.

4. Ibid., p. 86.

5. Geoffrey Galt Harpham, *The Ascetic Imperative in Culture and Criticism* (Chicago and London: The University of Chicago Press, 1987), pp. 27–8.

6. Kenneth E. Kirk, *The Vision of God* (New York: Harper & Row, 1966), p. 1.

7. Ibid., p. 54.

8. R. Newton Flew, *The Idea of Perfection in Christian Theology* (1934; repr., London: Oxford University Press, 1968), p. 158.

9. See Dennis Costa, *Irenic Apocalypse* (Saratoga, Calif.: Anma Libri, 1981), p. 24, for a discussion of how monasticism was used to replace martyrdom in the Christian consciousness.

10. Herbert B. Workman, *The Evolution of the Monastic Ideal* (London: Charles H. Kelly, 1913), p. 14.

11. Athanasius, *Life of Saint Anthony*, in *Early Christian Biographies*, ed. Roy J. Deferrari and trans. Sister Mary Emily Keenan (Fathers of the Church, 1952), p. 179.

12. Ibid., p. 153.

13. Ibid., p. 154.

14. Dmitri Obolensky, *The Bogomils* (Cambridge: Cambridge University Press, 1948), p. 3.

15. Kirk, *The Vision of God*, p. 58.

16. Workman, *Evolution*, p. 22.

17. Pachomius, as quoted in Workman, *Evolution*, p. 88.

18. Harpham, *The Ascetic Imperative*, p. 22.

19. John Passmore, *The Perfectibility of Man* (New York: Charles Scribner's Sons, 1970), p. 25.

20. Palladius, *The Lausiac History*, trans. Robert T. Meyer (Westminster, Md.: Newman Press, 1965), p. 27.

21. Brown, *Late Antiquity*, pp. 95–96.

22. See, for example, Bernhard Lohse, *Askese und Mönchtum in der Antike und in der alten Kirche* (Munich and Vienna: R. Oldenbourg, 1969), Peter Nagel, *Die Motivierung der Askese in der alten Kirche und der Ursprung des Mönchtums* (Berlin: Akademie Verlag, 1966), and Geoffrey Galt Harpham, *The Ascetic Imperative*.

23. Interestingly enough, Gorky's *Mother*, which reflects the teachings of the "god-builders," also evidences belief in the possibility of a union between God and man. This union is very different from the one talked about by Anthony, of course.

24. For a discussion of how the widespread belief in the imminent end of the world generated ascetic behavior in the early Church, see Nagel, *Die Motivierung der Askese*, pp. 20–34.

25. Michael Barkun, *Disaster and the Millennium* (New Haven and London: Yale University Press, 1974), p. 1.

26. "The Church rejected the apocalyptic writings, viewing them as apocryphal in proportion to the degree in which it later found its centre of gravity in the Greek-speaking world." (Klaus Koch, *The Rediscovery of Apocalyptic*, trans. Margaret Kohl [London: SCM Press, 1972], p. 20). On this same question, see also Jean Daniélou, *The Theology of Jewish Christianity*, trans. John A. Baker (London: Darton, Longman & Todd, 1977). Daniélou states that "Hellenistic converts, not knowing what was valid in such conceptions [i.e., the doctrine of the millennium], rejected the millenarian doctrine *in toto*. . . ." (p. 378).

27. Even today apocalyptic teachings continue to be viewed with a degree of suspicion. One contemporary writer on apocalypticism, for example, has stated that "wherever theology is practiced in the sphere of influence of the Christian proclamation, apocalyptic thought and belief in the genuine sense cannot prevail. The basic Christian doctrine of God's becoming man, the incarnation of the Logos, the redemption of the cosmos, the dawning within history of the new eon, makes any dualism that totally rejects the world and history a heresy. Therefore, the Christian churches have always set themselves just as consistently against any apocalyptic fanaticism as against gnostic enthusiasm." (Walter Schmithals, *The Apocalyptic Movement*, trans. John E. Steely [Nashville and New York: Abingdon Press, 1975], p. 215).

28. Both religious and revolutionary apocalypticism should be viewed as closely related subcategories of "apocalyptic eschatology," which is distinguished by its "vision of retribution beyond the bounds of history." (John J. Collins, *The Apocalyptic Imagination* [New York: Crossroads, 1984], p. 9).

29. A. Kartashev, *Ocherki po istorii russkoi tserkvi* (Paris: YMCA Press, 1959), 1, pp. 223–24.

30. Igor Smolitsch, "Zur Frage der Periodisierung der Geschichte der russischen Kirche," *Kyrios* (1940–1941), p. 76.

31. Igor Smolitsch, *Russisches Mönchtum*, p. 67.

32. Ibid., p. 69.

33. Paul J. Alexander, *The Byzantine Apocalyptic Tradition*, trans. and ed. Dorothy deF. Abrahamse (Berkeley: The University of California Press, 1985), p. 64. Although Alexander uses the term "eschatology," his discussions of "eschatological" literature indicate that he is actually talking about "apocalypses."

34. N. Bonwetsch, "Die christliche vornicänische Litteratur (mit Einschluss der jüdisch-hellenistischen und apokalyptischen) in altslavischen Handschriften," in *Geschichte der altchristlichen Litteratur bis Eusebius*, ed. A. Harnack (Leipzig: J. C. Hinrichs'sche Buchhandlung, 1893), 1, pp. 886–917.

35. A. Rubinstein, "Observations on the Slavonic Book of Enoch," *Journal of Jewish Studies*, 13 (1962), p. 20.

36. *Novgorodskaia pervaia letopis' starshego i mladshego izvodov* (Moscow and Leningrad, 1950), pp. 61–62.

37. Amos Funkenstein discusses the connection between apocalyptic beliefs, which he sees as collective manifestations, and individual eschatology, under which fear of the Last Judgment should be classified, in "A Schedule for the End of the World: The Origins and Persistence of the Apocalyptic Mentality," in *Visions of Apocalypse: End or Rebirth?* ed. Saul Friedlander et al. (New York and London: Holmes & Meier, 1985), p. 54.

38. F. Buslaev, "Izobrazhenie strashnago suda po russkim podlinnikam," in *Istoricheskie ocherki russkoi narodnoi slovesnosti i iskusstva* (St. Petersburg, 1861), 2, p. 144.

39. N. Berdyaev, *The Beginning and the End*, trans. R. M. French (Gloucester, Mass.: Peter Smith, 1970), pp. 203 and 200.

40. V. Sakharov, *Eskhatologicheskiia sochineniia i skazaniia v drevne–russkoi pis'mennosti i vliianie ikh na narodnye dukhovnye stikhi* (Tula, 1879).

41. See N. Kazakova and Ia. Lur'e, *Antifeodal'nye ereticheskie dvizheniia na Rusi XIV–nachala XVI veka* (Moscow and Leningrad, 1955), pp. 394–414 for a discussion of these texts.

42. A particularly interesting discussion of the Old Believer movement and its connection with millennial beliefs is given in Michael Cherniavsky,

"Old Believers and the New Religion," in *The Structure of Russian History*, ed. Michael Cherniavsky (New York: Random House, 1970), pp. 140–188.

43. Sakharov, *Eskhatologicheskiia sochineniia*.

44. These forms are analyzed by K. Chistov in *Russkie narodnye sotsial'no-utopicheskie legendy XVII–XIX vv* (Moscow, 1967).

45. Such folk legends are not, in any case, proper apocalypses in themselves. Rather, they represent an "apocalyptic fiction," "a modern equivalent of [an apocalypse], a kind of sacred text or version of *the Book* through which the character and the narrator and, by implication, the reader—all in their separate, self-enclosed realms—are made privy to a 'secret wisdom' from another time-space." (David M. Bethea, *The Shape of Apocalypse in Modern Russian Fiction* [Princeton: Princeton University Press, 1989], p. 33).

46. A. Klibanov cites a 1925 proclamation by the *molokane* announcing that "the world revolution is rapidly approaching and its coming is to be counted not in years but in months; God is speeding His work." ("Sectarianism and the Socialist Reconstruction of the Countryside," *Soviet Sociology* 8 [1970], p. 385).

47. Timothy Ware, *The Orthodox Church* (Baltimore: Penguin Books, 1963), p. 29.

48. Steven Runciman, *The Great Church in Captivity* (Cambridge: Cambridge University Press, 1968), p. 128.

49. Joan Mervyn Hussey, *Church and Learning in the Byzantine Empire 867–1185* (London: Humphrey Milford, 1937), p. 223.

50. Brown, *Late Antiquity*, p. 93.

51. Consider, for instance, the pathetic "Professor" of Joseph Conrad's *The Secret Agent*, who lives a life of extreme ascetic restraint while preparing for an anarchistic uprising in London.

CHAPTER 2

1. Another monument of the Kievan period, the eleventh-century *Tale of Varlaam and Ioasaf*, should perhaps also be mentioned as a work which contains an ascetic hero. On the one hand, however, the *Tale* is a translation of a version of the life of the Buddha. Although it was recast in Byzantium as a Christian *vita* well before it was translated, its Eastern provenance casts doubt on its suitability as a purely Russian example of literature about the ascetic hero. On the other hand, the actual plot structure of the *Tale* is rather weak. The bulk of the work is taken up by parables,

a fact which also adds to the difficulty of analysis from the perspective of the hero.

2. Unfortunately for any discussion of the history of asceticism in Russia, a central work of Old Russian hagiography, *The Life of Antonii Pecherskii*, has not survived. As is clear from information provided in *The Kievan Crypt Patericon*, Antonii led a severely ascetic life. For this reason George Fedotov posits him as the founder of the Russian ascetic tradition. The *Life* disappeared very early, however. For a discussion of the probable content as well as the history of the *Life*, see A. Shakhmatov, "Zhitie Antoniia i Pecherskaia letopis'," *ZhMNP* (1898), pp. 105–49. For another reconstruction of the content, see M. Priselkov, *Nestor letopisets: Opyt istoriko–literaturnoi kharakteristiki* (1923; repr., The Hague: Russian Reprint Series, 1967).

3. Likhachev, *Chelovek*, p.3.

4. Likhachev confirms for the Russian context the general rule that the saint stands outside all social structures. Ibid., pp. 26–29.

5. Ibid., p. 27.

6. Marvin Kantor, *Medieval Slavic Lives of Saints and Princes* (Ann Arbor: University of Michigan Department of Slavic Languages and Literatures, 1983), p. 1.

7. V. Kliuchevskii, *Drevnerusskiia zhitiia sviatykh kak istoricheskii istochnik* (1871; repr. The Hague and Paris: Mouton, 1968), p. 358.

8. D. Likhachev and A. Panchenko, *Smekhovoi mir drevnei Rusi* (Leningrad, 1976), p. 49.

9. The implications of the normative system are explored by Likhachev, *Poetika*, p. 90.

10. See, for instance, Margaret Church, *Time and Reality* (Chapel Hill: University of North Carolina Press, 1963), pp. 4–5, who distinguishes between writers who, seeing the outer world as separate from its observers, rely on the world (objective approach), and those who see the outer world as meaningful only in terms of the observer (subjective view). Hans Meyerhoff, however, connects the passage of time in the literary work to the hero's change and evolution over the course of the narrative. (Hans Meyerhoff, *Time in Literature* [Berkeley and Los Angeles: University of California Press, 1955], p. 2). If a hero like the ascetic fails to change, then the passage of time will, presumably, be less evident.

11. Likhachev, *Poetika*, p. 102.

12. For an overview of time in Old Russian literature, see ibid., pp. 209–34.

13. Karl Holl makes note of the Old Russian tendency to view the "higher world" as the true reality. He remarks that the Incarnation provides the basis for the belief that this higher world can come into touch with the lower, profane world. ("Die religiösen Grundlagen der russischen Kultur," in *Gesammelte Aufsätze zur Kirchengeschichte* [Tübingen: J. C. B. Mohr, 1928], 2, p. 419).

14. Mircea Eliade describes a similar phenomenon in the following words: ". . . neither the objects of the external world nor human acts, properly speaking, have any autonomous intrinsic value. Objects or acts acquire a value, and in so doing become real, because they participate, after one fashion or another, in a reality that transcends them." (*Cosmos and History: The Myth of the Eternal Return*, trans. Willard R. Trask [New York: Harper and Row, 1959], pp. 3–4).

15. Ibid., p. 86. "Great Time," according to Eliade, refers to the mythical time of the beginning of all things (Ibid., p. xi).

16. Likhachev provides a helpful discussion of character development in chapter 1 of *Chelovek*. He traces the beginning of a more modern approach to characterization to historical works of the seventeenth century in which the hero is shown to be an amalgam of vices and virtues which all influence his behavior simultaneously.

17. Ginzburg, *O literaturnom geroe*, pp. 34–35.

18. V. P. Adrianova-Peretts, for instance, argues that Kievan hagiography includes more "realistic" details than might be expected. She rejects the contention that the ideal is depicted as consistently as is usually claimed. For her discussion of realism in hagiography, see "Zadachi izucheniia 'agiograficheskogo stilia' Drevnei Rusi," *TODRL*, 20 (1964), pp. 41–71.

19. The text used will be the Kassian II redaction as prepared by D. Abramovich and reprinted in *Pamiatniki literatury drevnei Rusi: XII vek* (Moscow, 1980), pp. 412–623.

20. For a discussion of the genre-ensemble, an overarching super–genre whose constituent parts represent other genre categories in their own right, see D. Likhachev, "Drevneslavianskie literatury kak sistema," in *Slavianskie literatury* (Moscow, 1968), pp. 5–48.

21. The question of the genre of the KCP is taken up by D. Chizhevskii in "On the Question of Genres in Old Russian Literature," *HSS*, 2 (1956), p. 111. He writes that "paterika are collections of stories from the lives of saints, but include also 'fallen' hermits. These tales are not at all obliged to cover the whole life of the saint or sinner, but may treat only one isolated incident. Not infrequently the reports of the paterika are anonymous. . . ." Richard Warren Pope touches more specifically on the KCP and the

differences between it and the models it is based on in "O kharaktere i stepeni vliianiia vizantiiskoi literatury na original'nuiu literaturu vostochnykh i iuzhnykh slavian," in *American Contributions to the Seventh International Congress of Slavists*, ed. Victor Terras (The Hague and Paris: Mouton, 1973), 2, p. 486.

22. The fact that two distinct types of monks and, hence, two potentially different types of literary heroes lived in the Kievan Crypt Monastery has been noted before. To the best of my knowledge, however, there has been no study of the literary ramifications of this phenomenon. M. D. Priselkov, for instance, discusses the problem from the sociohistorical point of view. "The monastery was made up from the very first of two elements. First, there were the poor [monks] who were unable to make any kind of financial contribution and who brought nothing with them to the monastery other than a passionate impulse to ascetic feats. . . . The other faction was made up of those monastic brothers who placed a broad all–Russian significance on the cloister . . . or who were at least able to value and cherish the monastery's role in Russian life." (*Nestor letopisets*, pp. 35–36).

23. Many attempts have been made to establish the authorship and approximate date of each *slovo*. Among the pioneering studies are A. Shakhmatov, "Kievopecherskii paterik i Pecherskaia letopis'," *IORJaS*, 2 (1897), pp. 795–844, and D. Abramovich, "Izsledovanie o Kievo–Pecherskom Paterike, kak istoriko-literaturnom pamiatnike," *IORJaS*, 6 (1901), pp. 207–35. Other, more recent attempts include I. Eremin, "Literaturnoe nasledie Feodosiia Pecherskogo," *TODRL*, 5 (1947), pp. 159–84; Hans Reiter, *Studien zur ersten kyrillischen Druckausgabe des Kiever Paterikons* (Munich: Dr. Dr. Rudolf Trofenik, 1976); and Frauke Siefkes, *Zur Form des Žitije Feodosija* (Bad Homburg, Berlin, and Zurich: Verlag Gehlen, 1970). Richard Warren Pope has made a comparative linguistic analysis of the surviving texts in order to study the relationship between the major redactions and recreate the literary history of the work ("The Literary History of the *Kievan Caves Patericon* up to 1500," [Diss., Columbia University, 1970]). David Kirk Prestel ("A Comparative Analysis of the Kievan Caves Patericon," [Diss., University of Michigan, 1983]) and Friedrich Bubner ("Das Kiever Paterikon: Eine Untersuchung zu seiner Struktur und den literarischen Quellen," [Diss., Karl Ruprecht Universität, Heidelberg, 1969]) address genre considerations as well as the literary antecedents of the work.

24. E. Golubinskii (*Istoriia russkoi tserkvi* [Moscow, 1900–11], p. 762), however, suggests that Simon's letter to Polikarp has neither a logical nor an artistic connection with the *slova* that follow it. He claims that the literary merit of the KCP is considerably diminished by this interpolation of irrelevant material. T. Kopreeva, however, notes that both *poslaniia* serve to characterize Polikarp ("Obraz inoka Polikarpa po pis'mam Simona i Polikarpa," *TODRL*, 24 [1969], p. 112–16).

25. In general the traditions of the Kievan Crypt Monastery seem to link asceticism and excessive pride. The connection between the two is discussed in Leopold Karl Goetz, *Das Kiever Höhlenkloster als Kulturzentrum des vormongolischen Russlands* (Passau: M. Waldbauersche Buchhandlung, 1904), p. 117.

26. Russia followed the practice of Mount Athos in establishing monasteries which combined features of anchoritic and cenobitic life. For more detailed information on this topic, see N. F. Robinson, *Monasticism in the Orthodox Churches* (New York: AMS Press, 1971), p. 6.

27. Simon gives voice to the cenobitic vision of aesthetic perfection when he declares, "Perfection, brother, lies not in being praised by others but in conducting one's life properly and in keeping oneself pure. For this reason, brother, many bishops have been elevated from the Crypt Monastery by the Blessed Virgin, just as the apostles were sent out into the world by Christ, our God; and like bright luminaries they illuminated the entire Russian land with baptism." (p. 482)

28. Prestel characterizes Polikarp's address to Akindin as a variant of the exordial *topos*. ("Comparative Analysis," p. 49). Although this is most certainly the case, it does not change my contention that Polikarp is deliberately adding rhetorical touches to his letter. As D. Freydank has pointed out, the use of *topoi* is optional, and when an author avails himself of a *topos* he has some reason for doing so. ("Die altrussische Hagiographie als Gegenstand der Literaturwissenschaft," *Zeitschrift für Slawistik*, 23 [1978], p. 68).

29. Gudzy describes the effect of Simon's *slova* on Polikarp in the following manner: "All this material was supposed to impress Polikarp with a sense of the sanctity of the cloister where his modest position hung heavy on him. Evidently Simon's exhortation had its effect on Polikarp, and he in turn, in the form of an appeal to the crypt prior Akindinus, added to Simon's work a number of new tales from the lives of the Kiev–Crypt monks." (*History of Early Russian Literature*, trans. Susan Wilbur Jones [New York: MacMillan Co., 1949], p. 106).

30. George P. Fedotov, *The Russian Religious Mind* (Belmont, Mass.: Nordland Publishing Co., 1975), 1, p. 143. Fedotov connects the spirit of extreme asceticism evident in some segments of the KCP with the spiritual heritage of Antonii. Although Antonii may be the source of this, it is Polikarp who gives it literary expression.

31. As defined by V. Propp in *Morphology of the Folktale*, trans. Laurence Scott (Austin and London: The University of Texas Press, 1979), p. 21.

32. In discussing the tale of Moisei the Hungarian, Pope also notes its historical concreteness. He mentions the wealth of detail supplied about

the hero's private life and concludes that "through such details linking him to real contemporary historical figures, Polikarp gives Moses an identity and a social context within which the reader can visualize him." ("On the Comparative Literary Analysis of the Patericon Story [translated and original] in the Pre-Mongol Period," in *Canadian Contributions to the VIII International Congress of Slavists*, ed. Zbigniew Folejewski et al. [Ottawa: Canadian Association of Slavists, 1978], p. 10).

33. The young Christ's behavior towards his friends as depicted in the Gospel of Thomas sometimes verges on the sadistic and in many ways resembles Pimen's cruelty towards his fellow monks. For an English translation of the text of this Gospel, see David R. Cartlidge and David L. Dungan, *Documents for the Study of the Gospels* (Philadelphia: Fortress Press, 1980).

34. Theophylact's letter, in which he describes the Bogomils, is analyzed in Obolensky, *The Bogomils*, pp. 113–14.

35. For a more complete description of the moral teachings of the Bogomils, see Cosmas's *Sermon Against the Heretics*, as quoted in ibid., pp. 127–30.

36. Jaroslav Pelikan points out that the majority of Christian heresies emphasized doctrines which were unheard of in the Jewish tradition. (*The Emergence of the Catholic Tradition* [Chicago and London: The University of Chicago Press, 1971], p. 68).

37. Obolensky, *The Bogomils*, pp. 102–6.

38. Ibid., p. 278.

39. For further speculation on the Bogomil contribution to Old Russian culture, see A. Orlov, *Drevniaia russkaia literatura* (Moscow, Leningrad, 1945), pp. 20–21.

40. For a discussion of Isakii's *iurodstvo*, see Natalie Challis and Horace Dewey, "Divine Folly in Old Kievan Literature: The Tale of Isaac the Cave Dweller," *SEEJ*, 22 (1978), pp. 255–64, as well as the speculations of A. Panchenko in D. Likhachev and A. Panchenko, *Smekhovoi: mir Drevnei Rusi* (Leningrad, 1976), p. 93.

41. Chizhevskii concludes that Isakii finds salvation in his new way of life rather than in ascetic practices, but he posits that Isakii's adoption of humility, not his community service, saves him. ("Studien zur russischen Hagiographie: Die Erzählung vom hl. Isaakij," *Wiener Slavistisches Jahrbuch*, 2 [1952], 22–49).

42. Nestor's *Zhitie prepodobnaago ot'tsa nashego Feodosiia, igumena pecher'skago* is printed in *Pamiatniki literatury drevnei Rusi: XI–nachalo XII veka* (Moscow, 1978), pp. 305–91.

43. Fedotov characterizes Feodosii as "far removed from radicalism and onesidedness—sometimes even from consistency" (*Mind*, 1, p. 126); Smirnov writes that he combines contemplation, great feats [podvigi], and an outstanding practical and organizational talent (as quoted in Goetz, *Das Kiever Höhlenkloster*, p. 49), and Igor Smolitsch notes that his Life depicts not only the attempt to perfect the soul but also the necessity for work in the world (*Russisches Mönchtum, Das östliche Christentum*, Neue Folge, Heft 10/11 [Würzburg: Augustinus Verlag, 1953], p. 61).

44. Note, for instance, the ending of the *Life of Feodosii Pecherskii*. Feodosii senses that death is upon him and calls the brothers to his cell. He talks to them at length of the need to fulfill their duties conscientiously. The brothers are in some doubt as to why he is addressing them. "'[Maybe he] wants to hide from us in an unknown place and live alone?' For more than once he had planned to do just this, but he had always yielded to the entreaties of the prince and the nobles and especially to the entreaties of the brethren" (p. 386). Even the other characters in the work note the hero's vacillation, and up until the very moment of his death, they are unable to properly interpret what is happening.

45. The following conclusions apply only to those *slova* within the KCP which have an ascetic hero.

46. Mikhail Bakhtin "Forms of Time and of the Chronotope in the Novel," in *The Dialogic Imagination*, trans. Caryl Emerson and Michael Holquist (Austin: University of Texas, 1981), p. 84.

47. Ibid., p. 113.

48. Ibid., p. 122.

49. Ibid., p. 128.

50. Ibid., pp 121–22.

51. B. Tomashevskii, *Teoriia literatury* (Moscow, 1928), p. 157.

CHAPTER 3

1. Efrem, *Zhitie i terpenie prepodobnago ottsa nashego Avram'ia, prosvetivshagosia v" terpen'i mnoze, novago chiudotvortsa v" sviatykh" grada Smolenska* in *Pamiatniki literatury drevnei Rusi: XIII vek.* (Moscow, 1981), pp. 66–105. A detailed summary of the *Life* can be found in George Fedotov, *Sviatye drevnei Rusi* (Paris: YMCA Press, 1931). A discussion of the history of the text, its variants, and its sources is given in Fedotov, "*Zhitie i terpenie sv. Avraamiia Smolenskago*," *Pravoslavnaia mysl'*, 2 (1930), 127–47.

2. Fedotov, *Mind*, 1, p. 158.

3. Collins, *The Apocalyptic Imagination*, p. 10.

4. The division of eschatological doctrines into those which deal with the larger fate of the race and those which affect the individual alone has already been mentioned. This division, which is particularly characteristic of apocalypticism of the postapostolic age, seems largely irrelevant to Avraamii. For a more detailed discussion of the two types of eschatological doctrines, see Bernard McGinn, *Visions of the End* (New York: Columbia University Press, 1979), pp. 14–15.

5. Although Avraamii initially gives his wealth to the poor, this charitable act seems to have been borrowed directly from the *Life of Saint Anthony*. It is not particularly consistent with the rest of Avraamii's actions and has no other parallel in the *Life*. It should not be taken as an indication that Avraamii is interested in questions of social welfare.

6. "Glubinnyia" suggests to the modern reader the idea of secret "depths"; however, some students of the question have connected the word with "dove" and have posited a secret "sect of doves."

7. Fedotov, "Zhitie i terpenie," p. 146.

8. The immediacy of the end is not an essential ingredient to apocalypticism. Ware, for example, speaks for Church tradition when he says that "whether the end comes early or late, it is always imminent, always spiritually close at hand, even though it may not be temporally close." (*The Orthodox Church*, p. 267) John G. Gager also speaks for this view when he says that millennial dreams would not continue to persist if they were not understood to be at least partially fulfilled. ("The Attainment of Millennial Bliss Through Myth: The Book of Revelation," in *Visionaries and their Apocalypses*, ed. Paul D. Hanson [Philadelphia: Fortress Press, 1983], p. 146).

9. It is odd that Golubinskii criticizes the *Life* as being poor in external events (*Istoriia*, p. 772). This one scene alone lends the *Life* much more vividness than many other hagiographic works possess in their entirety.

10. This is a definition of the grotesque as given in Wolfgang Kayser, The *Grotesque in Art and Literature*, trans. Ulrich Weisstein (Bloomington: Indiana University Press, 1963), p. 21.

11. Prestel, who accepts Likhachev's linkage of genre and extra–literary function, writes that while both the patericon and the life seek to edify, the patericon concentrates more heavily on didacticism and the life on praising the saint. ("Comparative Analysis," p. 46).

CHAPTER 4

1. Fedotov notes that in the period immediately following the Tatar invasion, the clergy, the class which supplied the majority of Old Russian literary figures, was engaged primarily in the essential task of protecting the people from complete destruction. Therefore, the most basic religious concerns, not to mention literary ones, were neglected. (*Mind*, 2, p. 195). Charles J. Halperin also recognizes a change in cultural activity. He points to the fact that the economic basis for cultural life was severely eroded by the initial Mongol devastation as well as by heavy taxation. An unknown, but probably quite large, number of manuscripts perished in fires. Halperin is unwilling to posit as radical a change as Fedotov, however, because, as he rightly points out, many of Old Russia's men of letters survived the invasion, and the quality of literature produced shortly after it remained quite high. (*Russia and the Golden Horde* [Bloomington: Indiana University Press, 1985], 120–21). Halperin notwithstanding, however, chronicle accounts and tales from the period indicate an awareness on the part of literary figures that the invasion had wrought a major change in their lives.

2. Although the Kievan Crypt Monastery, for example, allowed individual monks to immure themselves in the caves as anchorites, it was established primarily to foster community life. The welfare of the community was Feodosii's major concern, and Bishop Simon's tales give evidence that this concern was shared by the founder's successors.

3. A valuable discussion of the transition from cenobitic to anchoritic monasticism and of the historical events connected with this transition is provided by Smolitsch, *Russisches Mönchtum*, pp. 77–86.

4. ". . . the Hesychasts believed that through the uncreated light, through the divine energy, man, having risen above 'material duality,' might achieve 'mental paradise,' might become deified, not only in soul and mind but also in body. He might become God through grace and comprehend the entire world from within. . . ." G. Prokhorov, "Isikhazm i obshchestvennaia mysl' v Vostochnoi Evrope v XIV veke," *TODRL* 23 (1968), p. 92.

5. Jostein Børtnes points out that the Greek Hesychasts were accused of spreading the Bogomil heresy and mentions that although Hesychasm is not Bogomilism by any stretch of the imagination, there were points of similarity between the two movements. Their geographical base was similar, and they emphasized inner peace and prayer at the expense of Church-imposed discipline and the sacraments. He also points out that the Russian version of Hesychasm showed a distinct evolution from its Greek prototype. (*Visions of Glory: Studies in Early Russian Hagiography*, trans. Jostein Børtnes and Paul L. Nielsen [Atlantic Highlands, N.J.: Humanities Press, 1988], p. 110). Prokhorov traces the evolution of Greek Hesychasm,

positing three distinct phases of development. He concludes that Russia simultaneously adopted both the first stage, in which the individual monk practices silent prayer on his own (a stage which coexists with the flowering of ascetic literature), and the third stage, which is more political. "Isikhazm i obshchestvennaia mysl'," p. 107.

6. "The Tatar–Mongol invasion was interpreted in Rus' as a cosmic catastrophe, as an incursion of other–worldly forces, as something as yet unseen and unapprehended." (D. Likhachev, *Kul'tura Rusi vremeni Andreia Rubleva i Epifaniia Premudrogo* [Moscow and Leningrad, 1962], p. 5).

7. Smolitsch, *Russisches Mönchtum*, p. 131.

8. For an account of the Judaizer heresy, see N. Kazakova and Ia. Lur'e, *Antifeodal'nye ereticheskie dvizheniia na Rusi XIV–nachala XVI veka* (Moscow and Leningrad, 1955).

9. According to the Jewish calendar, there were at least 1,500 more years before the 7,000 in question would be fulfilled (ibid., p. 135).

10. For detailed information on this "Gennadius" translation as well as on the number of biblical books existing in translation previous to it, see M. Rizhskii, *Istoriia perevodov Biblii v Rossii* (Novosibirsk, 1978).

11. D. Strémooukhoff is the first of several scholars to note the importance of the Gennadius translation of the Apocalypse of Ezra to the development of apocalyptic doctrines in Old Russia. See his "Moscow the Third Rome: Sources of the Doctrine," *Speculum*, 28 (1953), pp. 84–101.

12. See ibid., p. 91. Ezra actually identifies the third head with the fourth beast in Daniel and therefore only indirectly suggests that it signifies Rome.

13. Strémooukhoff discusses the vacillation in interpretations of the significance of Rome in ibid., p. 84.

14. Ibid., p. 88.

15. Hildegard Schaeder convincingly traces the correspondences between the rise of nationalistic feeling in Moscow and the disintegration of Byzantine influence, while A. Gol'dberg shows that Russians, who had always aspired to equality with Byzantium, actually began to feel confident that they had surpassed it in the fifteenth century. (Hildegard Schaeder, *Moskau das dritte Rom: Studien zur Geschichte der politischen Theorien in der slavischen Welt* [Hamburg: Frederichsen, de Gruyter and Co., 1929], p. 15, and A. Gol'dberg, "K predystorii idei 'Moskva—tretii Rim'," in *Kul'turnoe nasledie drevnei Rusi* [Moscow, 1976], pp. 111–16). For a very different view, see Ia. Lur'e, "O vozniknovenii teorii Moskva—tretii Rim," *TODRL*, 16 (1960), pp. 626–33.

206 Notes to Chapter 4

16. Strémooukhoff cites passages from Pskov chronicles which equate the rapidly expanding Muscovite empire with the reign of the Antichrist. ("Moscow the Third Rome," p. 93).

17. On this question, see chapter 3 of G. Florovskii, *Puti russkago bogosloviia* (Paris: YMCA Press, 1981).

18. N. Nikol'skii, *Kirillo–Belozerskii monastyr' i ego ustroistvo do vtoroi chetverti XVII veka (1397–1625)* (St. Petersburg, 1897), p. 2.

19. Fedotov writes that Sergii's spiritual heritage can be traced to monasteries in the South as well as to those in the North, but he also suggests that the tradition of contemplative prayer was much more frequently found in the North. (*Mind* 2, p. 247).

20. Ibid., p. 196.

21. "The disagreement between the Josephites and the Transvolgan movement can be summarized as follows: conquering the world by means of social labor within it vs. overcoming it through transfiguration and through the formation of a new man, through the creation of a new personality." (Florovskii, *Puti*, p. 22.) Although Iosif personally led a strict ascetic life, this may be more a reflection of his obsession with discipline than of any deeper urge towards personal perfection.

22. On this question, see G. Prokhorov, "Knigi Kirilla Belozerskogo," *TODRL*, 36 (1981), pp. 50–70.

23. "The basic cultural values (ideological, political, and religious) of medieval Russia were distributed in a bipolar field and divided by a sharp boundary without an axiologically neutral zone." (Iu. Lotman and B. Uspenskii, "Binary Models in the Dynamics of Russian Culture [to the End of the Eighteenth Century]," in *The Semiotics of Russian Cultural History*, trans. Robert Sorenson and ed. Alexander D. Nakhimovsky and Alice Stone Nakhimovsky [Ithaca and London: Cornell University Press, 1985], p. 31).

24. Likhachev defines the saint's life as the most representative genre of the fourteenth and fifteenth centuries. (*Chelovek*, p. 72.)

25. Likhachev, *Poetika*, pp. 126–7.

26. Although we must restrict ourselves here to analyzing only a small number of the lives of ascetics, many such lives exist. For summaries of them, see L. Dmitreev, *Zhitiinye povesti russkogo severa kak pamiatniki literatury XIII–XVII vv.* (Leningrad, 1973); Fedotov, *Mind*, 2; Kliuchevskii, *Drevnerusskiia zhitiia sviatykh*.

27. For a discussion of the depiction of the devil in Old Russian literature, see F. Buslaev, *Bes* (St. Petersburg, 1881).

28. Bakhtin, "Forms of Time and of the Chronotope," pp. 87–105.

29. Ibid., p. 120.

30. Ibid., pp. 121–22.

31. The northern ascetic tradition will be discussed on the basis of the lives of Sergii Radonezhskii and Kirill Belozerskii and the seventeenth–century life, or tale, of Ulianiia Osor'ina. These works have been chosen, not because they are the only lives of ascetics extant, but because they unquestionably belong to both the literary as well as to the religious tradition of Old Russia. They have also survived in numerous manuscript copies and can be assumed, therefore, to have appealed to a relatively large readership and to have exercised a good deal of influence on the development of subsequent literary works. The question of what genre *The Life of Ulianiia Osor'ina* belongs to is much debated. I will refer to it as a "life," because it is so designated by its author, not because of any genre judgment on my part.

32. Attempts by recent scholars to unravel the history of the *Life* include Julia Alissandratos, "Simmetricheskoe raspolozhenie epizodov odnoi redaktsii 'Zhitiia Sergiia Radonezhskogo'," in *American Contributions to the Ninth International Congress of Slavists*, ed. Paul Debreczeny (Columbus, Ohio: Slavica, 1983), pp. 7–17; Ortrud Appel, *Die Vita des hl. Sergij von Radonež: Untersuchungen zur Textgeschichte* (Munich: Wilhelm Fink Verlag, 1972); Ludolf Müller's introduction to *Die Legenden des heiligen Sergij von Radonež*, ed. D. Chizhevskii (1892; repr., Munich: Wilhelm Fink Verlag, 1967); and V. Zubov, "Epifanii Premudryi i Pakhomii Serb," *TODRL*, 9 (1953), pp. 145–58.

33. References are to *Zhitie i zhizn' prepodobnago ottsa nashego Sergiia*, in *Die Legenden des heiligen Sergij von Radonež*.

34. Sergii's given name is Varfolomei. In accordance with Church custom, he changes his name to that of the saint on whose feast day he receives the monastic tonsure.

35. The connection between this particular vision and ascetic practices is established quite explicitly. One of Sergii's disciples, who also witnesses the vision, admits that it has the effect of dissolving the link between his flesh and his spirit.

36. Sergii refuses ordination *three* times; he twice refuses the pleas of his disciples and once refuses Afanasii. He agrees to accept the status of priest only when the bishop chides him with his disobedience.

37. Much of what we know about Sergii as a historical figure comes from sources other than the *Life*. Many of his actual achievements (such as reestablishing the cenobitic way in Russia) are incompatible with the

ascetic paradigm, but the present discussion analyzes him as the hero of a specific literary text, not as a real–life person. Although Sergii certainly did contribute powerfully to the development of Russian culture, the power we see in the *Life* is not a social one. As Geoffrey Galt Harpham has described the ascetic way, ". . . the power situated in the eremite was not a product or function of culture but was universal ("in" everyone) and nonhuman. The eremite went to the desert to achieve a self constituted entirely by transcendence-of-self." (*The Ascetic Imperative*, p. 28).

38. This vignette about Sergii and the bear is not present in all variants of the *Life*. Those texts which Tikhonravov attributes to Pakhomii, for instance, substitute an elaborate sequence of demonic temptations. For a reprint of these texts, see *Die Legenden des heiligen Sergij von Radonež*.

39. Jostein Børtnes has written about the treatment of space in a series of frescoes in Volotovo, whose creation is roughly contemporaneous with that of the *Life*. He notes the tendency of the painter to place figures in different planes and create a three-dimensional effect unusual in Old Russian art. He attributes this glorying in space to an attempt to depict "man's way to deification through Christ's abasement" rather than to a Renaissance recognition of the beauty of the human body. (*Visions of Glory*, pp. 104–5). It is tempting to interpret the more realistic treatment of space in the *Life* as an analogous attempt to depict man's path to deification.

40. Likhachev, *Poetika*, p. 335.

41. The text of the *Life* used is found in *Pachomij Logofet. Werke im Auswahl* (Munich: Eidos Verlag, 1963)

42. For a discussion of the characterization of villains in Old Russian literature, see V. Adrianova–Peretts, "K voprosu ob izobrazhenii 'vnutrennego cheloveka' v russkoi literatury XI–XIV vekov," in *Voprosy izucheniia russkoi literatury XI–XX vekov* (Moscow and Leningrad, 1958), p. 15.

43. The text of the *Life of Ulianiia Osor'ina* used here is edited by M. Skripil' and found in *TODRL*, 6 (1948), pp. 256–323.

44. Skripil' discusses the relationship between the *Life* and the family chronicle in *Russkaia povest' XVII veka* (Moscow, 1954), p. 350.

45. For a discussion of the canonization of women in the Russian Orthodox Church, see F. Buslaev, "Ideal'nye zhenskie kharaktery drevnei Rusi," in *Istoricheskie ocherki russkoi narodnoi slovesnosti* (St. Petersburg, 1861), 2, pp. 240–45.

46. The events and significance of Nil's life are discussed in Fairy von Lilienfeld, *Nil Sorskii und seine Schriften* (Berlin: Evangelische Verlagsanstalt, 1963) as well as in George A. Maloney, *Russian Hesychasm* (The Hague

and Paris: Mouton, 1973) and Ia. Lur'e, "K voprosu ob ideologii Nila Sorskogo," *TODRL*, 13 (1957), pp. 626–32.

47. "Iosif was, above all, a proponent and a forceful advocate of communal life. . . . Iosif's outlook is defined completely by the idea of social service and the calling of the Church. Iosif's ideal constitutes a sort of populism." (Florovskii, *Puti*, p. 18). "The Transvolgan truth, the truth of contemplation and mental construction, lies specifically in a flight from the world. It must be immediately added that it constituted not only an attempt to surmount worldly passions and 'love of the world,' but also an attempt to forget the world, not just its vanity, but also its needs and sicknesses." (ibid., pp. 20–21).

48. "With the formation of a centralized Russian government, the literary formula, it would seem, not only does not become weaker but, on the contrary, becomes unusually elaborate . . . but the result of this type of growth of canons is the loss of their stability. In this connection we must note the following circumstance: the destruction of *literary* canons was taking place at the same time as the elaborate development of formulae in *real* life." (Likhachev, *Poetika*, p. 96).

49. Al'bert Opul'skii reinforces this when he writes that while the sixteenth century marks a highpoint in the quantity of lives produced, it also marks the death of the genre as a literary phenomenon because overstandardization of canons always destroys art. (Al'bert Opul'skii, "Problema khudozhestvennosti russkikh zhitii i ee izuchenie," *GRANI*, 120 [1981], pp. 189–90).

50. Chizhevskii, *History of Russian Literature*, (Westport, Conn.: Hyperion Press, 1981), p. 238.

51. Tomashevskii gives his theory of literary change in *Teoriia literatury*, pp. 156–57.

52. Tomashevskii discusses the possibility that devices that have outlived themselves may disappear at one point only to reappear in literature several generations later, when there is the appropriate motivation for them. (*Teoriia literatury*, p. 157).

53. Vatro Murvar, "Messianism in Russia: Religious and Revolutionary," *Journal for the Scientific Study of Religion*, 10 (1971), p. 284.

54. When Norman Cohn speaks of Soviet Communism, he says that it can be "best elucidated by reference to that subterranean revolutionary eschatology which so often sent tremors through the massive structure of medieval society." (*The Pursuit of the Millennium*, [Fairlawn, N.J.: Essential Books, 1957], p. xv).

55. *The Shape of Apocalypse*, p. 13. Bethea recognizes a shift from a

religious view of apocalypse towards the political. "It has long been maintained that as the idea of history as divinely inspired human activity with an imminent conclusion from without gave way to the idea of history as secular progress with an immanent conclusion here on earth the historical 'plot' was constantly modified to include an ever wider and disparate reality." (ibid., p. 37). The relationship between religious and revolutionary apocalypticism is also traced by Murvar in "Messianism," pp. 227–338.

CHAPTER 5

1. These terms are used by Rufus W. Mathewson, Jr. in *The Positive Hero in Russian Literature* (Stanford: Stanford University Press, 1975), p. 146.

2. This is Bakhtin's expression as used in the essay "Epic and Novel," in *The Dialogic Imagination*, trans. Caryl Emerson and Michael Holquist (Austin: University of Texas Press, 1981), p. 11.

3. Worringer, *Abstraction and Empathy*, p. 5.

4. Ibid., p. 45.

5. Edward Wasiolek, "Design in the Russian Novel," in *The Russian Novel from Pushkin to Pasternak*, ed. John Garrard (New Haven and London: Yale University Press, 1983), p. 54.

6. Ibid., p. 63.

7. In her study of the influence of hagiography on nineteenth–century Russian literature, Margaret Ziolkowski discusses several heroic types which were taken from saints' lives. She finds that the ones most frequently encountered in modern literature are the kenotic, the Josephite, and the holy fool (*iurodivyi*). Although none of these types corresponds entirely to the ascetic, the Josephite, perhaps, comes closest. Not surprisingly, Ziolkowski finds few examples of this type in the work of the "classic" writers. (*Hagiography and Modern Russian Literature* [Princeton: Princeton University Press, 1988]).

8. The division of medieval society into a laughing, life–affirming folk culture and a grim official culture is central to Bakhtin's arguments in *Rabelais and His World*, trans. Hélène Iswolsky (Bloomington: University of Indiana Press, 1984).

9. For a study of how the medieval tradition influenced the works of the great nineteenth-century writers, see Al'bert Opul'skii, *Zhitiia sviatykh v tvorchestve russkikh pisatelei XIX veka* (East Lansing, Mich.: Russian Language Journal, 1986), as well as Margaret Ziolkowski, *Hagiography and Modern Russian Literature*.

Notes to Chapter 5   211

10. Peter Burke discusses the withdrawal of Russia's upper classes from the old culture and suggests that it was complete by 1800. See his *Popular Culture in Early Modern Europe* (New York: Harper and Row, 1978), pp. 270–81.

11. Frye, *Fables of Identity*, pp. 19–20.

12. According to Donald Fanger's formulation, in "The Portrait," "the world as such needs to be redeemed by art." (*The Creation of Nikolai Gogol* [Cambridge, Mass., and London: The Belknap Press of Harvard University Press, 1979], p. 115). Fanger states clearly that he is referring to the 1842 version of the story. We should also note his reference to the need for redemption, a need which Worringer denies in totally naturalistic art.

13. Most students of Gogol view the 1842 "Portrait" as a considerable improvement over its original. Konstantin Mochul'skii, however, rightly points out that the original is much more revealing of Gogol's spiritual vision. (*Dukhovnyi put' Gogolia* [Paris: YMCA Press, 1976], p. 33), and V. Gippius notes that in this story "Gogol, for the first and only time in his art, offers us a religious type, a man who has 'turned completely into a flame.'" (*Gogol*, trans. and ed. Robert A. Maguire [Ann Arbor: Ardis, 1981], p. 53).

14. N. V. Gogol', *Sobranie sochinenii v shesti tomakh* (Moscow, 1952), 3, p. 281. Subsequent citations will be to this edition of the works.

15. Fanger, *The Creation of Nikolai Gogol*, p. 114. Mochul'skii, *Dukhovnyi put'*, p. 33. V. Gippius notes that, in general, Gogol's religious outlook was dualistic (*Gogol*, p. 15).

16. Simon Karlinsky, *The Sexual Labyrinth of Nikolai Gogol* (Cambridge, Mass., and London: Harvard University Press, 1976), p. 112.

17. Chertkov is not alone among Gogol's heroes in his unidimensionality. Fanger notes that "Gogol's most successful characters seldom aspire, achieve, change, or learn." (*The Creation of Nikolai Gogol*, p. 21). In comparing Gogol and Dostoevsky, he also states that "Gogol's characters depart no less sharply from the norm, though in a different direction: where Gogol *simplifies*, Dostoevsky intensifies." ("Influence and Tradition in the Russian Novel," in *The Russian Novel from Pushkin to Pasternak*, ed. John Garrard [New Haven and London: Yale University Press, 1983], p. 46, emphasis mine).

18. See G. W. Spence, *Tolstoy the Ascetic* (New York: Barnes and Noble, 1968).

19. References to the text are to L. N. Tolstoi, *Otets Sergii*. In *Sobranie sochinenii v dvadtsati tomakh* (Moscow, 1964), vol. 12.

212 Notes to Chapter 5

20. The similarity between the plots of "Father Sergius" and the *Life of Saint James* (*Zhitie Iakova Postnika*), in which a saint surmounts a great temptation only to fall to a lesser one, has been discussed in detail by R. Pletnev in "'Otets Sergii' i Chet'i Minei," *Novyi zhurnal*, 40 (1955), pp. 118–31.

21. For a discussion of the repetitive pattern which marks Sergius's quest for perfection, see Richard F. Gustafson, *Leo Tolstoy: Resident and Stranger. A Study in Fiction and Theology.* (Princeton: Princeton University Press, 1986), p. 415.

22. Julia Alissandratos identifies the *Life of Sergii Radonezhskii* as a second subtext of the story in "Leo Tolstoy's 'Father Sergius' and the Russian Hagiographical Tradition," *Cyrillomethodianum*, 8–9 (1984–85), pp. 158–60.

23. It is interesting that Bakhtin's assignment of laughter and folly to folk culture and of asceticism and humorlessness to official culture (*Rabelais*, p. 73.) seems to indicate that the *iurodivyi*, an essentially comic figure, (cf. Likhachev and Panchenko, *Smekhovoi mir*) should be regarded as the product of a folk outlook on life while the ascetic can be viewed as the product of institutionalized culture. Such a conclusion would surely please Tolstoy, who depicted a type of *iurodstvo* in the figure of Sergius and who tried to make all his later work accessible to even the most unsophisticated audiences.

24. Richard F. Gustafson has argued that "the history of Tolstoy's style is the story of his fiction becoming more and more emblematic" (*Leo Tolstoy*, p. xiii), which might appear to point towards an interpretation of a hero from the late period like Sergius as a unidimensional character type. L. Michael O'Toole, however, has suggested that although the narrative structure of "Father Sergius" is indeed very simple, the hero himself is distinguished by his paradoxical and complex characterization. (*Structure, Style and Interpretation in the Russian Story* [New Haven and London: Yale University Press, 1982], p. 68). Edward Wasiolek's assertion that Tolstoy's late works show the same strivings towards individualism as his early ones also seems to support the idea of a fairly complex hero in "Father Sergius." (*Tolstoy's Major Fiction* [Chicago and London: University of Chicago Press, 1978], p. 178).

25. F. M. Dostoevskii, *The Notebooks for The Brothers Karamazov*, trans. and ed. Edward Wasiolek (Chicago and London: University of Chicago Press, 1971), p. 24.

26. Linda Ivanits also points out that the introduction of Ferapont at the beginning of the "Laceration" ("*Nadryv*") section of the novel points towards a condemnation of asceticism. For Ivanits, Ferapont's asceticism

is a weapon with which to humiliate others while exalting oneself. ("Hagiography in *Brat'ja Karamazovy*: Zosima, Ferapont, and the Russian Monastic Saint," *Russian Language Journal*, 34 [1980], p. 114.

27. F. M. Dostoevskii, *Brat'ia Karamazovy*. In *Polnoe sobranie sochinenii v tridtsati tomakh* (Leningrad, 1976), 14, p. 154).

28. It *is* necessary to remember, of course, that this one "successful" hero, Rakhmetov, is very different from the heroes of the works that we have looked at here. In large part this is due to the fact that *What Is to Be Done*? itself is a very different piece of literature, one which is much closer to the non-naturalistic, unidimensional tradition than are the works discussed in this chapter. It is also very different in its approach to its ascetic, a man governed by social motivations rather than by religious ones.

29. Mention has already been made of Tolstoy's incorporation of at least two saints' lives into "Father Sergius." An inventory of Dostoevsky's personal library lists, among other titles, *Izbrannye zhitiia sviatykh kratko izlozhennye po rukovodstvu Chet'ikh-Minei, po mesiatsiam v dvenadtsati knigakh* (Moscow, 1860–61), indicating the author's keen interest in saints' lives. See L. Grossman, *Seminarii po Dostoevskomu. Materialy, bibliografii i komentarii* (Moscow, 1922) for a listing of the contents of Dostoevsky's library.

30. Ziolkowski, *Hagiography and Modern Russian Literature*, pp. 229–45.

31. Alissandratos, "'Father Sergius,'" p. 157.

32. Linda Ivanits analyzes Zosima's relation to real-life elders (*startsy*) and concludes that Dostoevsky makes a deliberate departure from his models in his characterization. Nevertheless, this departure does not, in my opinion, signify a complete rejection of Orthodox tradition, as is found in Tolstoy. For Ivanits's argument, see "Hagiography in *Brat'ja Karamazovy*."

33. Alastair Fowler, "The Life and Death of Literary Forms," *New Literary History*, 2 (1971), pp. 199–216.

34. The combination of earlier, religiously inspired motifs with more modern ones has also been studied by Nicholas Rzhevsky. He notes that nineteenth-century Russian writers were "heavily involved in the defense of human spirituality before the encroachments of science and the materialistic reductions of the individual. The eschatological projection of fictional characters into ultimate realms of existence, then, is traceable to a desperate struggle waged in the name of religiously mandated images of self and the role of self in society." (*Russian Literature and Ideology: Herzen, Dostoevsky, Leontiev, Tolstoy, Fadeyev* [Urbana, Chicago, and London: University of Illinois Press, 1983], p. 17).

CHAPTER 6

1. Clark, *Soviet Novel*, p. ix.

2. Ibid., pp. xi–xii.

3. We shall see, however, that certain elements of it still survive in Gorky's *Mother*.

4. Bethea, *The Shape of Apocalypse*, p. 37.

5. This development is not unique to nineteenth–century Russia. In a study of American social patterns, Jean B. Quandt notes that religiously motivated millennial doctrines were widespread. Toward the end of the nineteenth century, however, "what had once been defined solely in terms of evangelical Protestantism was . . . secularized in important ways. The process of secularization entailed a partial transfer of redemptive power from religious to secular institutions." ("Religion and Social Thought: The Secularization of Postmillennialism," *American Quarterly*, 25 [1973], p. 391).

6. Cohn, *The Pursuit of the Millennium*.

7. Ibid., p. 22.

8. I certainly do not mean to suggest that there were no millenarian peasant protests in Russia. A. Klibanov, for example, has documented numerous examples of millenarian expectations among the religious sectarians of Russia. (*History of Religious Sectarianism in Russia [1860s–1917]*, trans. Ethel Dunn and ed. Stephen P. Dunn [Oxford: Pergamon Press, 1982]). These sectarian movements do not seem to have left any traces in the literature read by the common people in late nineteenth-century Russia. Jeffrey Brooks divides the chapbooks read by the newly literate into several categories based on their subject matter, but none of them reflect millenarian concerns. (*When Russia Learned to Read: Literacy and Popular Literature, 1861–1917* [Princeton: Princeton University Press, 1985]).

9. Chernyshevsky can be taken as a case in point: ". . . the young Chernyshevsky's Christianity sprang not from a transcendental experience, but from a passionate belief in the Kingdom of God on earth. This belief easily underwent a process of secularization: from concluding after Feuerbach, that the secret of theology was anthropology, it was an easy step to interpreting the Kingdom of God on earth as a kingdom of emancipated human beings in full control of their fate." (Andrzej Walicki, *A History of Russian Thought from the Enlightenment to Marxism*, trans. Hilda Andrews–Rusiecka [Stanford: Stanford University Press, 1979], p. 187).

10. Joseph Frank also identifies Chernyshevsky as a pivotal figure in the melding of religious and social movements in nineteenth-century

Russia. Although his identification of the operative religious model as a kenotic one is questionable, we must agree with the overall thrust of his argument. ("N. G. Chernyshevsky: A Russian Utopia," *Southern Review*, 3 [1967], pp. 83–84).

11. On the question of the Marxist view of history as closed, see Ernest L. Tuveson, "The Millenarian Structure of *The Communist Manifesto*," in *The Apocalypse in English Renaissance Thought and Literature*, ed. C. A. Patrides and Joseph Wittreich (Ithaca, N.Y.: Cornell University Press, 1984), p. 325.

12. Friedrich Engels, *The Peasant War in Germany*, in *The German Revolutions*, ed. Leonard Krieger (Chicago and London: The University of Chicago Press, 1967), p. 54.

13. Bruce Mazlich also comes to the conclusion that the revolutionary ascetic acts as an individual, not as a member of the societal group he is supposed to represent. Using Freudian methods of analysis, he determines that actual, historical representatives of the class of revolutionary ascetics have few libidinal ties. They displace their capacity for loving individuals onto an abstract concept, the revolution. Thus, although they appear to be selfless men and women, dedicated entirely to others, they are, in fact, totally untouched by others' concerns. (*The Revolutionary Ascetic* [New York: Basic Books, Publishers, 1976]). E. Krasnoshchekova is, to the best of my knowledge, the first Soviet scholar to reach a similar conclusion, although her method of analysis is totally different. She refers to certain heroes of early Soviet novels as "fighting for the idea, not the man, and [thereby] condemning themselves to isolation from the masses . . . ." "Gumanizm i zhertvennost'," in *Metod i Masterstvo* (Vologda, 1971), 3, p. 56. Aileen Kelly also investigates the connection between literature and an ascetic revolutionary code. She notes that "to admit the existence of inner struggle or indulge in forbidden emotions and desires was, as he [the *intelligent*] was constantly reminded, to withdraw himself definitively 'from the ranks of the workers for progress.'" ("Self-Censorship and the Russian Intelligentsia," *Slavic Review*, 46 [1987], p. 196).

14. Sergei Bulgakov, "Heroism and Asceticism: Reflections on the Religious Nature of the Russian Intelligentsia," in *Landmarks*, trans. Marian Schwartz (New York: Karz Howard, 1977), p. 38.

15. Semen Frank, "The Ethic of Nihilism: A Characterization of the Russian Intelligentsia's Moral Outlook," in ibid., p. 169.

16. See, for example, Clark on this question. "The relationship of literary to extraliterary factors is always a complex one. Literature is, on the one hand, an autonomous series, having its own traditions and generating new forms within those traditions; on the other hand, it can never be completely independent of the extraliterary aspects of its own culture, for, if

it were, its signs would have no meaning. Literature interacts with *many* other aspects of culture, not just with politics and ideology. I say 'interacts with,' because literature never merely 'reflects' extraliterary matter; it always adapts it to fit its own traditions." (*Soviet Novel*, p. 7). Gary Saul Morson, in his *The Boundaries of Genre: Dostoevsky's Diary of a Writer and the Traditions of Literary Utopia* (Austin: University of Texas Press, 1981), argues for a primarily literary interpretation of *What Is to Be Done?* He views it as a utopia which consciously sets out to undermine the novelistic tradition and which should, accordingly, be read as metaliterature.

17. See Suleiman, *Authoritarian Fictions*.

18. Walter L. Reed, *Meditations on the Hero* (New Haven and London: Yale University Press, 1974), p. 192.

19. "The elements that make up the master plot come, at one level, from within literature itself. In general the master plot continues one strand of prerevolutionary literature: it reworks the prevailing myths and tropes of Russian radical fiction and rhetoric of the second half of the nineteenth and early twentieth centuries. Also carried over has been some influence from folk and religious literature (though pre-Soviet radicals used these sources, too)." (Soviet Novel, pp. 8–9).

20. See A. Sinyavsky, *On Socialist Realism*, trans. Max Hayward (New York: Vintage Books, 1965), p. 195.

21. D. S. Mirsky, *Contemporary Russian Literature: 1881–1925* (New York: Knopf, 1926), pp. 105–6.

22. Leon Trotsky, *Literature and Revolution*, (Ann Arbor: University of Michigan Press, 1960), p. 191.

23. As formulated by Herman Ermolaev in *Soviet Literary Theories, 1917–1934* (Berkeley: University of California Press, 1963), p. 193.

24. It is noteworthy that the contributors to the *Landmarks* collection began as Marxists but later turned towards ideas first enunciated by the Symbolists. This is, perhaps, a surface reflection of the deep underlying similarity between the two movements which has been posited here. It is also significant that Edward J. Brown has found a good deal of evidence for Gorky's "symbolist contamination." Although he specifically excludes works like *Mother* from his discussion, he finds that much of Gorky's work reflects Symbolist esthetics rather than realistic ones. ("The Symbolist Contamination of Gor'kii's 'Realistic' Style," *Slavic Review*, 47 [1988], pp. 227–38).

25. Bakhtin, "Epic and Novel," p. 35.

26. Clark, *Soviet Novel*, p. 29.

27. G. Žekulin explicitly identifies *What Is to Be Done?* with the Socialist Realist novel in "Forerunner of Social Realism: The Novel *What To
Do?* by N. G. Chernyshevsky," *Slavonic and East European Review*, 41 (1963),
pp. 467–83. Chernyshevsky cannot be satisfactorily identified with Soviet
writers, however, either from the perspective of his views on social problems or from that of literary technique. Richard Hare qualifies the Soviet
tendency to view Chernyshevsky as a fellow Marxist with the remark that
Chernyshevsky's "thought is far more complex, honest and far-sighted,
less *monolithic* in its points of contact with Marxism, less *dated* in its divergences from Marx, than many of his Soviet commentators appear to
realize, or are able to admit." (Richard Hare, *Pioneers of Russian Social Thought*
[New York: Vintage Books, 1964], p. 210.) Clark also points out important differences between *What Is to Be Done?* and the Socialist Realist novel.
(*Soviet Novel*, p. 55).

28. Georg Lukács, *Der Russische Realismus in der Weltliteratur* (Neuwied
and Berlin: Luchterhand, 1964), p. 138.

29. See Randall's arguments in favor of an interpretation of *What Is
to Be Done?* as a self-consciously Victorian novel in *N. G. Chernyshevskii*
(New York: Twayne Publishers, Inc., 1967).

30. The fact that *What Is to Be Done?* had to be completed in a very
short period of time and was published only once in the author's lifetime, at that, owing to an oversight on the part of the censorship, makes
is easy to select a redaction. The version referred to here appears in N. G.
Chernyshevskii, *Sobranie sochinenii v piati tomakh* (Moscow, 1974), vol. 5.
Subsequent references will be to this edition.

31. Richard Freeborn suggests that although Rakhmetov is only pe-
ripherally involved in the main plot line of the novel, his biography nevertheless recapitulates many of the major issues which the novel seeks to
elucidate (*The Russian Revolutionary Novel: Turgenev to Pasternak* [New York:
Cambridge University Press, 1982], p. 25). I understand Freeborn to mean
that Rakhmetov is the figure through whom Chernyshevsky relates the
careers of the Kirsanovs and the Lopukhovs to the broader revolutionary
cause. Soviet critics often identify Rakhmetov as the novel's hero. See, for
example, A. Lebedev, *Geroi Chernyshevskogo* (Moscow, 1962).

32. See, for instance, Irina Paperno, who posits as the structuring
mechanism of the novel an "organization of the narrative world in terms
of oppositions of contrasting qualities, motions or personages." (Irina Paperno,
"The Individual in Culture: N. G. Chernyshevsky," [Diss., Stanford University, 1984, p. 251]). She further proposes a resolution of these contrasts
through "a system of transformations of one quality into another medi-
ated through an algorithm of carefully arranged mental devices. . . ." p.
300). She implies that evil characters do become good by analogy with

the "evangelical principle; 'the last shall become the first'. . . ." (p. 300)
Clark suggests that Rakhmetov, at least, is subject to change and that the
novel is open-ended because he disappears without a trace. (*Soviet Novel*,
p. 51). Herbert E. Bowman, likewise, sees the interconnectedness of the
groups. "Just as the head is a part of the body, so the elite of a society is
a part of the society which it articulates and raises to self-consciousness.
It is not the function of an elite to impose preconceived ideas or ideals,
but, on the contrary, to elucidate the self–interest of the unenlightened
masses, whom historical events are moving in directions which they, in
their relative blindness, are unable to observe." ("Revolutionary Elitism
in Cernysevskij," *American Slavic and East European Review*, 13 [1954], p.
196.

33. N. G. O. Pereira, *The Thought and Teaching of N. G. Černyševskij*
(The Hague: Mouton, 1975), p. 77.

34. William F. Woehrlin, *Chernyshevskii: The Man and the Journalist*
(Cambridge, Mass.: Harvard University Press, 1971), p. 131.

35. Michael R. Katz and William G. Wagner argue in their introduction
to a new translation of *What Is to Be Done?* that Chernyshevsky "remained
essentially an idealist." They point to his tendency to judge life according
to moral categories as well as the existence in his work of an implied ideal
by which the actions of others are judged. (*What Is to Be Done?*, trans.
Michael R. Katz [Ithaca, N.Y. and London: Cornell University Press, 1989],
p. 20). In her book *Chernyshevsky and the Age of Realism: A Study in the
Semiotics of Behavior* (Stanford: Stanford University Press, 1988), Irina A.
Paperno asks of Chernyshevsky the man, "Which comes first, physical
sensation or metaphor? What are we dealing with, the sublimation of
physiological phenomena or the materialization of cultural phenomena?
Apparently, for Chernyshevsky constructs had more reality and substan-
tiality than did sensual phenomena" (p. 72).

36. "Indeed, the more he dwells on the majestic figure of Rakhmetov,
the more *all* the principles of Chernyshevsky's philosophy go flying out
the window. For Rakhmetov is nothing if not a prodigy of self-discipline,
whose 'firmness of will' is a living refutation of Chernyshevsky's denial
in theory that anything such as 'will' existed in human nature." (Joseph
Frank, "N. G. Chernyshevsky," p. 78.) ". . . Chernyshevsky portrayed an
elite that served society largely by shaping it in accordance with the elite's
own view of social justice. As a result, much like the Christian precepts
from which he drew his sustenance, Chernyshevsky's ideas contained the
potential for authoritarianism as well as for liberation. The tension between egoism and altruism, evident in his life and explored in his fictional characters, thus remains unresolved." (Katz and Wagner, introduction
to *What Is to Be Done?*, p. 20).

37. F. C. Barghoorn points out that Rakhmetov is cut off from his fellow men not only by his austerities but also by the fact that he is a member of the aristocracy. The other positive characters all come from lower classes. ("The Philosophic Outlook of Chernyshevski: Materialism and Utilitarianism," *American Slavic and East European Review*, 11 (1947), p. 56.

38. A reading of any recently written biography of Newton dispels both the idea that the *Observations* were written in Newton's old age and the idea that Newton was ever insane. See, for instance, Frank E. Manuel, *The Religion of Isaac Newton* (Oxford: Clarendon Press, 1974), p. 14.

39. For Newton's belief in the imminence of apocalypse, see *Observations on the Prophecies of Daniel and the Apocalypse of St. John* (London: J. Darby and T. Browne, 1733). For a history of Russia's fascination with the conflict between rationality and irrationality, see Alexander Vucinich, *Science in Russian Culture 1861–1917* (Stanford: Stanford University Press, 1970).

40. Initiation is, most probably, symbolized by Rakhmetov's triumph over the bed of nails. This completely unmotivated and unexplained incident represents the victory of the rational hero over an irrational act and symbolizes the greater societal victory to come.

41. Clark, *Soviet Novel*, p. 51.

42. The relationship between Rakhmetov and the other positive characters of the novel might be equated to the relationship between those who seek for utopian solutions to life's dilemmas and those who search for millenarian ones. Michael Barkun has suggested that "'utopia' and 'millennium' are to one another as microcosm is to macrocosm. What the utopian community hopes to achieve within a small and self-sufficient group [i.e., the sewing shop] the millenarian movement anticipates on a cosmic scale. In the most general sense, millenarians look to a coming world transformation." (*Crucible of the Millennium: The Burned-over District of New York in the 1840s* [Syracuse, N.Y.: Syracuse University Press, 1986], p. 11).

43. Freeborn notes that *What Is to Be Done?* is marked by "a clear assumption that the novel had the power to prescribe for the future as well as interpret the present or the past. . . ." (*The Russian Revolutionary Novel*, p. 245).

44. Frank Kermode, *The Sense of an Ending* (London, Oxford and New York: Oxford University Press, 1967), p. 39.

45. Evgenii Lampert explains this by the fact that Chernyshevsky "was concerned not so much with things happening in nature as with things happening in human nature." (Evgenii Lampert, *Sons Against Fathers* [Oxford:

Clarendon Press, 1965], p. 217). I would suggest that this results rather
from Chernyshevsky's obsession with history, the ultimate realm of time.
Total concentration on historical change precludes an equal concentration
on the accurate depiction of day-to-day surroundings.

46. Katerina Clark, "Political History and Literary Chronotope: Some
Soviet Case Studies," in *Literature and History: Theoretical Problems and Russian
Case Studies*, ed. Gary Saul Morson (Stanford: Stanford University Press,
1986), p. 232.

47. Ibid.

48. Chernyshevsky is often said to have an exclusively monist outlook, meaning that he denies the spiritual side of life and accepts only
the material. (See A. Lavretskii, *Belinskii, Chernyshevskii, Dobroliubov v bor'be
za realizm* [Moscow, 1968], p. 218). When I emphasize his dualism, I understand the term to refer to his tendency to divide the phenomena of
reality into polar categories, for example, evil and dissoluteness vs. virtue and purity or present vs. future.

49. Franco Venturi, *Roots of Revolution*, trans. Francis Haskell (New
York: Alfred Knopf, 1960), p. 133.

50. Ibid., p. 137.

51. For an account of Gorky's contribution to the god–building
movement, see Nina Gourfinkel, *Gorky*, trans. Ann Feshbach (Westport,
Conn.: Greenwood Press, Publishers, 1975).

52. Irwin Weil, *Gorky: His Literary Development and Influence on Soviet Intellectual Life* (New York: Random House, 1966), p. 59.

53. At the Congress, Gorky makes the statement that "God, in the
conception of primitive man, was not an abstract concept, a fantastic being, but a real personage, armed with some implement of labour, master
of some trade, a teacher and fellow-worker of men. God was the artistic
generalization of the achievements of labour, and the 'religious' thought
of the toiling masses should be placed in quotation marks, since it represented a purely artistic creativeness." (Maxim Gorky, "Soviet Literature,"
in *Problems of Soviet Literature*, ed. H. G. Scott [1935; rpt. Westport, Conn.:
Hyperion Press, 1981], p.30). He goes on in the same speech to suggest
that the hero of the new Soviet literature should be labor, and we are well
within our rights to assume that he understands labor as connected inti-
mately with the question of God.

54. As quoted in V. Vorob'ev, *M. A. Gor'kii o sotsialisticheskom realizme*
(L'vov, 1959), pp. 53–54.

55. A. Artiukhin, *Formirovanie estetiki sotsialisticheskogo realizma v 20ye
gody* (Saratov, 1978), p. 137.

56. References are to the text published in M. Gor'kii, *Sobranie sochinenii v vosemnadtsati tomakh*, 4. The novel was first published, in English, in 1906 in the United States and England. It came out in Russian in installments from July through August 1907 in Berlin in *Vorwärts*. Only the first part of the novel was released in a severely censored form in Russia. (See Gerhard Habermann, *Maksim Gorki*, trans. Ernestine Schlant [Frederick Ungar Publishing Co., 1971], p. 69).

57. Critics disagree on the degree of difference between Nilovna and Pavel. Freeborn, for instance, suggests that there is a close identification of the mother with her son and that this, in effect, puts an end to the traditional theme of generational conflict first explored in *Fathers and Sons*. (See *The Russian Revolutionary Novel*, p. 265.) Others do not find the issue to be quite so simple. "Gorky's povest' is built on an examination of the relations between a son and a mother. The recurring problem of generations, of 'fathers and sons,' is presented more than once in it." (*Geroi khudozhestvennoi prozy* ed. N. Balashov et al. [Moscow, 1973], p. 21).

58. Rolf–Dieter Kluge, *Vom kritischen zum sozialistischen Realismus: Studien zur literarischen Tradition in Russland 1880 bis 1925* (Munich: List Verlag, 1973), p. 168.

59. Soviet critics often try to fit Nilovna into the procrustean bed of the "typical" positive hero. For example, "several critics, falling into error, have talked about the atypicalness of the image of Nilovna. V. Vorovskii considered that mothers similar to Nilovna could exist in life only as individual phenomena. In the opinion of the critic, they were not typical for the given surroundings at the given moment." (A. Ovcharenko, *O polozhitel'nom geroe v tvorchestve M. Gor'kogo 1892–1907* [Moscow, 1956, p. 544.]) Ovcharenko, of course, implies that he feels otherwise.

60. "Retarding moments, insofar as they are not brought on by the power of the antagonist, are, with a few exceptions, completely absent, resulting in a linear, unidimensional structure." (Rolf–Dieter Kluge, "Gor'kij, *Die Mutter*," in *Der russische Roman*, ed. Bodo Zelinskij [Düsseldorf: Bagel, 1979], p. 247).

61. For a careful study of the evolution of the novel from its first appearance in *Krasnaia Nov'* to its final reworking in 1958, see Robert L. Busch, "Gladkov's *Cement*: The Making of a Soviet Classic," *SEEJ*, 22 (1978), pp. 348–61.

62. Maurice Friedberg, "New Editions of Soviet Belles Lettres: A Study in Politics and Palimpsests," *The American Slavic and East European Review*, 13 (1954), p. 85.

63. Friedberg, for instance, attributes much of the change in the portrayal of Dasha to changes in the official Soviet view of morality in the thirties.

This would argue for treating Dasha as an ascetic of the period which is consciously Socialist Realist in its techniques. See Friedberg, "New Editions," p. 86.

64. References to the text are to F. *Gladkov, Sobranie sochinenii v vos'mi tomakh* Moscow, 1958, 2, a late, "ascetic" version.

65. Gladkov would probably not agree with this assessment. In a letter to Berta Brainina, in which he compares the experiences of his heroes with his own real-life ones, he writes: "Do not think, however, that we were ascetics; we were set apart by a devilish joy and capacity for life." (Quoted in Berta Brainina, *"Tsement"* F. Gladkova [Moscow, 1965], p. 49).

66. Gladkov's autobiography, as quoted by M. Pakhomova, *Avtobiograficheskie povesti F. V. Gladkova i traditsii M. Gor'kogo* [Leningrad, 1966], pp. 20–21).

67. Soviet critics have also pointed out Gladkov's tendency to transform his heroes into representatives of an unchanging, timeless order. For example, ". . . in the characters of the positive heroes, it was necessary to embody not transitory, but rather, abiding traits. . . ." (A. Volozhenin, *Fedor Gladkov. Zhizn' i tvorchestvo* [Moscow, 1969], p. 98).

68. I understand the proletarian novel to be one which is informed by "the belief in the possibility and need for a class literature of the proletariat and faith in the proposition that 'hegemony' belongs to that literature as a historic right . . . ." (Edward J. Brown, *The Proletarian Episode in Russian Literature, 1928–32* [New York: Columbia University Press, 1953], p. 219). The proletarian novel is much narrower in its outlook as well as in its poetics than the novels under discussion.

69. This term is used by Robert A. Maguire in reference to *Cement* in *Red Virgin Soil: Soviet Literature in the 1920s* (Princeton: Princeton University Press, 1968), p. 322.

70. For a discussion of the issue of the particular and the general in 1920s literature, see Robert A. Maguire, "Literary Conflicts in the 1920s," *Survey,* 18 (1972), pp. 98–127.

71. Novels which reject fragmentation and particularism in favor of Marxian wholeness provide a perfect home for a superhero. As Mathewson puts it, "at the heart of [Marx's and Engels's] indictment of the present system is a vision of man crippled, fragmented, shriveled by the conditions of economic existence. . . . But if epochs of great social metamorphosis provided the richest soil for large–scale individuals, there was a hope that the transition to socialism might produce men of equivalent *stature,* if not identical qualities [to the Renaissance man]." (*The Positive Hero,* pp. 138–39).

72. See Clark, *Soviet Novel*, p. 136, for a description of this shift.

CHAPTER 7

1. A. Zhdanov, "Soviet Literature—the Richest in Ideas, the Most Advanced Literature," in *Problems of Soviet Literature*, ed. H. G. Scott (1935; rpt. Westport, Conn.: Hyperion Press, 1981), p. 22.

2. Richard Stites, *The Women's Liberation Movement in Russia: Feminism, Nihilism, and Bolshevism 1860–1930* (Princeton: Princeton University Press, 1977), pp. 376–88.

3. Robert Russell, *Valentin Kataev* (Boston: Twayne Publishers, 1981), p. 10.

4. Ibid., pp. 37–38.

5. Wasil G. Fiedorow, "V. P. Kataev vs. Socialist Realism: An Interpretation," (Diss., Indiana University, 1973), p.49.

6. Robert Russell notes at least two religiously inspired poems, "K tebe, Khristos" and "V khrame." (*Valentin Kataev*, p. 27).

7. Various critics have explained Margulies's unsuccessful search for food as an example of his eccentricity (cf. for example, Robert Russell, *Valentine Kataev* [Boston: Twayne Publishers, 1981], p. 78, and T. Sidel'nikova, *Valentin Kataev; Ocherk zhizni i tvorchestva* [Moscow, 1957], p. 93). They attribute the fact that he is so likeable to this humorous eccentricity.

8. Soviet critics have written that the novel contains too many "details" and "meaningless episodes" (cf. B. Brainina, *Valentin Kataev* [Moscow, 1954], pp. 16–17). I assume that they would consider this vision one such meaningless episode. It has meaning for the career of the ascetic, however, but Kataev leaves its spiritual dimensions unanalyzed.

9. References are to *Vremia vpered!* as published in *V. Kataev, Sobranie sochinenii v deviati tomakh* (Moscow, 1969), 3.

10. Nadezhda Mandelshtam, for example, chides Kataev for adapting his art to the standards of the time but concludes that "of all the writers who were allowed to survive and live in comfort, only Katayev did not lose his love of poetry and feeling for literature." (*Hope Against Hope*, trans. Max Hayward [New York: Atheneum, 1970], p. 336). Wasil G. Fiedorow notes that Kataev usually shuns the heroic in his work, which also suggests that he may have compromised his artistic vision with *Time Forward!* (Wasil G. Fiedorow, "V. P. Kataev vs. Socialist Realism: An Interpretation," [Diss., University of Indiana, 1973], p. 7).

11. Kataev has stated that Mayakovsky supplied him with the title for *Time Forward!*

12. L. Skorino bears witness to the fact that few of Kataev's contemporaries grasped this understanding of time when she writes that even his friends criticized his use of "dynamism." (L. Skorino, *Pisatel' i ego vremia: Zhizn' i tvorchestvo V. P. Kataeva* [Moscow, 1965], p. 250).

13. Kermode, *The Sense of an Ending*, p. 39.

14. Ibid., p. 39.

15. S. Tregub, the Soviet critic who seems most intensely devoted to Ostrovsky's work (cf. *Geroi nashego vremeni* [*Ot Pavla Korchagina k Olegu Koshevomu*] [Moscow, 1948]; *Nikolai Ostrovskii* [Moscow, 1939]; *Zhivoi Korchagin* [Moscow, 1968]), actually insists that the point of departure for any serious study of *How the Steel Was Tempered* must be the absolute identity of Nikolai Ostrovsky and Pavel Korchagin.

16. I have only been able to find one Soviet critic who sets out to discuss the artistic merits of the novel rather than its ideological message. Although he claims that Ostrovsky has literary talent, however, he too ends up by discussing the novel's ideology. (cf. V. Litvinov, "Tsel'nost': O khudozhestvennykh osobennostiakh romana *Kak zakalialas' stal'*," *Voprosy literatury*, 9 [1982], pp. 21–56).

17. Soviet critics refrain from criticizing Ostrovsky for his lack of organization but point to it covertly. L. Timofeev, for example, notes that Ostrovsky manages to incorporate some 250 separate episodes and 200 distinct characters into a novel of 400–odd pages. (cf. *O khudozhestvennykh osobennostiakh romana N. Ostrovskogo Kak zakalialas' stal'* [Moscow, 1956], p 11).

18. By 1966 *How the Steel Was Tempered* had already seen 313 Soviet editions. (As reported by Iu. Andreev, *Revoliutsiia i literatura* [Leningrad, 1969], p. 354.)

19. Ernest J. Simmons discusses the question of the novel's popularity and its connection with Ostrovsky's personal suffering in "The Organization Writer (1934–46)," in *Literature and Revolution in Soviet Russia 1917–62*, ed. Max Hayward and Leopold Labedz (London: Oxford University Press, 1963), pp. 74–98.

20. Korchagin/Ostrovsky actually admits that his asceticism is counterproductive. At the end of the novel, he talks about his misguided "Spartanism," which has deprived society of one of its most ardent champions (p. 299). References are to N. Ostrovskii, *Kak zakalialas' stal'* in *Romany, Rechi, Stat'i, Pis'ma* (Moscow, 1949), pp. 3–305.

21. In an era in which materialism was a byword, Gorky wrote of Ostrovsky that "the life of this man is a living illustration of the triumph of the spirit over the body." (Quoted in A. Karavaeva, *Kniga, kotoraia oboshla ves' mir* [Moscow, 1970], p. 54). This obviously applies to Korchagin as well.

22. Clark, "Political History and Literary Chronotope," p. 233.

23. Vera S. Dunham, *In Stalin's Time: Middleclass Values in Soviet Fiction* (Cambridge and New York: Cambridge University Press, 1976), p. 18.

24. Ibid.

25. Ibid. p. 49.

26. Claude Lévi–Strauss, *The Raw and the Cooked*, trans. John and Doreen Weightman (New York and Evanston: Harper & Row, 1969), p. 13.

CONCLUSION

1. Boris Pasternak, *Doktor Zhivago* (Ann Arbor: University of Michigan Press, 1959), p. 258.

2. S. Bulgakov, "Heroism and Asceticism: Reflections on the Religious Nature of the Russian Intelligentsia" in *Landmarks*, trans. Marian Schwartz (New York: Karz Howard, 1977), p. 40.

3. On the question of Soviet hippies and their idiosyncratic approach to asceticism, see John Bushnell, "An Introduction to the Soviet *Sistema*: The Advent of Counterculture and Subculture," *Slavic Review*, 49 (1990), pp. 272–77.

4. N. Berdyaev, "Philosophic Truth and the Moral Truth of the Intelligentsia," in *Landmarks*, trans. Marian Schwartz (New York: Karz Howard, 1977), p. 5.

5. Boris Shragin, "Introduction II," in ibid., p. xxxiv.

6. I am indebted to my colleague Valery Petrochenkov for bringing the following examples of asceticism in contemporary Russian literature to my attention.

7. A. Kim, *Otets-les, Novyi mir*, no. 4 (1989), p. 21.

WORKS CITED

PRIMARY LITERATURE

Athanasius. *Life of Saint Anthony*. In *Early Christian Biographies*. Ed. Roy J. Deferrari. Trans. Sister Mary Emily Keenan, 133–216. Fathers of the Church, 1952.

Chernyshevskii, N. *Chto delat'?* In *N. G. Chernyshevskii, Sobranie sochinenii v piati tomakh*. Vol.5. Moscow, 1974.

Dostoevskii, F. *The Notebooks for the Brothers Karamazov*. Trans. & Ed. Edward Wasiolek. Chicago and London: University of Chicago Press, 1971.

———. *Brat'ia Karamazovy*. In *F. M. Dostoevskii, Polnoe sobranie sochinenii v tridtsati tomakh*. Vol. 14. Leningrad, 1976.

Efrem. *Zhitie i terpenie prepodobnago ottsa nashego Avram'ia, prosvetivshagosia v terpen'i mnoze, novago chiudotvortsa v sviatykh grada Smolen'ska*. In *Pamiatniki literatury drevnei Rusi. XIII vek*. Moscow, 1981.

Epifanii. *Zhitie i zhizn' prepodobnago ottsa nashego Sergiia*. In *Die Legenden des heiligen Sergij von Radonež*. Ed. D. Chizhevskii. 1892; Reprint. Munich: Wilhelm Fink Verlag, 1967.

Gladkov, F. *Tsement*. In *F. Gladkov, Sobranie sochinenii v vos'mi tomakh*. Vol. 2. Moscow, 1958.

Gogol', N. "Portret." In *N. V. Gogol', Sobranie sochinenii v shesti tomakh*. Vol. 3. Moscow, 1952.

Gor'kii, M. *Mat'*. In *M. Gor'kii, Sobranie sochinenii v vosemnadtsati tomakh*. Vol. 4. Moscow, 1963.

Kallistrat. *Povest' ob Uliianii Osorinoi*. *TODRL* 6 (1948), 256–323.

Kataev, V. *Vremia vpered!* In V. *Kataev, Sobranie sochinenii v deviati tomakh*. Vol. 3. Moscow.

Kim, A. *Otets–les*. *Novyi mir*, no. 4 (1989), 5–48, no. 5 (1989), 42–155, no. 6 (1989), 111–45.

Nestor. *Zhitie prepodobnaago ot'tsa nashego Feodosiia, igumena pecher'skago*. In *Pamiatniki literatury drevnei Rusi. XI–nachalo XII veka*. 305–91. Moscow, 1978.

Nikolaeva, O. *Invalid detstva*. *Iunost'*, no. 2 (1990), 34–61.

Novgorodskaia pervaia letopis' starshego i mladshego izvodov. Moscow and Leningrad, 1950.

Ostrovskii, N. *Kak zakalialas' stal'*. In N. *Ostrovskii, Romany, Rechi, Stat'i, Pis'ma*. 3–309. Moscow, 1949.

Pakhomii. *Zhitie pr. Kirilla Belozerskago*. In *Pachomij Logofet. Werke im Auswahl*. Munich: Eidos Verlag, 1963.

Palladius. *The Lausiac History*. Trans. Robert T. Meyer. Westminster, Md.: Newman Press, 1965.

Pasternak, B. *Doktor Zhivago*. Ann Arbor: University of Michigan Press, 1959.

Paterik" pecherskyi. In *Pamiatniki literatury drevnei Rusi. XII vek*. 412–623. Moscow, 1980.

Tolstoi, L. *Otets Sergii*. In L. N. *Tolstoi, Sobranie sochinenii v dvadtsati tomakh*. Vol. 12. Moscow, 1964.

SECONDARY LITERATURE

Abramovich, D. "Izsledovanie o Kievo-Pecherskom Paterike, kak istoriko–literaturnom pamiatnike." *IORJaS* 6 (1901), 207–35.

Adrianova–Peretts, V. P. "K voprosu ob izobrazhenii 'vnutrennego cheloveka' v russkoi literatury XI–XIV vekov." In *Voprosy izucheniia russkoi literatury XI–XX vekov*. 15–24. Moscow and Leningrad, 1958.

———. "Zadachi izucheniia 'agiograficheskogo stilia' Drevnei Rusi." *TODRL* 20 (1964), 41–71.

Alexander, Paul J. *The Byzantine Apocalyptic Tradition*. Trans. and Ed. Dorothy deF. Abrahamse. Berkeley: University of California Press, 1985.

Alissandratos, Julia. "Leo Tolstoy's 'Father Sergius' and the Russian Hagiographical Tradition." *Cyrillomethodianum*, 8–9 (1984–85), 149–63.

————. "Simmetricheskoe raspolozhenie epizodov odnoi redaktsii 'Zhitiia Sergiia Radonezhskogo.'" In *American Contributions to the Ninth International Congress of Slavists*. Ed. Paul Debreczeny, 7–17. Columbus, Oh: Slavica, 1983.

Andreev, Iu. *Revoliutsiia i literatura*. Leningrad, 1969.

Appel, Ortrud. *Die Vita des hl. Sergij von Radonež: Untersuchungen zur Textgeschichte*. Munich: Wilhelm Fink Verlag, 1972.

Artiukhin, A. *Formirovanie estetiki sotsialisticheskogo realizma v 20e gody*. Saratov, 1978.

Bakhtin, Mikhail. "Epic and Novel." In *The Dialogic Imagination*. Trans. Caryl Emerson and Michael Holquist, 3–40. Austin: University of Texas, 1981.

————. "Forms of Time and of the Chronotope in the Novel." In *The Dialogic Imagination*. Trans. Caryl Emerson and Michael Holquist, 84–258. Austin: University of Texas, 1981.

————. *Rabelais and his World*. Trans. Hélène Iswolsky. Bloomington: University of Indiana Press, 1984.

Barghoorn, F. C. "The Philosophic Outlook of Chernyshevski: Materialism and Utilitarianism." *American Slavic and East European Review* 11 (1947), 42–56.

Barkun, Michael. *Crucible of the Millennium: The Burned-over District of New York in the 1840s*. Syracuse: Syracuse University Press, 1986.

————. *Disaster and the Millennium*. New Haven and London: Yale University Press, 1974.

Berdyaev, N. *The Beginning and the End*. Trans. R. M. French. Gloucester, Mass.: Peter Smith, 1970.

Bethea, David M. *The Shape of Apocalypse in Modern Russian Fiction*. Princeton: Princeton University Press, 1989.

Bonwetsch, N. "Die christliche vornicänische Litteratur (mit Einschluss der jüdisch–hellenistischen und apokalyptischen) in altslavischen Handschriften." In *Geschichte der altchristlichen Litteratur bis Eusebius*. Ed. A. Harnack, 886–917. Leipzig: J. C. Hinrichs'sche Buchhandlung, 1893.

Børtnes, Jostein. *Visions of Glory: Studies in Early Russian Hagiography*. Trans.

Jostein Børtnes and Paul L. Nielsen. Atlantic Highlands, N.J.: Humanities, 1988.

Bowman, Herbert E. "Revolutionary Elitism in Černyševskij." *American Slavic and East European Review* 13 (1954), 185–99.

Brainina, B. "*Tsement*" *F. Gladkova*. Moscow, 1965.

———. *Valentin Kataev*. Moscow, 1954.

Brombert, Victor. "The Idea of the Hero." In *The Hero in Literature*. Ed. Victor Brombert, 11–21. Greenwich, Conn.: Fawcett Publications, 1969.

Brooks, Jeffrey. *When Russia Learned to Read: Literacy and Popular Literature, 1861–1917*. Princeton: Princeton University Press, 1985.

Brown, Edward J. *The Proletarian Episode in Russian Literature, 1928–32*. New York: Columbia University Press, 1953.

———. "The Symbolist Contamination of Gor'kii's 'Realistic' Style." *Slavic Review* 47 (1988), 227–38.

Brown, Peter. *The Making of Late Antiquity*. Cambridge, Mass. and London: Harvard University Press, 1978.

Bubner, Friedrich. "Das Kiever Paterikon: Eine Untersuchung zu seiner Struktur und den literarischen Quellen." Diss., Karl Ruprecht Universität, Heidelberg, 1969.

Bulgakov, Sergei. "Heroism and Asceticism: Reflections on the Religious Nature of the Russian Intelligentsia." In *Landmarks*. Trans. Marian Schwartz, 23–63. New York: Karz Howard, 1977.

Burke, Peter. *Popular Culture in Early Modern Europe*. New York: Harper and Row, Publishers, 1978.

Busch, Robert L. "Gladkov's Cement: The Making of a Soviet Classic." *SEEJ* 22 (1978), 348–61.

Bushnell, John. "An Introduction to the Soviet *Sistema*: The Advent of Counterculture and Subculture." *Slavic Review* 49 (1990), 272–7.

Buslaev, F. *Bes*. St. Petersburg, 1881.

———. "Ideal'nye zhenskie kharaktery drevnei Rusi." In *Istoricheskie ocherki russkoi narodnoi slovesnosti*. 2: 238–68. St. Petersburg, 1861.

———. "Izobrazhenie strashnago suda po russkim podlinnikam." In *Istoricheskie ocherki russkoi narodnoi slovesnosti i iskusstva*. 2: 133–54. 1861. Reprint. Paris and the Hague: Mouton, 1969.

Campbell, Joseph. *The Hero with a Thousand Faces*. Princeton: Princeton University Press, 1968.

Cartlidge, David R. and David L. Dungan, eds. *Documents for the Study of the Gospels.* Philadelphia: Fortress Press, 1980.

Cawelti, John G. *Adventure, Mystery, and Romance: Formula Stories as Art and Popular Culture.* Chicago: University of Chicago Press, 1976.

Challis, Natalie, and Horace Dewey. "Divine Folly in Old Kievan Literature: The Tale of Isaac the Cave Dweller." *SEEJ* 22 (1978), 255–64.

Cherniavsky, Michael. "Old Believers and the New Religion." In *The Structure of Russian History.* Ed. Michael Cherniavsky, 140–88. New York: Random House, 1970.

Chistov, K. *Russkie narodnye sotsial'no-utopicheskie legendy XVII–XIX vv.* Moscow, 1967.

Chizhevskii, D. *History of Russian Literature.* Westport, Conn.: Hyperion Press, 1981.

———. "On the Question of Genres in Old Russian Literature." *HSS* 2 (1956), 105–15.

———. "Studien zur russischen Hagiographie: Die Erzählung vom hl. Isaakij." *Wiener Slavistisches Jahrbuch* 2 (1952), 22–49.

Church, Margaret. *Time and Reality.* Chapel Hill: University of North Carolina Press, 1963.

Clark, Katerina. "Political History and Literary Chronotope: Some Russian Case Studies." In *Literature and History: Theoretical Problems and Russian Case Studies.* Ed. Gary Saul Morson, 230–46. Stanford: Stanford University Press, 1986.

———. *The Soviet Novel: History as Ritual.* Chicago and London: University of Chicago Press, 1981.

Cohn, Norman. *The Pursuit of the Millennium.* Fairlawn, N.J.: Essential Books, 1957.

Collins, John J. *The Apocalyptic Imagination.* New York: Crossroads, 1984.

Costa, Dennis. *Irenic Apocalypse.* Saratoga, Calif.: Anma Libri, 1981.

Daniélou, Jean. *The Theology of Jewish Christianity.* Trans. John A. Baker. London: Darton, Longman and Todd, 1977.

Dmitreev, L. *Zhitiinye povesti russkogo severa kak pamiatniki literatury XIII–XVII vv.* Leningrad, 1973.

Dunham, Vera S. *In Stalin's Time: Middleclass Values in Soviet Fiction.* Cambridge and London: Cambridge University Press, 1976.

Eliade, Mircea. *Cosmos and History: The Myth of the Eternal Return.* Trans. Willard R. Trask. New York: Harper & Row, 1959.

Engels, Friedrich. *The Peasant War in Germany.* In *The German Revolutions.* Ed. Leonard Krieger, 19–119. Chicago and London: University of Chicago Press, 1967.

Eremin, I. "Literaturnoe nasledie Feodosiia Pecherskogo." *TODRL* 5 (1947), 159–84.

Ermolaev, Herman. *Soviet Literary Theories, 1917–1934: The Genesis of Socialist Realism.* Berkeley: University of California Press, 1963.

Fanger, Donald. *The Creation of Nikolai Gogol.* Cambridge, Mass. and London: Belknap Press of Harvard University Press, 1979.

———. "Influence and Tradition in the Russian Novel." In *The Russian Novel from Pushkin to Pasternak.* Ed. John Garrard, 29–50. New Haven and London: Yale University Press, 1983.

Fedotov, George P. *The Russian Religious Mind.* Vols. 1 and 2. Belmont, Mass.: Nordland Publishing Co., 1975.

———. *Sviatye drevnei Rusi.* Paris: YMCA Press, 1931.

———. "Zhitie i terpenie sv. Avraamiia Smolenskogo." *Pravoslavnaia mysl'* 2 (1930), 127–47.

Fiedorow, Wasil G. "V. P. Kataev vs. Socialist Realism: An Interpretation." Diss., University of Indiana, 1973.

Flew, R. Newton. *The Idea of Perfection in Christian Theology.* 1934; Reprint. London: Oxford University Press, 1968.

Florovskii, G. *Puti russkago bogosloviia.* Paris: YMCA Press, 1981.

Fowler, Alastair. "The Life and Death of Literary Forms." *New History.* 2 (1971), 199–216.

Frank, Joseph. "N. G. Chernyshevsky: A Russian Utopia." *Southern Review* 3 (1967), 68–84.

Frank, Semen. "The Ethic of Nihilism: A Characterization of the Russian Intelligentsia's Moral Outlook." In *Landmarks.* Trans. Marian Schwartz, 155–84. New York: Karz Howard, 1977.

Freeborn, Richard. *The Russian Revolutionary Novel: Turgenev to Pasternak.* New York: Cambridge University Press, 1982.

Freydank, D. "Die altrussische Hagiographie als Gegenstand der Literaturwissenschaft." *Zeitschrift für Slawistik* 23 (1978), 67–75.

Friedberg, Maurice. "New Editions of Soviet Belles Lettres: A Study in Politics and Palimpsests." *The American Slavic and East European Review* 13 (1954), 72–88.

Frye, Northrop. *Fables of Identity. Studies in Poetic Mythology.* New York: Harcourt, Brace and World, 1963.

Funkenstein, Amos. "A Schedule for the End of the World: The Origins and Persistence of the Apocalyptic Mentality." In *Visions of Apocalypse: End or Rebirth?* Ed. Saul Friedlander, et al.,44–60. New York and London: Holmes & Meier, 1985.

Gager, John G. "The Attainment of Millennial Bliss Through Myth: The Book of Revelation." In *Visionaries and Their Apocalypses.* Ed. Paul D. Hanson, 146–55. Philadelphia: Fortress Press, 1985.

Geroi khudozhestvennoi prozy. Moscow, 1973.

Ginzburg, L. *O literaturnom geroe.* Leningrad, 1979.

Gippius, V. *Gogol.* Ed. and Trans. Robert A. Maguire. Ann Arbor: Ardis, 1981.

Goetz, Leopold Karl. *Das Kiever Höhlenkloster als Kulturzentrum des vormongolischen Russlands.* Passau: M. Waldbauersche Buchhandlung, 1904.

Gol'dberg, A. "K predystorii idei 'Moskva—tretii Rim'." *Kul'turnoe nasledie drevnei Rusi.* 111–16. Moscow, 1976.

Golubinskii, E. *Istoriia russkoi tserkvi.* Moscow, 1900–11.

Gorkii, M. "Soviet Literature." In *Problems of Soviet Literature.* Ed. H. G. Scott, 27–69. 1935; Reprint. Westport, Conn.: Hyperion Press, 1981.

Gourfinkel, Nina. *Gorky.* Trans. Ann Feshbach. Westport, Conn.: Greenwood Press, Publishers, 1975.

Grossman, L. *Seminarii po Dostoevskomu. Materialy, bibliografii i komentarii.* Moscow, 1922.

Gudzy, N. *History of Early Russian Literature.* Trans. Susan Wilbur Jones. New York: MacMillan Company, 1949.

Gustafson, Richard F. *Leo Tolstoy: Resident and Stranger. A Study in Fiction and Theology.* Princeton: Princeton University Press, 1986.

Habermann, Gerhard. *Maksim Gorki.* Trans. Ernestine Schlant. New York: Frederick Ungar Publishing Co., 1971.

Halperin, Charles J. *Russia and the Golden Horde: The Mongol Impact on Medieval Russian History.* Bloomington: Indiana University Press, 1987.

Hanning, Robert W. *The Individual in Twelfth-Century Romance*. New Haven and London: Yale University Press, 1977.

Hare, Richard. *Pioneers of Russian Social Thought*. New York: Vintage Books, 1964.

Harpham, Geoffrey Galt. *The Ascetic Imperative in Culture and Criticism*. Chicago and London: University of Chicago Press, 1987.

Holl, Karl. "Die religiösen Grundlagen der russischen Kultur." In *Gesammelte Aufsätze zur Kirchengeschichte*. Vol. 2. Tübingen: J. C. B. Mohr, 1928.

Hussey, Joan Mervyn. *Church and Learning in the Byzantine Empire 867–1185*. London: Humphrey Milford, 1937.

Ivanits, Linda J. "Hagiography in *Brat'ja Karamazovy*: Zosima, Ferapont, and the Russian Monastic Saint." *Russian Language Journal* 34 (1980), 109–26.

Kantor, Marvin. *Medieval Slavic Lives of Saints and Princes*. Ann Arbor: University of Michigan Department of Slavic Languages and Literatures, 1983.

Karavaeva, A. *Kniga, kotoraia oboshla ves' mir*. Moscow, 1970.

Karlinsky, Simon. *The Sexual Labyrinth of Nikolai Gogol*. Cambridge, Mass., and London: Harvard University Press, 1976.

Katz, Michael R. and William G. Wagner. Introduction to *What Is to Be Done?* Trans. Michael R. Katz, 1–36. Ithaca, N.Y., and London: Cornell University Press, 1989.

Kayser, Wolfgang. *The Grotesque in Literature and Art*. Trans. Ulrich Weisstein. Bloomington: Indiana University Press, 1963.

Kazakova, N., and Ia. Lur'e. *Antifeodal'nye ereticheskie dvizheniia na Rusi XIV–nachala XVI veka*. Moscow and Leningrad, 1955.

Kelly, Aileen. "Self–Censorship and the Russian Intelligentsia." *Slavic Review* 46 (1987), 193–213.

Kermode, Frank. *The Sense of an Ending*. London, Oxford, and New York: Oxford University Press, 1967.

Kirk, Kenneth E. *The Vision of God*. New York: Harper & Row, 1966.

Klibanov, A. *History of Religious Sectarianism in Russia (1860s–1917)*. Trans. Ethel Dunn and Ed. Stephen P. Dunn. Oxford: Pergamon Press, 1982.

———. "Sectarianism and the Socialist Reconstruction of the Countryside." *Soviet Sociology* 8 (1970), 383–411.

Kliuchevskii, V. *Drevnerusskyia zhitiia sviatykh kak istoricheskii istochnik.* 1871; Reprint. The Hague and Paris, Mouton, 1968.

Kluge, Rolf–Dieter. "Gorkij, *Die Mutter.*" In *Der russische Roman.* Ed. Bodo Zelinsky, 242–64. Düsseldorf: Bagel, 1979.

―――. *Vom kritischen zum sozialistischen Realismus: Studien zur literarischen Tradition in Russland 1880 bis 1925.* Munich: List Verlag, 1973.

Koch, Klaus. *The Rediscovery of Apocalypse.* Trans. Margaret Kohl. London: SCM Press, 1972.

Kopreeva, T. "Obraz inoka Polikarpa po pis'mam Simona i Polikarpa." *TODRL* 24 (1969), 112–6.

Krasnoshchekova, E. "Gumanizm i zhertvennost'." In *Metod i masterstvo.* Vol. 3: 55–70. Vologda, 1971.

Lampert, Evgenii. *Sons Against Fathers.* Oxford: Clarendon Press, 1965.

Lavretskii, A. *Belinskii, Chernyshevskii, Dobroliubov v bor'be za realizm.* Moscow, 1968.

Lebedev, A. *Geroi Chernyshevskogo.* Moscow, 1962.

Lévi-Strauss, Claude. *The Raw and the Cooked.* Trans. John and Doreen Weightman. New York and Evanston: Harper & Row, 1969.

Likhachev, D. *Chelovek v literature drevnei Rusi.* Moscow, 1970.

―――. "Drevneslavianskie literatury kak sistema." In *Slavianskie literatury.* 5–48. Moscow, 1968.

―――. *Kul'tura Rusi vremeni Andreia Rubleva i Epifaniia Premudrogo.* Moscow and Leningrad, 1962.

―――. *Poetika drevnerusskoi literatury.* Moscow, 1979.

Likhachev, D., and A. Panchenko. *Smekhovoi mir drevnei Rusi.* Leningrad, 1976.

Lilienfeld, Fairy von. *Nil Sorskij und seine Schriften.* Berlin: Evangelische Verlagsanstalt, 1963.

Litvinov, V. "Tsel'nost': O khudozhestvennykh osobennostiakh romana *Kak zakalialas' stal'.*" *Voprosy literatury* 9 (1982), 21–56.

Lotman, Iu. and B. Uspenskii. "Binary Models in the Dynamics of Russian Culture (to the End of the Eighteenth Century)." In *The Semiotics of Russian Cultural History.* 30–66. Trans. Robert Sorenson and Ed. Alexander D. Nakhimovsky and Alice Stone. Ithaca, N.Y. and London: Cornell University Press, 1985.

Lukács, Georg. *Der russische Realismus in der Weltliteratur*. Neuwied and Berlin: Luchterhand, 1964.

Lur'e, Ia. "K voprosu ob ideologii Nila Sorskogo." *TODRL* 13 (1957), 182–213.

———. "O vozniknovenii teorii Moskva—tretii Rim." *TODRL* 16 (1960), 626–33.

Maguire, Robert A. "Literary Conflicts in the 1920s." *Survey* 18 (1972), 98–127.

———. *Red Virgin Soil: Soviet Literature in the 1920s*. Princeton: Princeton University Press, 1968.

Maloney, George A. *Russian Hesychasm*. The Hague and Paris: Mouton, 1973.

Mandelshtam, Nadezhda. *Hope Against Hope*. Trans. Max Hayward. New York: Atheneum, 1970.

Manuel, Frank E. *The Religion of Isaac Newton*. Oxford: Clarendon Press, 1974.

Mathewson, Rufus W., Jr. *The Positive Hero in Russian Literature*. Stanford: Stanford University Press, 1975.

Mazlich, Bruce. *The Revolutionary Ascetic*. New York: Basic Books, 1976.

McGinn, Bernard. *Visions of the End*. New York: Columbia University Press, 1979.

Meyerhoff, Hans. *Time in Literature*. Berkeley and Los Angeles: University of California Press, 1955.

Mirsky, D. S. *Contemporary Russian Literature: 1881–1925*. New York: Knopf, 1926.

Mochul'skii, K. *Dukhovnyi put' Gogolia*. Paris: YMCA Press, 1976.

Morson, Gary Saul. *The Boundaries of Genre: Dostoevsky's Diary of a Writer and the Traditions of Literary Utopia*. Austin: University of Texas Press, 1981.

Murvar, Vatro. "Messianism in Russia: Religious and Revolutionary." *Journal for the Scientific Study of Religion* 10 (1971), 277–338.

Newton, Isaac. *Observations on the Prophecies of Daniel and the Apocalypse of St. John*. London: J. Darby and T. Browne, 1733.

Nikol'skii, N. *Kirillo-Belozerskii monastyr' i ego ustroistvo do vtoroi chetverti XVII veka (1397–1625)*. St. Petersburg, 1897.

Obolensky, Dmitri. *The Bogomils*. Cambridge: Cambridge University Press, 1948.

Opul'skii, Al'bert. "Problema khudozhestvennosti russkikh zhitii i ee izuchenie." *GRANI* 120 (1981), 173–97.

———. *Zhitiia sviatykh v tvorchestve russkikh pisatelei XIX veka*. East Lansing, Mich.: *Russian Language Journal*, 1986.

Orlov, A. *Drevnerusskaia literatura*. 1945; Reprint. The Hague and Paris: Mouton, 1970.

O'Toole, L. Michael. *Structure, Style and Interpretation in the Russian Short Story*. New Haven and London: Yale University Press, 1982.

Ovcharenko, A. *O polozhitel'nom geroe v tvorchestve M. Gor'kogo 1892–1907*. Moscow, 1956.

Pakhomova, M. *Avtobiograficheskie povesti F. V. Gladkova i traditsii M. Gor'kogo*. Leningrad, 1966.

Paperno, Irina. "The Individual in Culture: N. G. Chernyshevsky. A Study in the Semiotics of Behavior." Diss., Stanford University, 1984.

———. *Chernyshevsky and the Age of Realism: A Study in the Semiotics of Behavior*. Stanford: Stanford University Press, 1988.

Passmore, John. *The Perfectibility of Man*. New York: Charles Scribner's Sons, 1970.

Pelikan, Jaroslav. *The Emergence of the Catholic Tradition (100–600)*. Chicago and London: University of Chicago Press, 1971.

———. *The Spirit of Eastern Christendom (600–1700)*. Chicago and London: University of Chicago Press, 1974.

Pereira, N. G. O. *The Thought and Teaching of N. G. Černyševskij*. The Hague: Mouton, 1975.

Perl, Jeffrey M. *The Tradition of Return: The Implicit History of Modern Literature*. Princeton: Princeton University Press, 1984.

Pope, Richard Warren. "The Literary History of the *Kievan Caves Patericon* up to 1500." Diss., Columbia University 1970.

———. "O kharatere i stepeni vliianiia vizantiiskoi literatury na original'nuiu literaturu vostochnykh i iuzhnykh slavian." In *American Contributions to the Seventh International Congress of Slavists*. Ed. Victor Terras, 469–93. The Hague and Paris: Mouton, 1973.

———. "On the Comparative Literary Analysis of the Patericon Story

(Translated and Original) in the Pre-Mongol Period." In *Canadian Contributions to the VIII International Congress of Slavists*. Ed. Zbigniew Folejewski, 1–24. Ottawa: Canadian Association of Slavists, 1978.

Prestel, David Kirk. "A Comparative Analysis of the Kievan Caves Patericon." Diss., University of Michigan, 1983.

Priselkov, M. *Nestor letopisets: Opyt istoriko-literaturnoi kharakteristiki*. 1923; Reprint. The Hague: Russian Reprint Series, 1967.

Prokhorov, G. "Isikhazm i obshchestvennaia mysl' v vostochnoi Evrope v XIV veke." *TODRL* 22 (1968), 86–108.

————. "Knigi Kirilla Belozerskogo." *TODRL* 36 (1981), 50–70.

Propp, V. *Morphology of the Folktale*. Trans. Laurence Scott. Austin and London: University of Texas Press, 1979.

Quandt, Jean B. "Religion and Social Thought: The Secularization of Postmillennialism." *American Quarterly* 25 (1973), 390–409.

Randall, Francis B. *N. G. Chernyshevskii*. New York: Twayne Publishers, 1967.

Reed, Walter L. *Meditations on the Hero*. New Haven and London: Yale University Press, 1974.

Reiter, Hans. *Studien zur ersten kyrillischen Druckausgabe des Kiever Paterikons*. Munich: Dr. Dr. Rudolf Trofenik, 1976.

Rizhskii, M. *Istoriia perevodov Biblii v Rossii*. Novosibirsk, 1978.

Robinson, N. F. *Monasticism in the Orthodox Churches*. New York: AMS Press, 1971.

Rubinstein, A. "Observations on the Slavonic Book of Enoch." *Journal of Jewish Studies* 13 (1962), 1–21.

Runciman, Steven. *The Great Church in Captivity*. Cambridge: Cambridge University Press, 1968.

Russell, D. S. *The Method and Message of Jewish Apocalyptic*. Philadelphia: Westminster Press, 1964

Russell, Robert. *Valentin Kataev*. Boston: Twayne Publishers, 1981.

Rybakov, B. *Iazychestvo drevnei Rusi*. Moscow, 1987.

Rzhevsky, Nicholas. *Russian Literature and Ideology: Herzen, Dostoevsky, Leontiev, Tolstoy, Fadeyev*. Urbana, Chicago, and London: University of Illinois Press, 1983.

Sakharov, V. *Eskhatologicheskiia sochineniia i skazaniia v drevne-russkoi pis'mennosti i vliianie ikh na narodnye dukhovnye stikhi.* Tula, 1879.

Schaeder, Hildegard. *Moskau das dritte Rom: Studien zur Geschichte der politischen Theorien in der slavischen Welt.* Hamburg: Friederichsen, de Gruyter and Co., 1929.

Schmithals, Walter. *The Apocalyptic Movement.* Trans. John E. Steely. Nashville and New York: Abingdon Press, 1975.

Shakhmatov, A. "Kievopecherskii paterik i Pecherskaia letopis'." *IORJaS* 2 (1897), 795–844.

———. "Zhitie Antoniia i Pecherskaia letopis'." *ZhMNP* (1898), 105–49.

Shragin, Boris. Introduction 2 to *Landmarks.* Trans. Marian Schwartz, xxxi–lv. New York: Karz Howard, 1977, xxxi–lv.

Sidel'nikova, T. *Valentin Kataev; ocherk zhizni i tvorchestva.* Moscow, 1957.

Siefkes, Frauke. *Zur Form des Žitije Feodosija.* Bad Homburg, Berlin, and Zurich: Verlag Gehlen, 1970.

Simmons, Ernest J. "The Organization Writer (1934–46)." *Literature and Revolution in Soviet Russia 1917–62.* Ed. Max Hayward and Leopold Labedz, 74–98. London: Oxford University Press, 1963.

Sinyavsky, A. *On Socialist Realism.* Trans. Max Hayward. New York: Vintage Books, 1965.

Skorino, L. *Pisatel' i ego vremia; Zhizn' i tvorchestvo V.P. Kataeva.* Moscow, 1965.

Skripil', M. *Russkaia povest' XVII veka.* Moscow, 1954.

Smolitsch, Igor. *Russisches Mönchtum. Entstehung, Entwicklung und Wesen.* Würzburg: Augustinus Verlag, 1953.

Spence, G. W. *Tolstoy the Ascetic.* New York: Barnes and Noble, 1968.

Stites, Richard. *The Women's Liberation Movement in Russia: Feminism, Nihilism, and Bolshevism 1860–1930.* Princeton: Princeton University Press, 1977.

Strémooukhoff, D. "Moscow the Third Rome: Sources of the Doctrine." *Speculum* 28 (1953), 84–101.

Suleiman, Susan Ruben. *Authoritarian Fictions: The Ideological Novel as Literary Genre.* New York: Columbia University Press, 1983.

Timofeev, L. *O khudezhestvennykh osobennostiakh romana N. Ostrovskogo Kak zakalialas' stal'.* Moscow, 1956.

Tomashevskii, B. *Teoriia literatury*. Moscow, 1928.

Tregub, S. *Geroi nashego vremeni (Ot Pavla Korchagina k Olegu Koshevomu)*. Moscow, 1948.

————. *Nikolai Ostrovskii*. Moscow, 1939.

————. *Zhivoi Korchagin*. Moscow, 1968.

Trotsky, Leon. *Literature and Revolution*. Ann Arbor: University of Michigan Press, 1960.

Tuveson, Ernest L. "The Millenarian Structure of The Communist Manifesto." In *The Apocalyptic in English Renaissance Thought and Literature*. Ed. C. A. Patrides and Joseph Wittreich, 323–41. Ithaca, N.Y.: Cornell University Press, 1984.

Venturi, Franco. *Roots of Revolution*. Trans. Francis Haskell. New York: Alfred Knopf, 1960.

Volozhenin, A. *Fedor Gladkov. Zhizn' i tvorchestvo*. Moscow, 1969.

Vorob'ev, V. M. A. *Gor'kii o sotsialisticheskom realizme*. L'vov, 1959.

Vucinich, Alexander. *Science in Russian Culture 1861–1917*. Stanford: Stanford University Press, 1970.

Walicki, Andrzej. *A History of Russian Thought from the Enlightenment to Marxism*. Trans. Hilda Andrews-Rusiecka. Stanford: Stanford University Press, 1979.

Ware, Timothy. *The Orthodox Church*. Baltimore: Penguin Books, 1963.

Wasiolek, Edward. "Design in the Russian Novel." In *The Russian Novel from Pushkin to Pasternak*. Ed. John Garrard, 51–63. New Haven and London: Yale University Press, 1983.

————. *Tolstoy's Major Fiction*. Chicago and London: University of Chicago Press, 1978.

Weil, Irwin. *Gorky: His Literary Development and Influence on Soviet Intellectual Life*. New York: Random House, 1966.

Woehrlin, William F. *Chernyshevskii: The Man and the Journalist*. Cambridge, Mass.: Harvard University Press, 1971.

Workman, Herbert B. *The Evolution of the Monastic Ideal*. London: Charles H. Kelly, 1913.

Worringer, Wilhelm. *Abstraction and Empathy: A Contribution to the Psychology of Style*. Trans. Michael Bullock. Cleveland and New York: World Publishing Co., 1967.

Žekulin, G. "Forerunner of Socialist Realism: The Novel 'What To Do?' by N. G. Chernyshevsky." *Slavonic and East European Review* 41 (1963), 467–83.

Zhdanov, A. "Soviet Literature—the Richest in Ideas, the Most Advanced Literature." In *Problems of Soviet Literature*. Ed. H. G. Scott. 1935; Reprint. Westport, Conn.: Hyperion Press, 1981.

Ziolkowski, Margaret. *Hagiography and Modern Russian Literature*. Princeton: Princeton University Press, 1988.

Zubov, V. "Epifanii Premudryi i Pakhomii Serb." *TODRL* 9 (1953), 145–58.

STUDIES OF THE HARRIMAN
INSTITUTE

Soviet National Income in 1937 by Abram Bergson, Columbia University Press, 1953.

Through the Glass of Soviet Literature: Views of Russian Society by Ernest Simmons Jr., ed., Columbia University Press, 1953.

Polish Postwar Economy by Thad Paul Alton, Columbia University Press, 1954.

Management of the Industrial Firm in the USSR: A Study in Soviet Economic Planning by David Granick, Columbia University Press, 1954.

Soviet Policies in China, 1917–1924 by Allen S. Whiting, Columbia University Press, 1954; paperback, Stanford University Press, 1968.

Literary Politics in the Soviet Ukraine, 1917–1934 by George S. N. Luckyj, Columbia University Press, 1956.

The Emergence of Russian Panslavism, 1856–1870 by Michael Boro Petrovich, Columbia University Press, 1956.

Lenin on Trade Unions and the Revolution, 1893–1917 by Thomas Taylor Hammond, Columbia University Press, 1956.

The Last Years of the Georgian Monarchy, 1658–1832 by David Marshall Lang, Columbia University Press, 1957.

The Japanese Thrust into Siberia, 1918 by James William Morley, Columbia University Press, 1957.

Bolshevism in Turkestan, 1917–1927 by Alexander G. Park, Columbia University Press, 1957.

Soviet Marxism: A Critical Analysis by Herbert Marcuse, Columbia University Press, 1958; paperback, Columbia University Press, 1985.

Soviet Policy and the Chinese Communists, 1931–1946 by Charles B. McLane, Columbia University Press, 1958.

The Agrarian Foes of Bolshevism: Promise and Defeat of the Russian Socialist Revolutionaries, February to October, 1917 by Oliver H. Radkey, Columbia University Press, 1958.

Pattern for Soviet Youth: A Study of the Congresses of the Komsomol, 1918–1954 by Ralph Talcott Fisher, Jr., Columbia University Press, 1959.

The Emergence of Modern Lithuania by Alfred Erich Senn, Columbia University Press, 1959.

The Soviet Design for a World State by Elliot R. Goodman, Columbia University Press, 1960.

Settling Disputes in Soviet Society: The Formative Years of Legal Institutions by John N. Hazard, Columbia University Press, 1960.

Soviet Marxism and Natural Science, 1917–1932 by David Joravsky, Columbia University Press, 1961.

Russian Classics in Soviet Jackets by Maurice Friedberg, Columbia University Press, 1962.

Stalin and the French Communist Party, 1941–1947 by Alfred J. Rieber, Columbia University Press, 1962.

Sergei Witte and the Industrialization of Russia by Theodore K. Von Laue, Columbia University Press, 1962.

Ukrainian Nationalism by John H. Armstrong. Columbia University Press, 1963.

The Sickle under the Hammer: The Russian Socialist Revolutionaries in the Early Months of Soviet Rule by Oliver H. Radkey, Columbia University Press, 1963.

Comintern and World Revolution, 1928–1943: The Shaping of Doctrine by Kermit E. McKenzie, Columbia University Press, 1964.

Weimar Germany and Soviet Russia, 1926–1933: A Study in Diplomatic Instability by Harvey L. Dyck, Columbia University Press, 1966.

Financing Soviet Schools by Harold J. Noan, Teachers College Press, 1966.

Russia, Bolshevism, and the Versailles Peace by John M. Thompson, Princeton University Press, 1966.

The Russian Anarchists by Paul Avrich, Princeton University Press, 1967.

The Soviet Academy of Sciences and the Communist Party, 1927–1932 by Loren R. Graham, Princeton University Press, 1967.

Red Virgin Soil: Soviet Literature in the 1920s by Robert A. Maguire, Princeton University Press, 1968; paperback, Cornell University Press, 1987.

Communist Part Membership in the U.S.S.R., 1917–1967 by T. H. Rigby, Princeton University Press, 1968.

Soviet Ethics and Morality by Richard T. DeGeorge, University of Michigan Press, 1969; paperback, Ann Arbor Paperbacks, 1969.

Vladimir Akimov on the Dilemmas of Russian Marxism, 1895–1903 by Jonathan Frankel, Cambridge University Press, 1969.

Soviet Perspectives on International Relations, 1956–1967 by William Zimmerman, Princeton University Press, 1969.

Kronstadt, 1921 by Paul Avrich, Princeton University Press, 1970.

Class Struggle in the Pale: The Formative Years of the Jewish Workers' Movement in Tsarist Russia by Ezra Mendelsohn, Cambridge University Press, 1970.

The Proletarian Episode in Russian Literature by Edward J. Brown, Columbia University Press, 1971.

Labor and Society in Tsarist Russia: The Factory Workers of St. Petersburg, 1855–1870 by Reginald E. Zelnik, Stanford University Press, 1971.

Archives and Manuscript Repositories in the U.S.S.R.: Moscow and Leningrad by Patricia K. Grimsted, Princeton University Press, 1972.

The Baku Commune, 1917–1918 by Ronald G. Suny, Princeton University Press, 1972.

Mayakovsky: A Poet in the Revolution by Edward J. Brown, Princeton University Press, 1973.

Oblomov and his Creator: The Life and Art of Ivan Goncharov by Milton Ehre, Princeton University Press, 1974.

German Politics Under Soviet Occupation by Henry Krisch, Columbia University Press, 1974.

Soviet Politics and Society in the 1970's, Henry W. Morton and Rudolph L. Tokes, eds., Free Press, 1974.

Liberals in the Russian Revolution by William G. Rosenberg, Princeton University Press, 1974.

Famine in Russia, 1891–1892 by Richard G. Robbins, Jr., Columbia University Press, 1975.

In Stalin's Time: Middleclass Values in Soviet Fiction by Vera Dunham, Cambridge University Press, 1976.

The Road to Bloody Sunday by Walter Sablinsky, Princeton University Press, 1976; paperback, Princeton University Press, 1986.

The Familiar Letter as a Literary Genre in the Age of Pushkin by William Mills Todd III, Princeton University Press, 1976.

Russian Realist Art. The State and Society: The Peredvizhniki and Their Tradition by Elizabeth Valkenier, Ardis Publishers, 1977; paperback, Columbia University Press, 1989.

The Soviet Agrarian Debate by Susan Solomon, Westview Press, 1978.

Cultural Revolution in Russia, 1928–1931, Sheila Fitzpatrick, ed., Indiana University Press, 1978; paperback, Midland Books, 1984.

Soviet Criminologists and Criminal Policy: Specialists in Policy-Making by Peter Solomon, Columbia University Press, 1978.

Technology and Society Under Lenin and Stalin: Origins of the Soviet Technical Intelligentsia by Kendall E. Bailes, Princeton University Press, 1978.

The Politics of Rural Russia, 1905–1914, Leopold H. Haimson, ed., Indiana University Press, 1979.

Political Participation in the U.S.S.R. by Theodore H. Friedgut, Princeton University Press, 1979; paperback, Princeton University Press, 1982.

Education and Social Mobility in the Soviet Union, 1921–1934 by Sheila Fitzpatrick, Cambridge University Press, 1979.

The Soviet Marriage Market: Mate Selection in Russia and the USSR by Wesley Andrew Fisher. Praeger Publishers, 1980.

Prophecy and Politics: Socialism, Nationalism, and the Russian Jews, 1862–1917 by Jonathan Frankel, Cambridge University Press, 1981.

Dostoevsky and The Idiot: *Author, Narrator, and Reader* by Robin Feuer Miller, Harvard University Press, 1981.

Moscow Workers and the 1917 Revolution by Diane Koenker, Princeton University Press, 1981; paperback, Princeton University Press, 1986.

Archives and Manuscript Repositories in the USSR: Estonia, Latvia, Lithuania, and Belorussia by Patricia K. Grimsted, Princeton University Press, 1981.

Zionism in Poland: The Formative Years, 1915–1926 by Ezra Mendelsohn, Yale University Press, 1982.

Soviet Risk-Taking and Crisis Behavior by Hannes Adomeit, George Allen and Unwin Publishers, 1982.

Russia at the Crossroad: The 26th Congress of the CPSU, Seweryn Bialer and Thane Gustafson, eds., George Allen and Unwin Publishers, 1982.

The Crisis of the Old Order in Russia: Gentry and Government by Roberta Thompson Manning, Princeton University Press, 1983; paperback, Princeton University Press, 1986.

Sergei Aksakov and Russian Pastoral by Andrew A. Durkin, Rutgers University Press, 1983.

Politics and Technology in the Soviet Union by Bruce Parrott, MIT Press, 1983.

The Soviet Union and the Third World: An Economic Bind by Elizabeth Kridl Valkenier, Praeger Publishers, 1986.

Russian Metaphysical Romanticism: The Poetry of Tiutchev and Boratynskii by Sarah Pratt, Stanford University Press, 1984.

Ruling Russia: Politics and Administration in the Age of Absolutism, 1762– 1796 by John LeDonne, Princeton University Press, 1984.

Insidious Intent: A Structural Analysis of Fedor Sologub's Petty Demon by Diana Green, Slavica Publishers, 1986.

Leo Tolstoy: Resident and Stranger by Richard Gustafson, Princeton University Press, 1986.

Workers, Society, and the State: Labor and Life in Moscow, 1918–1929 by William Chase, University of Illinois Press, 1987.

Andrey Bely: Spirit of Symbolism, John Malmstad, ed., Cornell University Press, 1987.

Government and Peasant in Russia, 1861–1906: The Prehistory of the Stolypin Reforms by David A. J. Macey, Northern Illinois Press, 1987.

The Making of Three Russian Revolutionaries: Voices from the Menshevik Past, edited by Leopold H. Haimson in collaboration with Ziva Galili y Garcia and Richard Wortman, Cambridge University Press, 1988.

Revolution and Culture: The Bogdanov-Lenin Controversy by Zenovia A. Sochor, Cornell University Press, 1988.

A Handbook of Russian Verbs by Frank Miller, Ardis Publishers, 1989.

1905 in St. Petersburg: Labor, Society and Revolution by Gerald D. Sochor, Cornell University Press, 1988.

Alien Tongues: Bilingual Russian Writers of the "First" Emigration by Elizabeth Klosty Beaujor, Cornell University Press, 1989.

Iuzovka and Revolution, Volume I: Life and Work in Russia's Donbass, 1869– 1924 by Theodore H. Friedgut, Princeton University Press, 1989.

248 Studies of the Harriman Institute

The Menshevik Leaders in the Russian Revolution: Social Realities and Political Strategies by Ziva Galili, Princeton University Press, 1989.

Russian Literary Politics and the Pushkin Celebration of 1880 by Marcus C. Levitt, Cornell University Press, 1989.

Russian Realist Art by Elizabeth Valkenier, Columbia University Press, 1989.

Russianness: In Honor of Rufus Mathewson, Robert L. Belknap, ed., Ardis Publishers, 1990.

Soldiers in the Proletarian Dictatorship: The Red Army and the Soviet Socialist State, 1917–1930 by Mark von Hagen, Cornell University Press, 1990.

Russia, Germany and the West from Khrushchev to Gorbachev by Michael Sodaro, Cornell University Press, 1990.

In Stalin's Time by Vera Dunham, Duke University Press, 1990.

Folklore for Stalin by Frank Miller, M. E. Sharpe, 1990.

Vasilii Trediakovsky: The Fool in the New Russian Literature by Irina Reyfman, Stanford University Press, 1990.

Ilya Repin and the World of Russian Art by Elizabeth Kridl Valkenier, Columbia University Press, 1990.

Autobiographical Statements in Twentieth-Century Russian Literature by Jane Gary Harris, Princeton University Press, 1990.

The Genesis of the Brothers Karamazov by Robert L. Belknap, Northwestern University Press, 1990.

Thinking Theoretically About Soviet Nationalities: Concepts, History, and Comparison in the Study of the USSR by Alexander J. Motyl, Columbia University Press.

Kronstadt 1921 by Paul Avrich, Princeton University Press, 1991.

INDEX

Accommodation relationship, 180, 186
Afanasii zatvornik, Tale of, 54–56
Akindin (*hegumen* of the Kievan Crypt Monastery), 39, 42, 54
Aleksandr (*Invalid detstva*), 187–88
Aleksei Mikhailovich (tsar), 28
Anchoritic monasticism: comparison with cenobitic, 21–22, 204n; in early Christianity, 16, 19–20, 22, 23, 208n; in Russia, 43, 46, 53, 78, 89
Andreev, Leonid, 134
Anthony, Saint: and dualism, 22; as founder of anchoritic monasticism, 18–21, 194n, 203n
Antichrist, 28, 80, 113, 115, 116, 125–26, 206n
Anti-hagiography, 124–25
Antipov. *See* Strel'nikov
Antonii Pecherskii, 55, 56–57, 58–59, 197n, 200n
Apocalypse: definition, 22–24, 66, 68; as extra-literary motivation, 7, 10, 11–12; in Old Russia, 26, 26–28, 78–82; and religious belief, 18, 194n, 195n, 203n; and revolutionary ideology, 6, 23–24, 105–06, 129–33, 134, 136; in specific works: *Doctor Zhivago,* 184; *The First Circle,* 185, *The Life of Avraamii Smolenskii,* 65–66, 68–72, 74; *The Life of Kirill Belozerskii,* 95–96; *The Life of Ulianiia Osor'ina,* 98; *Mahogany*

and *The Volga Falls to the Caspian Sea,* 164–66; *Mother,* 151; "The Portrait," 115–16; *Time Forward!,* 173; *What Is to Be Done?,* 141, 143, 144, 146
Apocalypse of Ezra, 79–80, 205n
Arabesques, 112
Ascetic imagery, 2, 111–12, 116
Atemporality, 10, 37–38, 41, 48–49, 189; in specific works: *Cement,* 156, 222n; *The Life of Avraamii Smolenskii,* 73; *The Life of Sergii Radonezhskii,* 90; *What Is to Be Done?,* 144–46
Athos. *See* Mount Athos
Augustine, Saint, 20
Autobiography: *How the Steel Was Tempered* as, 174
Avraamii Smolenskii, 1–2, 3, 7–8, 91, 106, 131, 133, 145, 150, 203n; *The Life of,* 33, 64, 65–76, 89

B

Berdyaev, N., 187
Bogomilism, 53–54, 69, 85, 152, 204n
Bogostroitel'stvo. See God-building
Boris and Gleb, The Life of, 67, 75
Brothers Karamazov, 109, 111, 117, 120–23, 124–26, 128
Bulgakov, Sergei, 132, 186